The Lake English Classics

Under the editorial supervision of LINDSAY TODD DAMON, A. B., Associate Professor of English in Brown University.

ADDISON—The Sir Roger de Coverley Papers—ABBOTT	30c
BUNYAN—The Pilgrim's Progress—LATHAM	30c
BURKE—Speech On Conciliation with America—DENNEY	25c
CARLYLE—Essay on Burns—AITON	25c
CHAUCER—Selections—GREENLAW	40c
COOPER—Last of the Mohicans—LEWIS	40c
COLERIDGE—The Ancient Mariner, LOWELL—Vision of Sir Launfal, } 1 vol.—MOODY	25c
DE QUINCEY—The Flight of a Tartar Tribe—FRENCH	25c
DICKENS—A Tale of Two Cities—BALDWIN	40c
DICKENS—A Christmas Carol, etc.,—BROADUS	30c
DRYDEN—Palamon and Arcite—COOK	25c
EMERSON—Essays and Addresses—HEYDRICK	35c
FRANKLIN—Autobiography—GRIFFIN	35c
GEORGE ELIOT—Silas Marner—HANCOCK	30c
GOLDSMITH—The Vicar of Wakefield—MORTON	30c
HAWTHORNE—The House of the Seven Gables—HERRICK	35c
HAWTHORNE—Twice-Told Tales—HERRICK AND BRUÈRE	40c
IRVING—Life of Goldsmith—KRAPP	40c
IRVING—The Sketch Book—KRAPP	40c
IRVING—Tales of a Traveller and parts of The Sketch Book—KRAPP	40c
LOWELL—Vision of Sir Launfal—See Coleridge	
MACAULAY—Essays on Addison and Johnson—NEWCOMER	30c
MACAULAY—Essays on Milton and Addison—NEWCOMER	30c
MILTON—L'Allegro, Il Penseroso, Comus, and Lycidas—NEILSON	25c
MILTON—Paradise Lost, Books I and II—FARLEY	25c
PALGRAVE—Golden Treasury—NEWCOMER	40c
POE—Poems and Tales, Selected—NEWCOMER	30c
POPE—Homer's Iliad, Books I, VI, XXII, XXIV—CRESSY and MOODY	25c
RUSKIN—Sesame and Lilies—LINN	25c
SCOTT—Lay of the Last Minstrel—MOODY and WILLARD	25c
SCOTT—Lady of the Lake—MOODY	30c
SCOTT—Marmion—MOODY AND WILLARD	30c
SCOTT—Ivanhoe—SIMONDS	45c
SHAKSPERE—The Neilson Edition—Edited with Introductions, Notes, and Word Indexes by W. A. NEILSON, Ph. D. As You Like It, Hamlet, Julius Caesar, Macbeth, Twelfth Night—each	25c
SHAKSPERE—Merchant of Venice—LOVETT	25c
STEVENSON—Treasure Island—BROADUS	25c
THACKERAY—Henry Esmond—PHELPS	50c
TENNYSON—Gareth and Lynette, Lancelot and Elaine, The Passing of Arthur, and other Poems—REYNOLDS	35c
TENNYSON—The Princess—COPELAND	25c

SCOTT, FORESMAN AND COMPANY

PUBLISHERS.   378-388 WABASH AVENUE, CHICAGO

The Lake English Classics

EDITED BY

LINDSAY TODD DAMON, A. B.

Professor of Rhetoric in Brown University

The Lake English Classics

SELECTIONS FROM
CHAUCER

EDITED, WITH AN INTRODUCTION, NOTES,
AND A GLOSSARY

BY

EDWIN A. GREENLAW, Ph.D.

(PROFESSOR OF ENGLISH LANGUAGE AND LITERATURE IN
ADELPHI COLLEGE)

CHICAGO
SCOTT, FORESMAN AND COMPANY
1907

COPYRIGHT, 1907,
BY SCOTT, FORESMAN AND COMPANY

PRESS OF
MARSH, AITKEN & CURTIS COMPANY
CHICAGO

PREFACE

In preparing this volume the editor has endeavored to reduce to a minimum the apparatus necessary to accompany the reading of selections from Chaucer. The introduction is by no means so long as it might have been made; the notes are not so complete as would be expected if the book were to be used by specialists in Middle English. The editor suggests that the first three sections of the introduction be read rapidly at the very outset; after some acquaintance has been gained with the text, these sections may be read again more carefully. The sections on Pronunciation, on Inflection, and on Versification should of course be mastered early; the best way seems to be to require them to be studied in connection with very short passages from the text, so that each principle may be immediately applied. Since the vocabulary of the Prologue is distinctly difficult some teachers may prefer to begin the reading with the comparatively easy Nun's Priest's Tale. In this way the language will seem less remote from the language of Shakspere, and attention may be centered upon the difficulties of pronunciation and metre.

A somewhat wider range of material is given in this volume than is customary. In addition to the Prologue a considerable number of the head-links and endlinks are included. It is hoped that the student will thus gain a better idea of the Canterbury Tales as a whole, and will also learn to appreciate some qualities of Chaucer not so prominent in the separate tales. Because of its intensity and compression, as well as for the subtle suggestions of the supernatural which it gives, the major portion of the Pardoner's Tale has been included. Selected lyrics are given in order to represent a side of Chaucer not found in the narrative poems.

The debt of the editor to others is very great. In the case of an author so exhaustively studied as Chaucer, there is little chance, or need, for originality. The researches of Professor Skeat, as embodied in the monumental Oxford Chaucer, have been of constant assistance. For invaluable suggestions the editor is indebted to Professor J. M. Manly of the University of Chicago, and to Professor J. L. Lowes of Swarthmore College.

E. A. G.

Brooklyn, New York, June, 1907.

CONTENTS

INTRODUCTION: PAGE
- I. England in Chaucer's Time 9
- II. Life of Chaucer 15
- III. Chaucer the Poet 22
- IV. Pronunciation 47
- V. Inflection 52
- VI. Versification 58
- VII. Bibliographical Note 61

TEXT:
- I. The Prologue 65
- II. The Knight's Tale 98
- III. The Monk's Tale (Selections) 180
- IV. The Nun's Priest's Tale 186
- V. The Pardoner's Tale (condensed) . . 211
- VI. Selections from Chaucer's Lyrics . . 230

NOTES 239

GLOSSARY 285

INTRODUCTION

I. ENGLAND IN CHAUCER'S TIME

The student of English history will recall that when Chaucer was born, about 1340, the third Edward was upon the English throne. Only a few years earlier, in 1328, the independence of Scotland had been grudgingly acknowledged by England, glorious fruit of that victory at Bannockburn (1314) which we remember best through Burns's stirring lines beginning "Scots wha hae wi' Wallace bled." About the time of Chaucer's birth, the troubles with France had increased to such an extent that the famed Hundred Years' War had begun. The great manufacturing cities of Flanders, such as Ghent, Bruges, Ypres, some of them named by Chaucer in the poems we are shortly to read, were in full sympathy with Edward, and it is likely that the poet's father was one of the Englishmen who went from time to time on missions to these cities. After the naval victory of Sluys (1340), Edward laid claim to the French throne, and the brilliant successes of Crecy (1346) and Calais (1347) made memorable the first decade of the poet's life. In the temporary peace which followed, English court life was brilliant with splendid entertainments at which knights and ladies and even priests frolicked in gay dress; but such gayety

seems tawdry when one remembers that amid the
revels the gaunt spectre of the Black Death stalked
unceasingly, until (1348) nearly two-thirds of England's
population had perished. Then to the fresh troubles
with Scotland and with France was added social discontent, culminating in riot and rebellion. France
suffered even more from the plague of English armies,
for the campaign of 1355-1356 so terribly devastated
that country that Edward was forced on his next
expedition to carry with him the provisions necessary
for the support of his army.

The next few years were filled with the vain efforts
of the English to hold their French possessions. At
home, repeated visitations of the Black Death had
fanned the discontent of the peasants to fury. The
church became more and more hateful to the people;
and the *Vision of Piers Plowman* (1362), appealing
to the peasants by its incisive attacks upon the corrupt
clergy and its crisp use of the imagery of the field;
the eloquence of Wycliffe, and the pitiable condition
of the brain-sick monarch, all added fuel to the flame.
John of Gaunt, Chaucer's powerful patron, became
the head of the anti-clerical party, not because of any
sincere desire to reform the abuses of the church, but
because he saw an opportunity to further his own selfish
schemes.

In 1377, when Chaucer was well on toward his
fortieth year, the ten year old Richard was crowned,
his reign extending until the year before the poet's
death. The opening years of the new king's reign were
troublous with wars abroad and peasant revolts at home.

INTRODUCTION

Wycliffe's disciples were preaching against the church; in 1379-1380 successive heavy taxes were laid upon the oppressed peasants. Then revolt came. In 1381 many outrages were committed on the landed estates of the nobility and murder was common. A hundred thousand men, led by Wat Tyler and Jack Straw, crowded the highways leading to London. Though badly frightened, and in spite of the protests of his court and the great danger to his life, the young king conferred with his rebellious subjects. But the relief which he promised was long in coming; the leaders of the peasants were executed, and even Wycliffe was forced into retirement until his death, in 1384. The Lollards, as his followers were called, went about the country complaining of the corruption of the clergy. Chaucer refers to them in one of the delightful little passages of wit among his Canterbury pilgrims.[1] When the Parson reproves the Shipman's profanity, Harry Bailly, the host, says:

> "O Jankin, be ye there?
> I smelle a loller in the wind," quod he,
> "How! good men," quod our hoste, "herkneth me,
> . . . . .
> For we shal han a predicacioun,
> This loller heer wil prechen us somwhat."
> "Nay, by my fader soule, that shal be nat,"
> Seyde the Shipman; "Heer he shal nat preche,
> He shal no gospel glosen heer ne teche.
> We leve alle in the grete god," quod he,
> "He wolde sowen som difficultee,
> Or springen cokkel in our clene corn."

---

[1] Prologue to *The Shipman's Tale*, ll. 10 ff.

Chaucer's *Prologue* and the various head-links and end-links to the *Canterbury Tales* give much information as to the social conditions of the time: some additional statements may be made.[1] The classes mixed freely; such excursions as the one to Canterbury were frequent. The roads were bad, and most travelers preferred riding horseback to the springless carts in vogue. In London, the streets were in wretched condition; there were no foot-paths or walks, and the street was raised in the middle to allow the filth to run into the ditches at the sides. For obvious reasons no one was allowed on the streets after curfew, and on the highways in the country travel was so dangerous because of bands of robbers that people often went by circuitous routes, over almost impassable roads. In London, huge signs were everywhere, always at least nine feet above the narrow roadway in order to allow men on horseback free passage. The stores were commonly in small booths on the outside of the houses. Recently it had become the fashion to add a second story, called a "solar," to the one room which in former times had constituted the house; this was used as a sleeping apartment, and was reached by a wooden or stone stair on the outside of the building. Sanitary conditions were bad enough, although pigs had recently been excluded from the streets. Filth diseases were common, the Black Death, already referred to, being the scourge of the century. There was no escape from its ravages by flight; many victims

---

[1] For a fuller account, see Traill's *Social England*, Vol. II, and Jusserand's *English Wayfaring Life*.

died within twenty-four hours, most within three days. In Chaucer's lifetime, the most deadly visitations were in 1348, 1361, 1368-9, 1375, 1382, 1390-1; but the poet happily escaped them all.

Yet in spite of bad roads, insanitary methods of living, terrible pestilences, and social discontent which led to peasant uprisings, it was a "merry England." The miracle plays, produced at such important centers as York and Chester, attracted thousands of spectators who were equally ready to weep at the sufferings of Christ or to laugh at the troubles of Noah with his shrewish wife. In some of the plays, notably the shepherd plays in the Wakefield series, great progress had been made toward the development of modern comedy, and the life which was represented attracted the peasants because it was closely imitative of their own rude, noisy lives. In the intervals between the presentation of the miracle plays, amusement was supplied by a motley crowd of pedlers, mountebanks, jugglers, pardoners, and quack doctors, who crowded the highways and furnished amusement wherever there was prospect of profit. On holidays the village green was filled with countrymen who gave eager ear to the harangues of some herbalist who claimed to have a panacea for all diseases. He denied all desire to profit; his sole object was to benefit sufferers. He told so many stories of his marvelous adventures, and enlivened his discourse with so many jests, that it is no wonder that his visit was considered a great event. His remedies, too, were eagerly bought, for it was an extremely superstitious age, and people were gullible to the last degree. Medicines were administered with great ceremony; to be most effective they were to be taken on sacred ground, while the patient was repeating psalms and paternosters, and, if possible, were to be drunk out of a church bell. Chaucer's physician was also an astrologer, careful of his "hours" and the "ascendent of his ymages." Even so great a man as John of Gaddesden, who was royal physician under Edward II., claimed to cure smallpox by wrapping his patient in red cloths and putting him on a red couch. The same learned practitioner professed to cure stone by pounding crickets and beetles mixed with oil and applying the lotion to the patient. When such remedies were counted good by the most learned of physicians, what wonder if the quack doctor, who was also a prince of entertainers, flourished in the land. Somewhat more dignified than such entertainers as these quacks and the jugglers and singers who went everywhere, were the minstrels. These last were important allies of literature, because in those days when there were no printed books and when one manuscript romance often cost the price of fifty oxen, they preserved in memory and told or sang the deeds of ancient heroes. No feast was complete without its quota of minstrels, more than four hundred having been employed upon at least one occasion. But their tales were tales of chivalry, and though they were perhaps analogous to what we in our day call "classics," they did not so truly represent the England of Chaucer's time as the Tales of Canterbury or the rude comedy scenes of the miracle plays.

To sum up, Chaucer's England was a nation just finding itself, composed of men and women eager to take part in adventurous deeds or to hear wonders from strange lands. It was an England torn by the dissensions and struggles which nearly always accompany a sudden and important development of national life; it suffered grievously in the efforts to establish habits of living suited to the rapidly increasing population, but it was, after all, an England fond of amusement and ready to develop means for the entertainment it craved. It saw the highest development of the old sacred drama, and in some respects anticipated the modern drama. It drew away from the hackneyed chivalric romances and set about creating a new literature, a literature which should express the lives of the people themselves. There were many men who did their part toward bringing this new literature into existence; some of them of no mean eminence. But far above them all in grasp of his art and in knowledge of life stands one man, Geoffrey Chaucer, the creator of the *Canterbury Tales*.

II. Life of Chaucer

Chaucer resembled Raleigh, Spenser, Sidney, and others of the brilliant Elizabethan period in that he was both literary man and courtier. His life, like theirs, has two aspects: on the one hand he is the poet; on the other the diplomat, the controller of the customs, the clerk of the king's works. And since perhaps it will be easier to get acquainted with him first through his life as a courtier and government official, we may consider briefly his business career.

Chaucer's family name is first found in English records in the middle of the thirteenth century; we read that Benedict le Chaucer was a merchant in London in 1252.[1] The name probably means "shoemaker" and it is supposed that the family came over from France. Robert le Chaucer, the poet's grandfather, was probably a vintner in London early in the fourteenth century and that he was in favor with the king is shown by the fact that he was for a time a collector of customs. After his death, about 1315, his widow married Richard le Chaucer, and in 1326 Richard and Mary Chaucer brought suit against Agnes de Westhale and others on a charge of abduction of Robert's son John, then a lad of fourteen. That this John Chaucer was the father of the poet is proved by a deed signed by Geoffrey. As has already been intimated, John was abroad in 1338 on a royal embassy to Flanders and Cologne. He was a vintner, and the family seem by this time to have been living in the ward of the vintners in London. The poet's mother was Agnes Chaucer, who, after her husband's death about 1366, married Bartholemew atte Chapel, also a London vintner. These facts seem to make it clear that the poet was born in London and received what education his parents were able to give him in that city.

Of the poet's early life very little is known. Even

---

[1] This sketch of Chaucer is chiefly based on the *Life Records of Chaucer*, Part IV, ed. by R. E. G. Kirk for the Chaucer Society, 1900.

the date of his birth is uncertain, but is supposed, from some testimony which he gave in 1386 in a celebrated law case, to have been somewhere near 1340. The old date of 1328 is absolutely discredited. His parents seem to have been far from wealthy. It is not probable that he inherited much property, for he lived in rented houses. His father was connected now and then with the court, and this leads to the supposition that perhaps the poet's parents planned a courtier's life for their offspring. The first references to Geoffrey are found in a fragment of an account book kept by the wife of the Duke of Clarence, by which it appears that Geoffrey Chaucer received several inexpensive articles of clothing "of his Lady's gift" on the fourth of April, 1357. In May of the same year there is the record of a small sum of money paid him; and in December he received another gratuity "for necessaries against the feast of the Nativity." Two years later we learn that he was in France; that he was armed as an Esquire, and that he was taken prisoner by the French. In 1360 he was ransomed by the king for £16. We next hear of him in 1366, and as he seems then to be receiving a small annuity from the king the inference is that he had spent the intervening years in the king's service. By 1366 he was apparently married to the sister of Katherine Swinford, at one time governess to the children of John of Gaunt and later his wife. From a patent (1366) it appears that Philippa Chaucer was a "Domicella" of Queen Philippa, and received an annuity of ten marks. The following year a similar patent was issued giving twenty marks annually to "our beloved Yeoman," Geoffrey Chaucer; this was paid until 1389. Later Chaucer was promoted to the rank of Esquire in the King's Household.

During the next few years Chaucer lived a busy life, with considerable travel, and with many marks of favor from the king. In 1369 we find him receiving from his royal master the sum of £10, "for wages and expenses at various times;" the next year royal letters of protection were issued for a journey he was to make abroad in the king's service; in 1372 he was commissioned, with two others, to treat with the Doge and citizens of Genoa for the establishment of a market somewhere on the English coast to which the Italian merchants might bring their goods for trading with the English. He was abroad until April of the next year, and he states in his account of receipts and expenditures that he went to Florence as well as to Genoa. There has been some interesting speculation as to whether he saw Petrarch. Be that as it may, it is certain that Italy made a deep impression upon him, and that his journey, with its resultant acquaintance with a remarkable literature, aroused in him an interest which exerted no small influence upon his own poetical work. The next year (1374) was also very important in Chaucer's life. In April he received a grant of a pitcher of wine daily; on the tenth of May he took a lease of "all the mansion above the gate of Aldgate, with the houses built thereupon and with a cellar under the gate on the east side." This property Chaucer was to keep in good repair, allowing free access to the City Chamberlain whenever that officer came to inspect it, and he was to hold it for the term of his life. On the eighth of June he received the post of Controller of the Custom and Subsidy of Wools, Hides and Wool-fells in the Port of London "during the king's pleasure." The patent stipulated that he was to do all the work himself, no deputy being allowed, and that he was to receive £10 a year. That the office was not in those days very burdensome is proved by the fact that a single boatman was thought to be the only assistant Chaucer would need to prevent smuggling and to make the collections. A few days after his appointment to this comfortable and honorable office, he received a grant of £10 for life from his patron, John of Gaunt, in return for services rendered that nobleman. It has been estimated that at this time Chaucer's income from all sources was nearly £64 a year, a sum equivalent to upwards of a thousand pounds to-day.

During the next few years Chaucer went abroad on missions to Flanders, to France, and to Italy. The new king, Richard II., confirmed him in his office of Controller, and in 1382 he was given the additional office of Controller of the Petty Customs in the Port of London. That he found his duties irksome is shown by the fact that he several times petitioned the king for leave of absence and finally (1385) for a permanent deputy; this last request was granted, and for a short time Chaucer enjoyed a leisure which eleven years of clerical work had made impossible before. Another honor was soon his, for he was knight of the shire for Kent in 1386.

But like those whose "tragedies" he recounts in his

Monk's Tale, Chaucer was destined to suffer Fortune's frown as well as her smile. The difficulties of Richard with his nobles have already been referred to. John of Gaunt was in Spain from 1386 to 1389, and in his absence the Duke of Gloucester obtained a temporary ascendency. The king's power was taken from him and given to a board of regents; soon afterward Chaucer lost his offices and his pensions. The records show that the poet was often forced to borrow money, and it seems clear that he was very poor. About the same time his wife died. It is thought that perhaps the pilgrimage to Canterbury was taken about this time, but Chaucer had often been in Kent on business and had plenty of opportunity to observe the curious pilgrimages one of which he so marvelously describes. A temporary recovery from his political misfortunes took place in 1389 when Richard, who had freed himself from the regents, appointed him Clerk of the King's Works. In this new position he had charge of the royal residences and was given power to employ deputies and workmen and to purchase material. As he was granted £30 a year, he was once more free from financial worries. He was very active in his new office, and his records show that he surveyed the "coast" of the Thames between Greenwich and Woolwich, repaired the collegiate chapel of St. George, and served as sub-forester of the Forest of North Petherton. In 1390 he had personal experience of the dangerous conditions of travel in England, for he was several times robbed of money which was in his charge as Clerk. The following year he lost his office again. The next few years were apparently difficult ones, for though he received several grants of money and one pension, he seems to have found it hard to collect what was due him, being forced repeatedly to borrow small sums. When the new king, Henry IV., came to the throne in 1399 the poet immediately addressed to him the *Compleynt to his Purs*, with the result that his old pension was confirmed and a new one, more liberal than the old, was granted. Still there was difficulty in obtaining the money due him, and the poet was continually borrowing small amounts. In 1399 he rented a dwelling in the garden of St. Mary's Chapel, but he was not destined to live there very long, for on the 25th of October, 1400, he died. To him belongs the proud distinction of being the first poet to be buried in the famous north transept of Westminster Abbey.

Such is the bare outline of a long and busy life, so far as its external relations are concerned. For the most part, our knowledge is based upon old account books and state patents, meagre material enough for reconstructing the biography of one of the greatest of Englishmen. He held honorable positions, and enjoyed the favor of three monarchs and the patronage of one of the most powerful of English nobles. But useful as this life of his was, it would not merit our study to-day were it simply the life of Geoffrey Chaucer, sometime Controller of the Customs and Clerk of the King's Works. That which makes every scrap of evidence concerning him interesting to us is a side of his life which no doubt seemed to his friends, perhaps to himself, the least important. For the life and works of Chaucer, like the life and works of every great poet, teach us the truth of the saying of Spenser,

> For deeds doe die, however noblie donne,
> And thoughts of men do as themselves decay;
> But wise wordes, taught in numbers for to runne,
> Recorded by the Muses, live for ay.

III. CHAUCER THE POET

It is probable that Chaucer had very little formal schooling, though some have attempted to prove that he was a student at Oxford. As already outlined, the records of his life show that when very young he entered the service of one of the noble families of the court, and that very soon afterwards he adopted the career of a courtier; thus there seems to have been little time for going to school. But all this does not mean that Chaucer was a man of little education; nothing could be farther from the truth. We get an idea of the way in which he employed his leisure by some lines in one of the later books, *The Hous of Fame*, which tell us that when he had completed the work of the day in the custom house, he would spend the evenings in hard study, so that he is accused of knowing nothing of "Loves folk" or of anything else that God has made;

> And noght only fro fer contree
> That ther no tyding comth to thee,
> But of thy verray neyghebores,
> That dwellen almost at thy dores,
> Thou herest neither that ne this;
> For whan thy labour doon al is,
> And hast y-maad thy rekeninges,
> In stede of reste and newe thinges,

> Thou gost hoom to thy hous anoon;
> And, also domb as any stoon,
> Thou sittest at another boke,
> Till fully daswed is thy loke,
> And livest thus as an hermyte,
> Although thyn abstinence is lyte.[1]

The effects of this hard study are everywhere apparent in his writings. He was well versed in the science of his time, and however absurd much of this learning seems to us to-day, no one will deny that its mastery must have required a considerable time. His treatise on the astrolabe, as well as innumerable references throughout his works, prove his familiarity with mediæval astrology, which was an extraordinarily complex science; while the Nun's Priest's Tale, not to speak of numberless passages elsewhere, shows that he knew well the theories of the physiologists of his time. His acquaintance with theological matters ranged from the "Sermon Books" or collections of *exempla*, to the most abstruse works on theology; the Parson's Tale and his translation of Boethius are illustrations of this, while the Pardoner's Tale, as will be pointed out in the notes, is very similar to a mediæval sermon. His works everywhere show his familiarity with the historians counted authoritative in his day. Turning to the subjects which we should expect would prove especially attractive to a literary man, we find that he knew well the most important Latin authors, although he had no knowledge of Greek at first hand. With the romances and other literature popular during the Middle Ages he was

---

[1] ll. 647 ff.: *daswed*, dazed.

familiar, and the love allegory, with the curious institution called the Court of Love, he knew and made use of in his poems. In his first period he was influenced by French models, and he was personally acquainted with some talented writers of that country. His two journeys to Italy would have served to awaken his interest in the literature of the land of Petrarch and Dante, had any special stimulus been necessary. The Italian period, second in the record of Chaucer's literary development, shows his acquaintance with the great Italian writers, though his knowledge was by no means complete, for he gives no evidence of having appreciated the depth of Dante's mind, he made no use of Boccaccio's *Decamerone*, and of Petrarch he used only that writer's Latin translation of Boccaccio's story of Griselda and a sonnet.

But to name a complete list of the authors and books contributing to Chaucer's education, while it would impress one with the extent of his learning, would be only confusing at this point.[1] A word ought to be said, however, on the subject of a mediæval author's originality, or his relation to his "sources." In Chaucer's time and earlier, originality was felt to have small place in literature. The romances of the time were repeated and repeated, and the author who added to or subtracted from the story as it appeared in his source was felt to be doing an unwarranted thing, deserving the condemnation of those who followed him, because he did not "tell it right." And Chaucer, although he allowed

---

[1] For a delightful essay upon the subject, see Professor Lounsbury's *Studies in Chaucer*, chapter on "The Learning of Chaucer."

himself more freedom in this respect than was usual, often says that he cannot tell certain things because he does not find them in his source, or apologizes for the introduction of something unpleasant on the ground that he has no right to omit anything found in the authority he is following:

> For this ye knowen al so wel as I,
> Whoso shal telle a tale after a man,
> He moot reherce as ny as evere he can,
> Everich a word, if it be in his charge,
> Al speke he never so rudeliche and large;
> Or elles he moot telle his tale untrewe.

Thus it happens that what would to-day be denounced as plagiarism of the rankest sort was in the Middle Ages counted an author's chief virtue. This is why the subject of "sources," often unimportant in the study of a modern author, becomes significant in tracing the development of the mind and art of a fourteenth century poet.[1]

It follows from what has been said above, that the mediæval writer attached very little importance to being known as the author of a certain work. The greater number of poems and romances belonging to this period are anonymous; the chief duty of the author was to tell his story with the utmost fidelity. Since this was the case, it is fortunate that

---

[1] Yet Chaucer should not be classed with the oftentimes unintelligent repeaters of romances and ballads, who were content to re-tell old stories with small attention to artistic presentation. With Chaucer and the contemporary French poets who influenced him, true originality was felt to consist in the workmanship which the poem displayed, not in originality of theme.

scholars have been able to identify with comparative certainty almost all the works written by Chaucer; a few have been lost, and a few others are doubtfully his. The matter of chronology is in by no means so satisfactory a state. A few references to historical events; the enumeration, by Chaucer himself, of some of his works in the prologue of another; contemporary references by other English poets the dates of whose works happen to be known—these are the chief means of arriving at conclusions regarding dates. Of course, the tests of rhyme and metre, and of comparative amateurishness or maturity of performance, are also to be taken into consideration.

Chaucer's earliest poems show that he was at first working under the influence of French models. The prayer to the Virgin entitled *An A. B. C.*, a poem consisting of eight line stanzas beginning with the letters of the alphabet taken successively, is a paraphrase from the French and shows that Chaucer was trying experiments in verse forms. To the same period belong the *Compleynt unto Pite* and some short lyrics probably lost; and we know that Chaucer translated from the French the famous allegorical poem of the thirteenth century, *Le Roman de la Rose*.[1] An English version of the poem, in almost eight thousand lines, has come down to us, and it is thought that the first part of this is Chaucer's. The allegorical element

---

[1] It is really two poems. The first part, by Guillaume de Lorris, abounds in the sentimentalities of the conventional love allegory; the second, by Jean de Meun, is really a fierce satire which attacks the chivalric ideal, the church, women, and many of the social and economic views of the time.

in the French poem exerted great influence in its time, but possesses little interest now because of its sentimentality, its lack of real life, and its endless debates. There is a very slight plot: a lover falls asleep and has a dream of a garden in which is a Rose that he desires to secure. He is helped by Beauty, Wealth, Hospitality, etc., and is opposed by such qualities as Pride, Poverty, and Evil Report. After a long time he gets the Rose. Chaucer, like others who were influenced by this work, often made use of allegory, abstract qualities, the dream *motif*, and debates on the casuistry of love, but he did not do his best work until he got away from the imitation of this form. *The Boke of the Duchesse*, also cast in the form of a dream, is one of the few works by him that can be definitely dated; it was written to commemorate the death of the wife of Chaucer's noble patron, John of Gaunt, which took place in 1369. It is probable that the other works named in this paragraph were also all written before 1375.

In 1373, it will be remembered, Chaucer made the first of his two journeys to Italy. The effect was soon apparent, for in the *Lyf of St. Cecyle*, afterwards worked over and made one of the Canterbury Tales, he shows that he has studied Dante's great poem. Soon after this, he wrote a series of "tragedies," or stories in verse of famous men whose lives had begun in prosperity and ended in poverty or other misfortune. These tragedies, which afterwards became the Monk's Tale, were based on a book by Boccaccio (*De Casibus Virorum Illustrium*). Some scholars think that the story of Griseldis, afterwards the Clerk's Tale, which is based on one of Petrarch's translations from Boccaccio, also belongs in this period; and there is little doubt that he wrote at about the same time a first version of the story of Constance, afterwards the Man of Law's Tale.

Some minor works, such as the *Compleynt to his Lady*, the *Compleynt of Mars*, and the *Anelida and Arcite*, must be passed with a mere mention as works probably written about 1380. Somewhere about the same time must be placed Chaucer's prose translation of a famous work by the Roman senator and philosopher Boethius (died 525 A.D.) entitled *De Consolatione Philosophiae*. Boethius was one of Chaucer's favorite authorities, and we shall meet with references to him in the poems soon to be read. *Troilus and Criseyde*, perhaps written before 1376, though there are strong reasons for supposing it to belong somewhat later, is the most important of the works yet noted.[1] The poem is based upon one of Boccaccio's works (*Il Filostrato*), but two-thirds of it is Chaucer's own. It was in this story that Chaucer first gave evidence of his marvelous power of characterization, and in this respect the poem is one of the greatest before Shakspere.

In 1382, Chaucer wrote *The Parlement of Foules*, in

---

[1] On the date, one may consult the article by Dr. Tatlock in *Modern Philology*, Vol. I, pp. 317 ff., in which it is maintained that by 1376 *Troilus* had been completed; and also the paper by Professor Lowes in *Pub. Modern Lang. Association*, Vol. XIII, pp. 749 ff. Dr. Lowes thinks it was written somewhere near 1383-85.

honor of the betrothal of Richard II. and Anne of Bohemia. The poem, which shows the influence of Dante and Boccaccio, is cast in the form of a dream, but that Chaucer was mastering his instrument is proved by the greater ease of the verses and by the genial humor outcropping here and there. Sometime after 1382, also, belongs *The Legende of Good Women*, in which Chaucer tells of those who have been faithful to Love, even unto death. The poem tells us how Chaucer loves books above everything else, except in the month of May, when "Farewel my boke, and my devocioun." He spends the day in the meadows, chiefly in observation of the daisies, and at night he returns in his dreams to the scenes of the day. The god of Love appears, leading by the hand a beautiful woman who wears a crown of daisies. Following them is a company of nineteen ladies scarcely less beautiful than their queen, and in the distance are others, more numerous than can be counted. The god of Love sees Chaucer, who is reproved for being near such a company, for Chaucer has written much against women in his translation of the *Roman de la Rose* and the *Troilus*. As the poet is trembling with fear, the queen undertakes his defense by naming some works which he has written in praise of women,—the *Boke of the Duchesse*, *Palamoun and Arcite* (afterwards, it is supposed, *The Knight's Tale*), and the *Lyf of St. Cecyl*. The poet then attempts to defend himself but is prevented, and is told that he must write by way of penance a "glorious legende" in honor of women faithful in love. After this prologue the poet begins to tell stories of the nineteen ladies and their queen, and although he does not complete his task (only nine of the twenty legends were written), he proves that he has at last found the literary form in which he could do his best work, that of a collection of tales. Only one thing is lacking, a fatal lack to one of Chaucer's temperament; there is little or no opportunity for variety. The first tales are the best; after Chaucer has sung of the faithfulness of women in love for a little while, his vocabulary is too severely drawn upon, the freshness of his first enthusiasm has disappeared, and the last legends are poor enough.

Before beginning the consideration of Chaucer's greatest work, a few words may be said about *The Hous of Fame*, which some scholars think was written about 1384.[1] Once more he uses the dream form; in a vision he is borne to a magical temple on whose walls he sees depicted the story of Troy. Then the poet is transported by an eagle to the House of Fame, where he sees that fickle goddess bestowing favors without regard to deserts or to consistency. To some she grants fame; others who have performed the same works are refused the boon for which they pray. It is here that we find one of the autobiographical passages always so precious in the works of a poet. When some one asks Chaucer if he has come there to seek fame, he scornfully replies:

---

[1] Professor Lowes thinks it was written about 1379. See his article cited on page 28, note.

> "Nay, forsothe, frend," quod I;
> "I cam noght hider, graunt mercy,
> For no swich cause, by my heed;
> Suffyceth me, as I were deed,
> That no wight have my name in honde
> I woot myself best how I stonde."[1]

Just as the *Legende* marks Chaucer's mastery of the short verse-tale, the form with which he did his best work, so *The Hous of Fame* shows the tendency toward a rather cynical humor, a kindly satire, that also marks the maturity of his powers.

Chaucer was now ready to write his great work. He was at the summit of his worldly position and powers. At this time he was Controller of the Customs and also Controller of the Petty Customs; in 1385 he was granted the privilege of employing a deputy for the conduct of his offices. In the art of "making" he had passed the time of apprenticeship and was master of his craft. He had spent his leisure in arduous studies, so that now he had the breadth of learning necessary for him who is to do mature work. He was thoroughly familiar with the best contemporary literature, and he had experimented with verse forms and the usual devices of poets until he was ready to do original work. His experience at the court and in the custom house had made him a keen observer of men; thus he was fitted to characterize the procession of representatives of all classes who were to ride to Canterbury. He was democratic in tastes; free from undue prejudices; gifted with a vein of

---

[1] ll. 1873 ff.

kindly satire, and with a never failing humor which constantly illuminates his work. And, finally, he had mastered his instrument; he could make words say just what he intended. Under such favorable circumstances he turned, about 1385, to the writing of the *Canterbury Tales*.

THE CANTERBURY TALES

Perhaps it was when he was growing tired of his stories of "good women" that Chaucer hit upon the plan of writing a series of tales with a pilgrimage to Canterbury as the background which was to give them a certain unity. Years previously, as has already been noted, he had written a series of "tragedies" about the lives of famous men, once fortunate but ending their days in wretchedness. But this was a mere biographical dictionary, not a unified production. Then came the Legend, with its fanciful and graceful introduction, but with no other means of connecting its stories of women faithful to love and with no opportunity to characterize all sorts and conditions of persons such as a great novelist or dramatist must have. As has been pointed out, Chaucer had no desire to write original stories; mediæval canons of art forbade any such presumption. But if he could select here and there his favorite tales, re-tell them in condensed and vigorous form, and connect them in such a way as to preserve some unity, he could produce the great work which is the dream of every true literary craftsman, and for which, consciously or unconsciously, Chaucer had been for many years preparing.

It must not be supposed that the idea of collecting a number of stories and then relating them to each other by some means was original with Chaucer. Indeed, he was here, as elsewhere, merely following tradition, so binding upon the story tellers of his own and previous centuries. The ancient but ever-modern *Arabian Nights* is a familiar example of the type. Another collection immensely popular in the Middle Ages was called the *Seven Wise Masters*, in which a youth, trained by seven learned men, is saved from the machinations of a cruel step-mother by his former teachers. Every night the step-mother tells a story calculated to inflame the mind of the king against his falsely accused son; every day one of the wise men tells a tale showing the probable innocence of the youth and reflecting on the character of step-mothers. In this way a number of very old and very popular stories were connected, to the delight of generations of story loving people. Even more famous was the work of Chaucer's contemporary, Boccaccio, to whom the Plague suggested the idea of the *Decamerone*. In the great Italian collection, a party of ladies and gentlemen, forced on account of the scourge to quit Florence, hit upon the plan of beguiling the time of exile by telling, each day, a story apiece. Thus Boccaccio secured the frame-work for his collection, and the tales are bound together by comments and conversation on the part of the listeners.

Thus in a sense, Chaucer's plan of forming a collection of his favorite stories was merely a literary convention of the time. It is clear, however, that he was not indebted for his plan to the author of the *Decamerone*, as has sometimes been held. No traces can be found of a possible influence of the famous Italian collection upon the English work, and none of Chaucer's tales has any of the *novelle* of the *Decamerone* for its direct source. Indeed, it is quite possible that Chaucer never saw the *Decamerone*. We have seen how common was the device of connecting a number of stories by some simple plot; we have seen, also, that Chaucer had twice before made collections of his own; we do not need to seek further for the source of the idea in Chaucer's mind, or to think that he was imitating the *Decamerone* or any other particular collection.

In the working out of his plan, moreover, Chaucer was far superior to any of his predecessors. In a collection like that of the *Seven Wise Masters*, the stories had to be of such a nature as to point the moral intended by the narrator, thus preventing entire freedom of choice. In the *Decamerone* the persons comprising the exiled company were of the same class; such a kaleidoscopic view of society as is given in the Prologue to the *Canterbury Tales* was therefore impossible, and the art with which the English poet in many cases fits the tale to the rank and manner of life and thinking of the narrator was obviously not open to Boccaccio. Thus, while we may read with interest almost any of the separate tales as an individual piece of literary art, we shall miss what is perhaps the most distinctive part of the work if we leave out of account the general framework or plot which serves to connect the stories. For here it is that Chaucer gives the very best proof of his craftsmanship. It was a most happy stroke of genius which suggested to him the idea of describing one of the pilgrimages then so popular, working in the stories he desired to relate as if they were the means of whiling away the tedious hours of a long and difficult journey. By this means he gains an air of reality which is one of the never-failing charms of the *Canterbury Tales*. The work appears to be a transcript from life, and in a sense such is indeed the case.

Pilgrimages of every kind were extremely common in Chaucer's time.[1] They were made to satisfy vows taken in order to secure relief from diseases which the soothsayers and physicians could not cure, or in consequence of religious vows, or in expiation of sins. Sometimes, no doubt, such journeys were taken in order to secure change of scene, much as one goes now to the mountains or the sea-shore. In days when there were no newspapers and no printed books, life became very monotonous, and a pilgrimage was much more valuable in breaking up this sameness of life than is the summer vacation trip of to-day. The most famous English pilgrimages were those to Walsingham and to Canterbury, but many went to France, to Italy, and to Jerusalem for the same purposes. Pilgrimage towns were crowded with inns and churches, and the churches were filled with relics reputed to have the power of performing marvelous cures. Rich and poor, nobles and villeins, men and women, went on these

---

[1] For a mass of interesting material upon the subject of pilgrimages, one may consult Jusserand, *English Wayfaring Life*, pp. 238 ff.

journeys. Caste distinctions were forgotten; the pilgrimage was a democratic institution.

In the Prologue to his great work, Chaucer tells us of a compact entered into by a company of pilgrims on their way to the shrine of Thomas à Becket. After they have enjoyed their suppers at the Tabard Inn and have paid their reckonings, their good host, Harry Bailly by name, proposes that they beguile the tedium of the slow journey to Canterbury by telling stories. According to the plan proposed, which was promptly adopted by the party, each pilgrim was to tell two stories on the way to the shrine and two on the return journey; the host was to be the umpire, and the winner of the contest was to have a fine supper at the Tabard at the expense of the others. This plan, if it had been carried out, would have resulted in a collection of about one hundred and twenty tales. It is probable that Chaucer had a number of the tales already written when, in 1386 or 1387, he went actively to work upon the great collection. No doubt he had other material in mind as well, so that the project did not seem too great for accomplishment. But Chaucer's fatal habit of proposing to himself plans so large that he could not accomplish them, already evident from the number of unfinished works he had up to this time produced, finds additional illustration in the fact that only twenty-four tales were written. This number sufficed to cover the journey from London to Canterbury, and thus the collection is not altogether lacking in unity or completeness.

With the help of some hints scattered here and there through the tales, and with the more considerable service afforded by the scraps of dialogue and comment which connect some of them, scholars have been able to arrange the stories in about the order which the poet intended, and even to assign the days of the month on which they were told. Apparently about three days were required by the pilgrims for their journey, and though this may seem unreasonable for the short distance (about fifty-seven miles), there are precedents for such slow traveling, and it must be remembered that Chaucer expressly tells us in the Prologue that his pilgrims were not very good riders and that some of them were poorly mounted. The road, too, in spite of the fact that it was one of the most frequented in the kingdom, was very bad, and progress was necessarily slow. There is abundant evidence that Chaucer's pilgrims were not unreasonably long on the way.[1]

Not long ago, an inn was still standing on the site of the Tabard in Southwark, and no doubt part of the very road used by the pilgrims is still in use. The start was made at daybreak, and by the time the Miller had finished his tale they had reached Deptford, at about half-past seven. This was unusually rapid progress, but nevertheless the first day's halting place was probably Dartford, about fifteen miles from London. Since Chaucer did not complete his work, the only tales

---

[1] Much interesting information may be gained from *The Road from London to Canterbury*, edited for the Chaucer Society by Henry Littlehales, 1898. The student should at least consult the maps given therein, if the work is accessible.

belonging to the first day are those of the Knight, the Miller, the Reeve, and the unfinished tale of the Cook. The next day, which scholars suppose to have been April 18, 1386, entertainment is first provided by the Man of Law, who tells of Constance, of the false accusations directed against her, of wicked mothers-in-law, and of her happiness after she had been tried by suffering. Next the Shipman tells a rather disreputable story, quite in keeping with his character, and in contrast the Prioress relates a story drawn from church lore and bearing upon the persecution of the Christians by the Jews. Afterwards,

> Whan seyd was al this miracle, every man
> As sobre was, that wonder was to see,
> Til that our hoste japen[1] tho[2] bigan,
> And than at erst he loked upon me,
> And seyde thus, "What man artow?" quod he;
> "Thou lokest as thou woldest finde an hare,
> For ever upon the ground I see thee stare.
> Approche neer, and loke up merily.
> Now war yow, sirs, and lat this man have place;
> He in the waast is shape as wel as I;
> This were a popet[3] in an arm t' enbrace
> For any womman, smal and fair of face.
> He seemeth elvish by his contenaunce,
> For unto no wight dooth he daliaunce."

Thus introduced to the company, Chaucer begins a delightful parody on some of the conventional metrical romances of the time, but he is not suffered to proceed; the host calls it "rym doggerel" and maintains that he does nothing but waste their time. After some

---
[1] *To joke.* [2] *Then* [3] *Puppet.*

INTRODUCTION

protest Chaucer tells a long prose tale about Melibeus and his wife Prudence; after which the Monk recounts a number of "tragedies" or histories of men who fell from prosperity to bad fortune. These are so much alike that Harry Bailly once more loses patience and orders the Nun's Priest to entertain the pilgrims. The tale of the cock and the hen follows, and by the time it is ended they are near Rochester, thirty miles from London.

The story-telling is continued by the Pardoner, whose tale is followed by the Wife of Bath's story of a loathly damsel who afterwards became a beautiful maiden. The Friar's tale, next in order, reflects on the character of the "Sompnour," who retorts in kind. Of better type is the tale of Patient Griselda told by the Clerk, who is followed by the Merchant with the ancient Eastern story of January and May. Apparently the next entertainer was the Squire, the one

> . . . that left half told
> The story of Cambuscan bold.

Though there is no very good evidence to support it, scholars generally have held the view that the Squire began the last day's story-telling. At any rate, by the time this story had been told, together with the Franklin's tale of magic and love, and the Second Nun's miracle story, the company had covered five miles since leaving Ospringe, forty-seven miles from London, where the second night had been passed:[1]

---

[1] Some scholars think that a stop was made at Rochester, about half-way between Dartford and Ospringe, and that four days, or three

The record of the last day is very incomplete. Besides the tales by the Squire, the Franklin, and the Second Nun, if we reckon all these as assigned to that day, we have only the stories told by the Canon's Yeoman, the Manciple, and the Parson. The Canon, accompanied by his yeoman, joined the company about five miles from Ospringe, but the servant is so talkative about his master's affairs that the Canon flees in shame. Then the coast is clear for the yeoman's tale of alchemy, which exposes the villainy of his former master. Several tales are lacking here, for by the time the Manciple has finished his story of the talking bird it is about four in the afternoon. The end of the journey is near, and the Parson quite appropriately delivers a homily calculated to bring their minds into a proper frame for the visit to the sacred town.

This hasty survey makes clear how far short Chaucer came of carrying out his original design. We do not even have the two tales which each pilgrim was to tell on the way to Canterbury, to say nothing

---

and a half, perhaps, were required for the entire journey. Though this has been the generally accepted view, recent research seems to make the view here adopted, viz., a three-days' journey, more tenable. The reference to Rochester in the Monk's Prologue by no means compels us to believe that the company stopped there for the night. Dartford and Ospringe were the usual stopping places on the journey from London to Canterbury, if it be safe to draw conclusions from the scanty records of such pilgrimages. On the stop at Ospringe, see Skeat, *Oxford Chaucer*, Vol. V, p. 415. See also Dr. Tatlock's interesting discussion on "The Duration of the Canterbury Pilgrimage," in *Pub. Mod. Lang. Association*, Vol. XIV, p. 478. It is hardly necessary to remark that the unequal distribution of the tales among the three days is due to the fact that Chaucer never completed his work. He was filling in here and there, when the interruption came which turned his mind to other things.

of the return journey. Neither do we have any account of the experiences of the company at the shrine, or any story of the award of the prize and of the supper that was served at the Tabard upon their return. We suffer a very great loss because of this incompleteness, for the excellence of the Prologue and the various connecting links proves what Chaucer could have done had he completed the original design. The extremely irregular arrangement of the tales is of course due to the facts that in some cases Chaucer used old material, narrative poems which he had written long before, and also that in the stories written expressly for the *Canterbury Tales,* he suited, for the most part, the story to the narrator, and not unnaturally wrote those first which he liked best.

But however incomplete the poem is, we cannot fail to appreciate the perfection of the plan. Through the Prologue and the connecting links we become acquainted with each pilgrim, and since these men and women came from all walks of life, the opportunity for skilful characterization was immense. To realize how fully Chaucer grasped it, one has only to read a few hundred pages written by preceding or contemporary authors. The Canterbury pilgrimage is in a sense an epitome of the pilgrimage of life. Nowhere in our literature, before Chaucer's day, had there been such a transcript of actual life. Here was the true democracy toward which England was gradually working. Viewed through the mist of years, the march of the deathless nine and twenty becomes a stately progress.

Knight, and Squire, and Shipman; the fat and complaisant Monk and the garrulous Wife of Bath; that rascally pair, the Sompnour and the Pardoner; the meek and lovable Parson of a town,—these and many more strike hands in a common fellowship, and they represent, in a way, the English nation that was to be. We know not their names, save Harry Bailly and the elvish wight who tells the story, but for us they live as truly as any characters we ever met in our literary journeyings. Thus to create is to give proof of the highest genius.

CHAUCER AS A LITERARY ARTIST

The distinguishing marks of Chaucer as a poet are his power of characterization and his rare humor. The first is not attained by what may be called the dramatic method, that is, he does not let us see how a man or a woman acts under stress of circumstance and thus allow us to draw our own conclusions as to the character. Nor do we find, except perhaps in *Troilus*, the development of a character such as Shakspere gives us in Macbeth or Lear. Chaucer's method is more akin to portraiture. But in painting his portraits he does not confuse by over-description; it is the supreme power which he exhibits of selecting the significant attribute or element in descriptions which makes the portrait so wonderfully vivid. By comparing his method with that of such a poet as Crabbe one understands how far superior Chaucer is in the power to make a real personality stand forth by means of a few quick, sure strokes. There is no need to give examples; the Prologue supplies abundant material for the study of this element in his style.

As to his humor, that is what endears him more than anything else, perhaps, to the modern reader. It is a sly, quiet, roguish humor; nothing of an attempt to make the reader burst into guffaws of laughter, nothing of the grotesque or exaggerated, nothing obtrusive or conscious. He often laughs at himself, as in the lines,

> Till that the brightë sun had lost his hue
> For the orisont had reft the sun his light
> (This is as much to sayn as "it was night").

So sly is his humor that one must needs be on guard lest one miss it. Take for example the frequent incursions which he makes into the mock-heroic or the inflated-didactic, in which, after reaching the climax of rhetoric, he suddenly catches himself, pauses, and gravely remarks, "Now will I turn to my tale again." It is as much as to say, "You see I can do this sort of thing because it's fashionable, but I know it's ridiculous as well as you, so we'll have it over as soon as possible and get back to business." His humor is inextricably mingled with the peculiar satire which marks him as the earliest of modern English authors. It is not a biting satire; the butts of his ridicule do not turn and writhe in agony. Rather is it, as an eminent critic has said, as if his victims were put in the sun of his raillery, until they cast aside one by one their disguises and stand revealed, hardly conscious as to whether they are abused or not. Here, too, Chaucer's wit is so sly as to be almost impalpable. The portraits in the Prologue abound in examples, and the tale of the Nun's Priest is a delicious compound of raillery and good sense, all incidental to a story told transcendently well.

In observing Chaucer's humor and power of characterization, one is struck by the ease with which he does it all. There is a total absence of that strain which is characteristic of so many writers. He seems utterly unconscious of ever saying anything particularly well. This is partly due to the evenness of his temperament. He has no violent passions; one is almost tempted to say that he never feels very deeply. Of course we find pathetic passages in his works,—one can never be a true humorist without some mastery of pathos. There is the famous description of the death of Arcite, who grieves that he must soon be laid in the cold grave,

> Allone,—withouten any companye.

And there is the touching scene in the Man of Law's Tale in which Constance is compelled to put to sea, alone except for the helpless little son. He comes nearer to genuine passion, when, in the Frankeleyns Tale, Dorigen, long separated from her husband, walks up and down the rock-girt shore, a prey to a thousand fears when she sees the cruel rocks on which his ship may perchance be destroyed:

> I woot wel clerkës wol seyn, as hem leste,
> By arguments, that al is for the beste,
> Though I ne can the causes nat y-knowe,
> But thilkë god, that madë wind to blowe,
> As kepe my lord! this my conclusioun;

> To clerkës lete I al disputisoun.
> But woldë god that alle thise rokkës blake
> Were sonken into hellë for his sake!
> Thise rokkës sleen myn hertë for the fere.

Such passages are the exception rather than the rule. For the most part, he avoids the tragic elements in life, or when he cannot, but must face a disagreeable situation whether or no, he has recourse to a series of exclamations which perhaps satisfy his sense of what is expected of a poet under such circumstances, but which leave real pathos and tragedy untouched. He is the poet of merry England, distinguished for his wholesome and sane view of life; he has no time or inclination for the tragic.

Perhaps it is because of this easy-going temper that he shows so little indignation against the abuses of his day, capital as these were. His keen insight detects the evils of the church, the pretense of caste, the charlatanry of science, but he has no zeal for reforming the world. He is by no means a Wycliffe or a Luther. For similar reasons, we find little of that fine lyric rapture which marks the poets of the Romantic movement. He is not morbid like Byron, or introspective like Wordsworth, or a dreamer of dreams like Shelley. He is not, like Dante and Milton, concerned with the mysteries of heaven and hell. He does not care to indulge in conjectures about the future; he cannot tell us about Arcite's experiences after death:

> His spirit chaunged hous, and wente ther,
> As I cam nevere, I can nat tellen wher.

The Puritans conceived life as a pilgrimage from this world to the next; so did Chaucer, but, as Lowell long ago pointed out, it is the scenery of life, not the mysteries of life in which he is interested. It is instructive to compare the pilgrimage described by Bunyan with the Canterbury Pilgrimage. There are plenty of ethical lessons in Chaucer, but they are incidental, to be extracted or left severely alone at the reader's pleasure. In this he is like Shakspere, not a conscious moralist, but a poet whose work, because it is genuine poetry, is sufficiently moral. He is interested in this world, in its abundant life, in its infinite variety. He looks about him and rejoices, because he sees that life, on the whole, is good.

When he finds a man who can teach him more of life than he knew before, his delight is unbounded. Therefore he has an intellectual sympathy even for rascals like the Manciple and the Pardoner; a sympathy for the Monk, who loves hunting above the precepts of Saint Augustine; for the Doctor, whose study is but little on the Bible, and for the Man of Law, who seems always busier than he is. One of the most striking scenes in the poem is that in which the Pardoner is represented as so carried away by his enthusiasm that after exposing all his shameless practices he actually begins to harangue the pilgrims themselves as he harangues his dupes. One can picture the scene: the surprise of the knight; the deep impression upon the unlearned members of the company; the scorn of big Harry Bailly, who becomes so furious that his words are unprintable; while in the background stands the poet himself, his eyes dancing with his pleasure in the astonishing situation but losing no detail. Chaucer seems to take the same delight in such persons and situations as the physician takes in a case which appeals to the utmost to his professional skill. The physician calls it a "beautiful case," though his patient may be mortally ill, and he seems heartless in his enthusiasm. So Chaucer may seem absolutely unmoral in the admiration which he is at no pains to conceal for the master-rogues among the morally deformed and diseased. But his sympathy is intellectual, not moral. His portraits of a "poore Persoun of a Town" and of the Clerk of Oxenford serve to remind us how many-sided were his interests, how keen his enthusiasm for all phases of life. Optimism is his constant companion. There is evil in life, but there is also good, and the good out-balances the evil. To quote his own words in *Troilus:*

> For thilkë ground, that bereth the wedës wikke,
> Bereth eek thise holsom herbës, as ful ofte
> Next the foulë netle, rough and thikke,
> The rosë waxeth swote and smothe and softe;
> And next the valey is the hil a-lofte;
> And next the derkë night the gladë morwe;
> And also joye is next the fyn[1] of sorwe.

IV. Pronunciation

In the centuries that have passed since Chaucer's time many changes have taken place in the pronunciation of English words. Not a few of our present vowel

---

[1] *End.*

sounds have been known only since the seventeenth century, while if actors should pronounce the text of Shakspere's plays as the great dramatist himself would have done, the average man would find it practically impossible to understand the words. In Chaucer's time, not only were the vowel sounds still more remote from present usage, but the language preserved some traces of the Anglo-Saxon inflectional endings, so that the scansion of verses is materially affected. Anglo-Saxon, while not so highly inflected as Latin, preserved the characteristics of the Germanic group of languages. Owing to a variety of causes which cannot be treated here, the constant tendency, after the Norman Conquest, was to level the inflectional endings to -e (for the genitive, -es). In Modern English these final syllables, always pronounced in Chaucer's time, have fallen off. Often the letter remains, as for example the -e of *come*, but it is not pronounced. When Chaucer was read by Englishmen of the sixteenth and seventeenth centuries, they attempted to pronounce the words according to their own standards, not giving the proper emphasis to the final syllables, with the result that he seemed uncouth and unmusical. One has only to read the first few lines of the Prologue, before studying this chapter any further, pronouncing them as one would pronounce lines from Tennyson, to be satisfied as to the apparent lack of any consideration for metre. Indeed, in the sixteenth century it was seriously supposed by a group of English students of which the youthful Spenser was a member, that Chaucer deliberately wrote his lines of uneven length and irregular accent, and that he observed some such laws of quantity as those which governed the writing of Latin verse. So they tried to determine his laws of "quantity" and to write verse of a similar character, with the most lamentable results.

In the latter part of the nineteenth century, a great revival of interest in Chaucer manifested itself in England and in the United States. Some of the profoundest of modern scholars have studied his works as faithfully as Shakspere has been studied, with the result that now we know his language, his pronunciation, and the laws of his verse almost as well as if we had been taught by the master himself. For a complete discussion of these difficult problems, one must look elsewhere; the aim here is to present the subject of pronunciation and metre in the very simplest possible form.[1] The student will find it convenient to prepare a small card having on it the vowel and consonant sounds, and to keep this as a bookmark, pronouncing the text aloud from the first and referring to the card when necessary. A little time spent in this way at the outset, especially if supplemented by careful reading aloud by the teacher, will enable the beginner to read his Chaucer with pleasure and advantage.

---

[1] The teacher should, of course, be familiar with the discussions on these subjects in Skeat's *Oxford Chaucer*, Vol. VI. Professor Hempl's *Chaucer's Pronunciation*, now unfortunately out of print, will be most helpful if the teacher can secure a copy from some library. The great authority on the subject is the book by A. J. Ellis, on *Early English Pronunciation*, very useful for the teacher, but entirely too technical for the beginner.

THE VOWELS

In accented syllables the vowels have approximately the following values:

a as in the first syllable of *aha*, never as in *cat*.

ā as in *art, father*.

ai, ay as in *aisle*.

e as in *met*.

ē (open) as in *there*.

ē (close) as in *they*.

i, y as in *fin*.

ī, ȳ as in *machine*.

ei, ey as in *they*.

o as in *hot;* except in words in which the vowel has in modern English the sound of *o* in *son, company,* etc., where it has the sound of *u* in *put, full,* German *dumm*.

ō (open) as in *orb*.

ō, ōō (close) as in *coke*

oi, oy as in *noise*.

u as in *put*.

ū as in German *grün*. To make this sound, round the lips as in whistling, then try to pronounce the *ē* in modern English *green*.

au, aw as in *count*.

eu, ew, as *ē* (open) + *u* as in *fool*. The sound is very similar to the dialectic pronunciation of *cow, now, town,* etc. (i.e., *caow, naow, taown*). To make this sound, pretend to mock a person who uses such pronunciation. In a few common words derived from the French (*vertu, vertuous, Jhesu,* etc.), the *u* has the same sound.

ou, ow as *o* in *lord* (= open *o*) + *u* (*moon*). But *ou, ow*, are often written for *u* or *o*, under the influence of French spelling. In such cases, the sound is as *ou* in *soup*. This spelling is frequent in suffixes (*-cioun, -sioun, -ous*, etc.), and is also found in such words as *hous, flour, ground, amount, croune, doute*, etc.

In unaccented syllables, final *-e* has the sound of *a* in *idea*.

REMARK 1. Vowels are open or close, according as the mouth opening is larger in the one sound than in the other. (For these and other phonetic distinctions consult Emerson, *History of the English Language*, ch. XII.) The modern English spelling for what in Chaucer's time was open *e* is usually *ea*, as in *clean, steal, deal, heat*, etc.; close *e* is usually *ee, e*, as in *steel, we*, etc. Again, in modern English Chaucer's open *o* is usually written *oa*, as in *oak, road, boat*, etc., though it may be *o* as in *stone*; close *o*, on the other hand, changed into *oo*, as in *moon, root, fool, tooth, food*, etc. Thinking of the modern spelling of Chaucer's word will therefore help the student to decide whether the open or the close pronunciation is to be given $\bar{e}, \bar{o}$.

REMARK 2. Where *w* is used as a vowel, as in *yelw*, etc., it has the sound of *u* in *put*.

REMARK 3. In unaccented syllables, vowels may be pronounced as in accented syllables, if the secondary stress be strong. The same remark applies, as a rule, to prefixes. Syncope often takes place, as in *ev(e)re, nev(e)re, op(e)nen, ar(e)n*. Elision will be treated under scansion.

THE CONSONANTS

In general, the consonants were pronounced as in modern English. The most important variations may be noted as follows: (1) *r* was strongly trilled; (2) *s* between vowels had the sound of *z;* (3) *f* between vowels had the sound of *v;* (4) every letter was sounded; the *k* in *know* and the *-l* of *-lk* were not silent; (5) *-gh* had the sound of German *-ch*, as in *Buch* (*ch* in Chaucer was always sounded as in *rich*, never as in *machine* or in *chemist*); (6) *s* or *c* or *t* before *e* or *i* never had the modern sound *-sh*; *-sion, -tion*, etc. = *si* + *on, ti* + *on*, etc.; (7) *g* was as in *gay*, except before *e* and *i* in words derived from French, where it was as in *gin*.

V. INFLECTION

The name Anglo-Saxon or Old English is given to the English language as spoken during the years preceding the Norman Conquest; Middle English is the designation of the language from the Conquest to the latter part of the fifteenth century; Modern English dates from the end of the Middle English period. It should be understood that no arbitrary dates can be assigned for these transitions. In Anglo-Saxon times the language was near enough to its Teutonic ancestry to preserve a fairly well developed system of inflection. Since the Norman Conquest, however, with the great changes which it brought, and in consequence of a tendency operative in all languages, these inflectional endings have been sloughed off, until only a few words and phrases remain to show us that our language was ever inflected. In Chaucer's time, however, words were still inflected to a certain extent. It is impossible to read Chaucer's verse without taking these forms into consideration.[1]

NOUNS

An Anglo-Saxon noun belonging to the first declension was inflected as follows:

   Sing. N., A. dom   *Pl.* N., A. domas
            G. domes   G. doma
            D. dome   D. domum

By Chaucer's time these case endings remained only as a syllabic *-e* or *-es*. In the genitive singular the *-es* remained, and in the plural the nominative *-as* had changed to *-es* and was used in all the cases. Some further observations upon Chaucer's forms may be made:

(1) The genitive singular, as already noted, usually ends in *-es*; as *lordes werre* (*Prol.* 47). But (a) if the Anglo-Saxon form of the word had some other genitive ending than *-es*, or had none at all, the word in Chaucer often has none. Examples are *fader soule* (*Prol.* 81); *lady grace* (*Prol.* 88). (b) Proper names in *-s* do not take the ending: *Epicurus owne sone* (*Prol.* 336).

(2) The dative singular is sometimes marked by *-e*. This is true particularly in phrases which have been

---

[1] The student of Chaucer should know something of the history of the English language. By all odds the best brief account is to be found in Greenough and Kittredge's *Words and Their Ways in English Speech*, chapters VII, VIII, IX. A more detailed account may be found in one of the works on the subject, such as Emerson's *History of the English Language*. Selected chapters from this may be made the subject of special reports at the discretion of the teacher.

used so frequently that they have become "petrified"; as, *to reste* (*Prol.* 30).[1]

(3) All cases of the plural usually terminate in *-es* or *-s*. To this rule, however, as in modern English, there are a few exceptions:

(a) A number of plurals in *-n*, *-en*, are found, sometimes the remnants of an old Anglo-Saxon plural in *-an*, and sometimes by analogy, as, *asschen, eyen, fon, ton, shoon*. These forms are common in Spenser and Milton; in modern English examples are, *children, oxen, brethren*, etc.

(b) In some nouns, usually because of the influence of the Anglo-Saxon forms, no plural termination is found: *deer, folk, yeer, thing*, etc.

(c) As in modern English, a few examples of vowel change are noted: *teeth, men, gees*, etc.

ADJECTIVES

(1) The definite form of the adjective (i.e., one preceded by the definite article, a possessive pronoun, or a demonstrative) ends in *-e* in all cases, singular and plural; the indefinite form is uninflected in the singular, but takes *-e* in the plural.

(2) But in adjectives of more than one syllable the *-e* is often omitted.

(3) The vocative case of adjectives always ends in

---

[1] It is rather more accurate to say that the dative in Chaucer had no inflectional termination, but preserved an *-e* in certain inherited phrases, such as *to toune, to bedde*, etc. Chaucer was not consciously inflecting. For a full discussion, cf. Kittredge, *Observations on the Language of Chaucer's Troilus*, pp. 36-38.

-e.[1] Adjectives modifying proper names usually also take -e.

(4) As a rule, the comparative is formed as in modern English; sometimes -re is found, as in *ferre* (farther). Vowel change, as in the modern *elder*, is also found, as in *lenger*, *strenger*, etc.

(5) The superlative takes -est.

ADVERBS

Most adverbs in Chaucer end in -e; some have -ely (*trewely*, *softely*, etc.). In a few instances, also, adverbs formed by the addition of the genitive termination -es to nouns and adjectives remain in Chaucer: as, *needes*,[2] *whiles*, *his thankes* (for his part = willingly).

PRONOUNS

(1) The first person nominative is either *I* or *Ich;* genitive, *min* or *my;* the other cases are as in modern usage.

(2) The second personal pronoun is inflected:

Sing.	N. thou	*Pl.*	N. ye
	G. thin, thi		G. your(e)
	D., A. the, thee		D., A. yow, you

(3) The genitive of the neuter third person singular is *his; its* did not come into use until the seventeenth century, the King James version of the Bible (1611)

---

[1] The student should carefully note all the forms in which the syllabic *-e* is preserved, as the bearing upon versification is important. A list of these uses may be made from this grammatical introduction; e.g., "petrified" dative; vocative adjective; plural adjective, etc.

[2] Cf. the modern "He must needs go," in which *needs* is really an old genitive = he must go of necessity, or necessarily.

using the form *his*. The plural third person has nominative *they* (a Northern form); genitive *here, hir, her;* dative and accusative *hem*.

VERBS

Weak verbs in Chaucer have in the present singular the terminations *-e, -est, -eth;* in the plural *-en* or *-e*. The termination is always syllabic. In the preterit singular, the endings are *-ede, -edest, -ede;* plural, *-eden* or *-ede*. The final *e* in *-ede* was probably dropped in colloquial use, and does not appear uniformly in the MSS. A few verbs show contracted forms, such as *sit* for *sitteth; stont* for *stondeth; rist* for *riseth*. We also find *-de, -te* in the preterit (*kepen, kepte; heren, herde; letten, lette*, etc.); and in a few cases vowel change; as, *leden* (lead), preterit *ladde; leven* (leave) *lafte; tellen, tolde; sellen, solde; sechen, soughte*.

Strong verbs have vowel-change in the preterit; usually these changes are preserved in modern English, and separate lists need not be given.[1] The student should observe, when he comes upon them in his reading, just what forms Chaucer uses for his preterites and participles in strong verbs. It should be noted here, however, that the first and third persons preterit singular of strong verbs do not take a final *-e*, but this termination marks the plurals; as, *ryden;* pret. sing., *rood* or *rod;* pret. pl., *rode* or *riden*, ppl., *riden*. Except in a few cases, the second person preterit ends in *-e*.

---

[1] Except where differences are noted in what follows, the terminations of the strong verbs are the same as in the case of the weak verbs.

The present subjunctive of both weak and strong verbs terminates in *-e*. This is syllabic, and should be carefully noted as one of the uses of syllabic *-e* in scansion. A syllabic *-e* is sometimes the termination, also, of the imperative (*love, telle*); but in most cases the imperative has no inflectional ending. Usually the plural imperative ends in *-eth*. The infinitive ends in *-en*, sometimes *-e*. Present participles end in *-ing*, as in modern English; strong past participles in *-en* or *-e;* weak past participles in *-ed, -d*. Frequently an initial *y-* or *i-* is found (cf. Milton's *yclept*); this is from the Anglo-Saxon participial prefix *ge-*.

A few anomalous verbs, such as *ben, been* (to be), *may, shal, wil, witen* (to know), etc., are found in Chaucer as in modern English. The forms are usually similar to those with which the student is familiar, and will be noted in the glossary.

For the convenience of the student the following table of inflectional endings is inserted:

Weak Verbs

PRESENT INDICATIVE
Sing. 1. -e
      2. -est
      3. -eth
Pl.   -en, -e

PRETERIT INDICATIVE
Sing. 1. -ede, -de, -te
      2. -edest, -dest, -test
      3. -ede, -de, -te
Pl.   -ede(n), -ed, -de(n), -te(n)

PRESENT SUBJUNCTIVE
Sing. -e
Pl.   -e, -en

PRETERIT SUBJUNCTIVE
Sing. -ede, -de, -te
Pl.   -ede(n), -de(n), -te(n)

PRESENT IMPERATIVE

Sing. -e   *Pl.* -eth, -e

PARTICIPLES

Present, -ing(e)   *Past,* -ed, -d, -t

Strong Verbs

Present Indicative and Subjunctive, same as in weak verbs.

PRETERIT INDICATIVE

Sing. 1. —   *Pl.* -e, -en
      2. -e
      3. —

PRETERIT SUBJUNCTIVE

Sing. -e   *Pl.* -e, -en

PRESENT IMPERATIVE

Sing. —   *Pl.* -eth, -e

PARTICIPLES

Present, -ing(e)   *Past,* -e, -en, -n

VI. Versification

The following laws govern the scansion of Chaucer's verse:

(1) The majority of the Canterbury Tales are written in five accent iambic lines, rhyming in couplets. There are thus ten syllables in the normal line, the stresses usually coming upon alternate syllables; but many lines contain eleven syllables, and, less frequently, lines having only nine are found. In most lines having eleven

syllables, the addition is found in the last foot, is unaccented, and is generally due to the presence of a final *-e*. The student should exercise great care not to omit this final syllable; *soote*, *roote* (*Prol.*, ll. 1, 2), etc., are dissyllabic. In lines having but nine syllables, the first foot lacks the unstressed syllable. Examples are *Prol.* 170, 247, 294, 371, 391. There are about twenty such lines in the *Knight's Tale*.

(2) As often in modern verse, a final vowel preceding an initial vowel in the next word is elided. Elision is also frequent before pronouns beginning with *h* and before forms of the auxiliary verb *have*.

The drŏghte ŏf Marche hăth pĕrced tŏ thĕ rootĕ.
—Prol. 2.

But,

Ĭn ălle hăste cŏm tŏ mē, hĕ saȳdĕ.
—N. P. T. 187.

Often words are contracted, or two words are pronounced, frequently written, as one: *whether* becomes *wher*; *ne am*, *ne is*, *ne hadde*, etc., become *nam*, *nis*, *nadde*, etc. *Evere*, *nevere*, etc., are dissyllabic, as in

Thăn ĕv(e)rĕ Cătoŭn wăs, sŏ mŏot Ĭ theĕ.
—N. P. T. 156.

Fŏr hĭm wăs lĕv(e)r(e) hăve ăt hĭs bĕddĕs heĕd.
—Prol. 293.

This tendency to slur an unstressed *-e-*, especially in the syllables *-er*, *-eth*, *-el*, etc., is also shown by the lines:

> She gád(e)reth floures párty whýt(e) and réde.
> —K. T. 195.

> The hóte som(e)r (h)adde máad his hew(e) ál broun.
> —Prol. 394.

> By wát(e)r he sente hem hóm to év(e)rý lond.
> —Prol. 400.

Other examples, if at all difficult, will be cited in the notes.

(3) Care must be taken not to adopt the modern method of pronouncing words, thereby often eliding a syllable. Unless some other rule interferes, each vowel in Chaucer marks a syllable. It will not do to pronounce *dayesye* as a dissyllable; it is *day + es + y + e*, with a secondary accent on *-y-*. Words in *-yë* are especially frequent at the ends of lines, and both syllables must be fully sounded. Again, final *-es*, *-en*, and *-ed* must be pronounced, as in *nedës, escapën, entunëd*. Sometimes *-ede* is found in weak preterits, and this may show syncopation of the first *-e-:*

> So hót(e) he lóv(e)de, that by níghtertálë.
> —Prol. 97.

But this rule, like most of the others just cited for elision, is permissive only, not absolute:

> And óf manhód him lákkede right naúght.
> —Prol. 756.

Comments on the metrical forms of the selections from the lyrics will be found at the proper places in the notes.

VII. Bibliographical Note

The best brief biography is the *Chaucer Primer*, by A. W. Pollard, published by Macmillan & Co. Somewhat longer is the volume on Chaucer by A. W. Ward in the English Men of Letters Series. For criticism, convenient references are the chapters on Chaucer in Courthope's *History of English Poetry*, Vol. I, and in Ten Brink's *History of English Literature*. In Jusserand's *Literary History of the English People*, Vol. I, the English translation of which is published by the Putnams, is a most delightful chapter. Lowell's essay, in the Riverside edition of his works, Vol. III, remains one of the best critical discussions yet written. Professor Lounsbury's *Studies in Chaucer*, in three volumes, is a mine of interesting material for the Chaucer enthusiast. Some of it is too difficult for the beginner, but selected topics may be assigned with profit, especially in the chapter on "Chaucer's Learning." Dr. R. K. Root's *The Poetry of Chaucer* (Houghton, 1906), contains much useful material in a convenient form.

As for texts, the standard authority is the great Oxford Chaucer, edited by Professor W. W. Skeat, and published in six volumes by the Clarendon Press. There is a convenient one-volume edition of this text, with a rather limited introduction but with an excellent glossary. The only other standard single volume text is the "Globe Chaucer," published by Macmillan & Co.

Much interesting supplementary material is available. Perhaps the best single volume is Jusserand's *English Wayfaring Life in the XIV Century*. a copy of which should be in every school library. Tudor Jenks's *In the Days of Chaucer* (Barnes), is a readable book, but of elementary type and no great value. *The Road from London to Canterbury*, edited by Henry Littlehales for the Chaucer Society, is interesting, as is also the chapter on roads and travel in *Glimmerings in the Dark*, by F. S. Merryweather.

On the philological questions which any serious study of Chaucer is sure to involve, a number of important works may be named. Professor Hempl's little book, *Chaucer's Pronunciation*, if available, will help materially. The most exhaustive study of Middle English pronunciation is A. J. Ellis's *Early English Pronunciation*, published by the Early English Text Society. It is entirely too technical for the beginner, but the teacher may consult it with profit. Ten Brink's *Language and Metre of Chaucer* is of course a standard work; it is available in an English translation (Macmillan). Professor Kittredge's *Observations on the Language of Chaucer's Troilus* (Ginn) is a most useful reference book for teachers. For students, the most convenient Middle English Grammar is found in Emerson's *Middle English Reader* (Macmillan, 1905). The same author's *History of the English Language* is readable and scholarly. Greenough and Kittredge's *Words and their Ways in English Speech* (Macmillan) contains an excellent brief history of the language together with a vast amount of interesting material upon the histories of words.

Some important recent magazine articles bearing upon questions discussed in this book may be named. An article on "The Duration of the Canterbury Pilgrimage," by Dr. J. S. P. Tatlock, is printed in the *Publications of the Modern Language Association* for June, 1906. Important studies in Chaucerian chronology are those by Dr. Tatlock, *Modern Philology*, Vol. I, and by Dr. J. L. Lowes in the *Publications*, Vol. XX, p. 749. Other articles are referred to in the introduction and notes. In general, the teacher should be on the lookout for new material on Chaucer in such journals as *Modern Philology, Modern Language Notes,* and the *Publications of the Modern Language Association.*

SELECTIONS FROM CHAUCER

THE PROLOGUE

HERE BEGYNNETH THE BOOK OF THE TALES OF CANTERBURY

Whan that Aprille with his shoures soote
The droghte of Marche hath perced to the roote
And bathed every veyne in swich licour,
Of which vertu engendred is the flour;
Whan Zephirus eek with his swete breeth   5
Inspired hath in every holt and heeth
The tendre croppes, and the yonge sonne
Hath in the Ram his halfe cours y-ronne,
And smale fowles maken melodye,
That slepen al the night with open yë,   10
So priketh hem nature in hir corages:
Than longen folk to goon on pilgrimages,
And palmers for to seken straunge strondes,
To ferne halwes, couthe in sondry londes;
And specially, from every shires ende   15
Of Engelond, to Caunterbury they wende,
The holy blisful martir for to seke,

---

9. E., *foweles*; Pt., Ln., *foules*.

10. E., *eye*. The scribes were often confused in the use of the two forms of this word.

12. E., *thanne*; Pt., Ln., *than*; E., *pilgrimage*, clearly a mistake, as the rhyme shows.

13. E., *Palmeres*.

That hem hath holpen whan that they were seke.
  Bifel that in that sesoun on a day,
20 In Southwerk at the Tabard as I lay,
  Redy to wenden on my pilgrimage
  To Caunterbury with ful devout corage,
  At night were come into that hostelrye
  Wel nyne and twenty in a compaignye,
25 Of sondry folk, by aventure y-falle
  In felawshipe, and pilgrims were they alle,
  That toward Caunterbury wolden ryde.
  The chambres and the stables weren wyde,
  And wel we weren esed atte beste.
30 And shortly, whan the sonne was to reste,
  So hadde I spoken with hem everychon,
  That I was of hir felawshipe anon,
  And made forward erly for to ryse,
  To take our wey, ther as I yow devyse.
35   But natheles, whyl I have tyme and space,
  Er that I ferther in this tale pace,
  Me thinketh it acordaunt to resoun
  To telle yow al the condicioun
  Of ech of hem, so as it semed me,
40 And whiche they weren, and of what degree;
  And eek in what array that they were inne:
  And at a knyght than wol I first biginne.

  A Knyght ther was, and that a worthy man,
  That fro the tyme that he first bigan

---

19. E., *Bifil.*
23. E., *were*, rest *was.*
26. E., *felaweship, pilgrimes.*
32. E., *felaweship.*
35. E., *nathelees.*
40. E., *were*; Hl., *weren.*

PROLOGUE

To riden out, he lovede chivalrye, 45
Trouthe and honour, fredom and curteisye.
Ful worthy was he in his lordes werre,
And therto hadde he riden, no man ferre,
As wel in cristendom as in hethenesse,
And ever honoured for his worthinesse. 50
At Alisaundre he was, whan it was wonne;
Ful ofte tyme he hadde the bord bigonne
Aboven alle naciouns in Pruce.
In Lettow hadde he reysed and in Ruce,
No Cristen man so ofte of his degree. 55
In Gernade at the seege eek hadde he be
Of Algezir, and riden in Belmarye.
At Lyeys was he, and at Satalye,
Whan they were wonne; and in the Grete See
At many a noble armee hadde he be. 60
At mortal batailles hadde he been fiftene,
And foughten for our feith at Tramyssene
In lystes thryes, and ay slayn his foo.
This ilke worthy knyght hadde been also
Somtyme with the lord of Palatye, 65
Agayn another hethen in Turkye:
And evermore he hadde a sovereyn prys.
And though that he were worthy, he was wys,
And of his port as meeke as is a mayde.
He never yet no vileinye ne sayde 70
In al his lyf, unto no maner wight.

---

45. E., *chivalrie*; *curteisie*.
49. Hn., omits *in*; rest insert.
53. E., *nacions*.
60. E., Hn., *armee*; Cp., Ln., *arme*; Hl., *ariue*; Cm., *aryue* (u = v).
68. E., Hn., Cm., *were*, rest *was*.

He was a verray, parfit, gentil knyght.
But for to tellen yow of his array,
His hors weren goode, but he was nat gay.
75 Of fustian he wered a gipoun
Al bismotered with his habergeoun.
For he was late y-come from his viage,
And wente for to doon his pilgrymage.

With him ther was his sone, a yong Squyer,
80 A lovyer, and a lusty bacheler,
With lokkes crulle, as they were leyd in presse.
Of twenty yeer of age he was, I gesse.
Of his stature he was of evene lengthe,
And wonderly delyvere, and greet of strengthe.
85 And he hadde been somtyme in chivachye,
In Flaundres, in Artoys, and Picardye,
And born him wel, as of so litel space,
In hope to stonden in his lady grace.
Embrouded was he, as it were a mede
90 Al ful of fresshe floures, whyte and rede.
Singing he was, or floyting, al the day;
He was as fresh as is the monthe of May.
Short was his gowne, with sleves longe and wyde.
Wel coude he sitte on hors, and faire ryde.
95 He coude songes make and wel endyte,
Juste and eek daunce, and wel purtreye and wryte.
So hote he lovede, that by nyghtertale
He sleep namore than doth a nyghtingale.

---

74. E., Pt., *weren*; Hl., Ln., *was*; rest *were*.
92. E., *in*, rest *is*.
98. E., *slepte*; so all but Hl., Cp., *sleep*.

PROLOGUE

Curteys he was, lowely and servisable,
And carf bitorn his fader at the table.   100

A Yeman hadde he, and servaunts namo
At that tyme, for him liste ryde so;
And he was clad in cote and hood of grene;
A sheef of pecok arwes bright and kene
Under his belt he bar ful thriftily,   105
(Wel coude he dresse his takel yemanly;
His arwes drouped noght with fetheres lowe,)
And in his hand he bar a mighty bowe.
A not-heed hadde he, with a broun visage.
Of wode-craft wel coude he al the usage.   110
Upon his arm he bar a gay bracer,
And by his syde a swerd and a bokeler,
And on that other syde a gay daggere,
Harneised wel, and sharp as poynt of spere;
A Cristofre on his brest of silver shene.   115
An horn he bar, the bawdrik was of grene;
A forster was he, soothly, as I gesse.

Ther was also a Nonne, a Prioresse,
That of hir smyling was ful simple and coy;
Hir gretteste ooth was but by Seynte Loy;   120
And she was cleped madame Eglentyne.
Ful wel she song the service divyne
Entuned in hir nose ful semely;
And Frensh she spak ful faire and fetisly,

---

101. E., *seruantz*.
104. All have *bright* exc. Cm., *bryghte*.
115. E., *-phere*; Hn., *-fre*.
120. Pt., only has *seynte*, rest *seint*.

THE CANTERBURY TALES

125 After the scole of Stratford-atte-Bowe,
For Frensh of Paris was to hir unknowe.
At mete wel y-taught was she withalle;
She leet no morsel from hir lippes falle,
Ne wette hir fingres in hir sauce depe.
130 Wel coude she carie a morsel, and wel kepe
Thát no drope ne fille upon hir brest.
In curteisye was set ful muchel hir lest.
Hir over lippe wyped she so clene,
That in hir coppe ther was no ferthing sene
135 Of grece, whan she dronken hadde hir draughte.
Ful semely after hir mete she raughte,
And sikerly she was of greet disport,
And ful plesaunt, and amiable of port,
And peyned hir to countrefete chere
140 Of court, and been estatlich of manere,
And to ben holden digne of reverence.
But, for to speken of hir conscience,
She was so charitable and so pitous,
She wolde wepe if that she sawe a mous
145 Caught in a trappe, if it were deed or bledde.
Of smale houndes had she, that she fedde
With rosted flesh, or milk and wastel breed.
But sore wepte she if oon of hem were deed,

---

131. E. *brist.*
132. E., *muchel*; so Hn., Ln.; Cm., *meche*; Cp., *moche.*, Pt., *mochel.*
132. E. *list.*   133. E., *hire.*
134. Hl., om. *ther*, rest ins.
137. E., *desport*; so Hn., rest *dis-*.
140. E. *to been*; Hn., Hl., om. *to*.
144. E., *saugh*; Cp., Hn., Hl., *sawe.*
146. Pt., Ln., *had*, rest *hadde*
148. E. *wepte*; so all but Ln., *wepped.* Skeat reads *weep.*

PROLOGUE

Or if men smoot it with a yerde smerte;
And al was conscience and tendre herte.   150
Ful semely hir wimpel pinched was:
Hir nose tretys; hir eyen greye as glas;
Hir mouth ful smal and therto softe and reed,
But sikerly she hadde a fair forheed,—
It was almost a spanne brood, I trowe;   155
For, hardily, she was nat undergrowe.
Ful fetis was hir cloke, as I was war.
Of smal coral aboute hir arm she bar
A peire of bedes gauded al with grene,
And thereon heng a broche of gold ful shene,   160
On which ther was first write a crowned A,
And after, *Amor vincit omnia*. — (Love conquers all)

Another Nonne with hir hadde she,
That was hir chapeleyne, and Preestes thre.

A Monk ther was, a fair for the maistrye,   165
An outridere that lovede venerye;
A manly man, to been an abbot able.
Ful many a deyntee hors hadde he in stable:
And whan he rood men mighte his brydel here
Gynglen in a whistling wynd as clere,   170
And eek as loude as doth the chapel belle,
Ther as this lord was keper of the celle.
The reule of seynt Maure or of seynt Beneit,—
By-cause that it was old and som-del streit,
This ilke monk leet olde thinges pace,   175

---

151. E. *semyly, wympul*.
160. E., Hn., *brooch*, rest *broche*.
170. E., *whistlynge, als,* Hl., *whistlyng . . . so.* Cp., Hn., Pt., *as*.

And held after the newe world the space.
He yaf nat of that text a pulled hen
That seith that hunters been nat holy men;
Ne that a monk whan he is recchelees
180 Is likned til a fish that is waterlees;
This is to seyn, a monk out of his cloystre.
But thilke text held he nat worth an oystre.
And I seyde his opinioun was good.
What sholde he studie, and make himselven wood,
185 Upon a book in cloystre alwey to poure,
Or swynken with his handes, and laboure,
As Austyn bit? How shal the world be served?
Lat Austyn have his swynk to him reserved.
Therfore he was a pricasour aright;
190 Grehoundes he hadde, as swifte as fowel in flight;
Of priking and of hunting for the hare
Was al his lust, for no cost wolde he spare.
I seigh his sleves purfiled at the hond
With grys, and that the fyneste of a lond;
195 And for to festne his hood under his chin,
He hadde of gold wroght a ful curious pin;
A love-knot in the gretter ende ther was.
His heed was balled, that shoon as any glas,
And eek his face, as he hadde been anoynt.
200 He was a lord ful fat and in good poynt;

---

178. E., *beth*, so Ln.; Hn., *been*; Cm., *ben*; Cp., Pt., *be*.
179. E., Hn., *recchelees*, Cm., *rekeles*; Cp., *recheles.*; Hl., *cloysterlees*.
188. E., *owene swynk*; rest om.
190. E., *swift*; so rest exc. Hl., *swifte*.
193. E., *ypurfiled*; Hn., Cm. Ln., om. *y*.
196. E., *ywroght*; all but Hl. insert *ful*.
199. E., *it*; rest *he*.

PROLOGUE

His eyen stepe, and rollinge in his heed,
That stemed as a forneys of a leed;
His bootes souple, his hors in greet estat.
Now certeynly he was a fair prelat;
He was nat pale as a for-pyned goost.   205
A fat swan loved he best of any roost.
His palfrey was as broun as is a berye.

A Frere ther was, a wantown and a merye,
A lymytour, a ful solempne man.
In alle the ordres foure is noon that can   210
So muche of daliaunce and fair langage.
He hadde maad ful many a mariage
Of yonge wommen at his owne cost.
Unto his ordre he was a noble post.
Ful wel biloved and famulier was he   215
With frankeleyns overal in his contree;
And eek with worthy wommen of the toun,
For he hadde power of confessioun,
As seyde himself, more than a curat,
For of his ordre he was licentiat.   220
Ful swetely herde he confessioun,
And plesaunt was his absolucioun;
He was an esy man to yeve penaunce
Ther as he wiste to have a good pitaunce;
For unto a povre ordre for to yive   225

---

208. E.,-*towne*.
211. E., *muchel*; Hn., *muche*, so Ln.; Hl., *moche*.
213. E., *owene*.
215. E., *and*; rest *ful*.
217. Hn., Hl., *eek*; rest om.
224. Cm., Hl., *han*; E., *haue*.

Is signe that a man is wel y-shrive;
For if he yaf, he dorste make avaunt,
He wiste that a man was repentaunt:
For many a man so hard is of his herte,
230 He may nat wepe althogh him sore smerte;
Therfore, in stede of weping and preyeres,
Men moote yeve silver to the povre freres.
His tipet was ay farsed ful of knyves
And pinnes, for to yeven faire wyves.
235 And certeinly he hadde a mery note;
Wel coude he singe and pleyen on a rote;
Of yeddinges he bar utterly the prys.
His nekke whit was as the flour-de-lys.
Therto he strong was as a champioun.
240 He knew the tavernes wel in every toun,
And everich hostiler and tappestere
Bet than a lazar or a beggestere;
For unto swich a worthy man as he
Acorded nat, as by his facultee,
245 To have with seke lazars aqueyntaunce.
It is nat honest, it may nat avaunce
Fór to delen with no swich poraille,
But al with riche and sellers of vitaille.
And overal, ther as profit sholde aryse,
250 Curteys he was, and lowly of servyse.
Ther nas no man nowher so vertuous.

---

229. E., *harde*.   234. E., *yonge*; rest *faire*
235. E., *murye*; Hl., *mery*.
237. E., *outrely*; Pt., Hl., *uttirly, utturly*.
240. E., *al the*; rest *every*.
245. E., *sike*.   Pt., Ln., *seke*. Cf. l. 18.
248. E., *selleres*.   250. E., *lowely*.

He was the beste beggere in his hous,
For thogh a wydwe hadde noght a sho,
So plesaunt was his *In principio*,
Yet wolde he have a ferthing, er he wente: 255
His purchas was wel bettre than his rente.
And rage he coude as it were right a whelpe.
In love-dayes ther coude he muchel helpe.
For ther he was nat lyk a cloisterer,
With a thredbar cope, as is a povre scoler,   260
But he was lyk a maister or a pope.
Of double worsted was his semi-cope,
That rounded as a belle, out of the presse.
Somwhat he lipsed, for his wantownesse,
To make his English swete upon his tonge;   265
And in his harping, whan that he had songe,
His eyen twinkled in his heed aright,
As doon the sterres in the frosty night.
This worthy lymytour was cleped Huberd.

A Marchant was ther with a forked berd,   270
In motteleye, and hye on horse he sat,
Upon his heed a Flaundrish bever hat;
His botes clasped faire and fetisly.
His resons he spak ful solempnely,
Sowninge alway thencrees of his winning.   275
He wolde the see were kept for any thing
Bitwixe Middelburgh and Orewelle.

---

259. E., *cloystrer*.
260. E., *thredbare*.
262. E., *worstede*.
266. Pt., Ln., *had*, rest *hadde*.
271. E., *motlee*; Ln., *motteley*; Hl., *motteleye*.
272. E., *bevere*.
274. E., *hise*.

Wel coude he in eschaunge sheeldes selle.
This worthy man ful wel his wit bisette;
280 Ther wiste no wight that he was in dette,
So estatly was he of his governaunce,
With his bargaynes, and with his chevisaunce.
For sothe he was a worthy man withalle,
But sooth to seyn, I noot how men him calle.

285   A Clerk ther was of Oxenford also,
That unto logik hadde longe y-go.
As lene was his hors as is a rake,
And he nas nat right fat, I undertake;
But loked holwe, and therto sobrely.
290 Ful thredbare was his overest courtepy;
For he hadde geten him yet no benefice,
Ne was so worldly for to have office.
For him was levere have at his beddes heed
Twénty bookes, clad in blak or reed,
295 Of Aristotle and his philosophye,
Than robes riche, or fithele, or gay sautrye.
But al be that he was a philosophre,
Yet hadde he but litel gold in cofre;
But al that he mighte of his freendes hente,
300 On bookes and his lerninge he it spente,
And bisily gan for the soules preye
Of hem that yaf him wherwith to scoleye.
Of studie took he most cure and most hede.
Noght o word spak he more than was nede,

---

287. E., *and*; Hl., *at so*; rest *as*.
290. E., *overeste*.
300. E., *his*; so Hl., rest *on*.

PROLOGUE

And that was seyd in forme and reverence, 305
And short and quyk, and ful of hy sentence.
Sowninge in moral vertu was his speche,
And gladly wolde he lerne, and gladly teche.

A Sergeant of the Lawe, war and wys,
That often hadde been at the Parvys, 310
Ther was also, ful riche of excellence.
Discreet he was, and of greet reverence:
He semed swich, his wordes weren so wyse.
Justice he was ful often in assyse,
By patente and by pleyn commissioun; 315
For his science and for his heigh renoun
Of fees and robes hadde he many oon.
So greet a purchasour was nowher noon.
Al was fee simple to him in effect,
His purchasing mighte nat been infect. 320
Nowher so bisy a man as he ther nas,
And yet he semed bisier than he was.
In termes hadde he caas and doomes alle,
That from the tyme of king William were falle.
Therto he coude endyte, and make a thing, 325
Ther coude no wight pinche at his wryting;
And every statut coude he pleyn by rote.
He rood but hoomly in a medlee cote,
Girt with a ceynt of silk, with barres smale;
Of his array telle I no lenger tale. 330

A Frankeleyn was in his compaignye;

---

313. E., *hise*.   326. E., *pynchen*, so Hn.
324. E., *yfalle*, rest *falle*.

Whit was his berd as is the dayesye;
Of his complexioun he was sangwyn.
Wel loved he by the morwe a sope in wyn.
335 To liven in delit was ever his wone,
For he was Epicurus owne sone,
That heeld opinioun that pleyn delit
Was verraily felicitee parfit.
An housholdere, and that a greet, was he;
340 Seynt Julian he was in his contree.
His breed, his ale, was alwey after oon;
A bettre envyned man was nowher noon.
Withouten bake mete was nevere his hous,
Of fish and flesh, and that so plentevous,
345 It snewed in his hous of mete and drinke,
Of alle deyntees that men coude thinke.
After the sondry sesons of the yeer,
So chaunged he his mete and his soper.
Ful many a fat partrich hadde he in mewe,
350 And many a breem and many a luce in stewe.
Wo was his cook but if his sauce were
Poynaunt and sharpe, and redy al his gere.
His table dormant in his halle alway
Stood redy covered al the longe day.
355 At sessiouns ther was he lord and sire;
Ful ofte tyme he was knight of the shire.
An anlas and a gipser al of silk
Heng at his girdel, whyt as morne milk.

---

332. E., *heed*, rest *berd*; E., *a*; rest *the*.
336. E., *owene*.   341. E., *alweys*.
338. E., *verray*; Hl., *verraily*.   349. E., *muwe*.
340. E., *was he*; rest *he was*.   350. E., *stuwe*.

A shirreve hadde he been, and a countour;
Was nowher such a worthy vavasour. 360

An Haberdassher and a Carpenter,
A Webbe, a Dyere, and a Tapicer,—
And they were clothed alle in o liveree,
Of a solempne and greet fraternitee.
Ful fresh and newe hir gere apyked was; 365
Hir knyves were chaped noght with bras,
But al with silver, wroght ful clene and weel,
Hir girdles and hir pouches everydeel.
Wel semed ech of hem a fair burgeys,
To sitten in a yeldhalle on a deys. 370
Everich, for the wisdom that he can,
Was shaply for to been an alderman.
For catel hadde they ynogh and rente,
And eek hir wyves wolde it wel assente;
And elles certeyn were they to blame. 375
It is ful fair to been y-clept *ma dame*,
And goon to vigilyës al bifore,
And have a mantel roialliche y-bore.

A Cook they hadde with hem for the nones,
To boille the chiknes with the mary-bones, 380
And poudre-marchant tart, and galyngale.
Wel coude he knowe a draughte of London ale.
He coude roste, and sethe, and boille, and frye,
Maken mortreux, and wel bake a pye.

---

359. E., omits *a* before *countour*.
364. All but Hl. have *and a*. 370. E., *yeldehalle*.
366. Hl., *ichapud*. 376. E., *ycleped*.
380. Hl., om *the* before *chiknes*.
383. E., *boille*, so Cm., and Hl.; rest *broille*.

THE CANTERBURY TALES

385 But greet harm was it, as it thoughte me,
That on his shyne a mormal hadde he;
For blankmanger, that made he with the beste.

A Shipman was ther, woning fer by weste:
For aught I woot, he was of Dertemouthe.
390 He rood upon a rouncy as he couthe,
In a gowne of falding to the knee.
A daggere hanging on a laas hadde he
Aboute his nekke under his arm adoun.
The hote somer hadde maad his hewe al broun;
395 And, certeynly, he was a good felawe.
Ful many a draughte of wyn had he y-drawe
Fro Burdeux-ward, whyl that the chapman sleep,
Of nyce conscience took he no keep.
If that he faught, and hadde the hyer hond,
400 By water he sente hem hoom to every lond.
But of his craft to rekene wel his tydes,
His stremes and his daungers him bisydes,
His herberwe and his moone, his lodemenage,
Ther nas noon swich from Hulle to Cartage.
405 Hardy he was, and wys to undertake;
With many a tempest hadde his berd been shake.
He knew wel alle the havenes, as they were,
From Gootlond to the cape of Fynystere,
And every cryke in Britaine and in Spayne;
410 His barge y-cleped was the Maudelayne.

---

388. E., *wonynge*.
396. E., *drawe*; Cm., *idrawe*.
407. Hl., inserts *wel*; rest omit.
409. E., *Britaigne*.

With us ther was a Doctour of Phisik,
In al this world ne was ther noon hym lik
To speke of phisik and of surgerye;
For he was grounded in astronomye.
He kepte his pacient a ful greet del   415
In houres, by his magik naturel.
Wel coude he fortunen the ascendent
Of his images for his pacient.
He knew the cause of everich maladye,
Were it of hoot, or cold, or moiste, or drye,   420
And where engendred, and of what humour;
He was a verray parfit practisour.
The cause y-knowe, and of his harm the rote,
Anon he yaf the seke man his bote.
Ful redy hadde he his apothecaries,   425
To sende him drogges, and his letuaries,
For ech of hem made other for to wynne;
Hir frendschipe nas nat newe to bigynne.
Wel knew he the olde Esculapius,
And Deïscorides, and eek Rufus;   430
Old Ypocras, Haly and Galien;
Serapion, Razis, and Avicen;
Averrois, Damascien, and Constantyn;
Bernard, and Gatesden, and Gilbertyn.
Of his diete mesurable was he,   435
For it was of no superfluitee,
But of greet norissing and digestible.
His studie was but litel on the Bible.

---

421. E., *they engendred*; so Cm., and Hl.; Hn., ins. *it*.
424. E., *sike*.
430. E., *Risus*; Pt., *Rufus*.   431. E., *olde*.

In sangwin and in pers he clad was al,
440 Lyned with taffata and with sendal;
And yet he was but esy of dispence;
He kepte that he wan in pestilence.
For gold in phisik is a cordial,
Therfore he lovede gold in special.

445 A Good-wyf was ther of bisyde Bathe,
But she was somdel deef, and that was scathe.
Of cloth-making she hadde swiche an haunt,
She passed hem of Ypres and of Gaunt.
In al the parisshe wyf ne was ther noon
450 That to the offringe bifore hir sholde goon;
And if ther dide, certeyn so wrooth was she,
That she was out of alle charitee.
Hir coverchiefs ful fyne were of ground,
I dorste swere they weyeden ten pound,
455 That on a Sonday were upon hir heed.
Hir hosen weren of fyn scarlet reed,
Ful streite y-teyd, and shoos ful moiste and newe.
Bold was hir face, and fair, and reed of hewe.
She was a worthy womman al hir lyve,
460 Housbondes at chirche-dore she hadde fyve,
Withouten other compaignye in youthe,
—But therof nedeth nat to speke as nouthe,—
And thryes hadde she been at Jerusalem;
She hadde passed many a straunge streem;
465 At Rome she hadde been, and at Boloigne,

---
447. E., *swich*.
450. E., *bifore*; Cm., *tofore*; Pt., Cp., *toforn*; Ln., *toforne*.
453. E., *weren*.   455. E., *weren*.
457. E., Hn., Pt., *shoes*; Cp., *schoos*; Ln., *schoes*.

In Galice at Seynt Jame, and at Coloigne.
She coude muche of wandring by the weye:
Gat-tothed was she, soothly for to seye.
Upon an amblere esily she sat,
Y-wimpled wel, and on hir heed an hat 470
As brood as is a bokeler or a targe;
A foot-mantel aboute hir hipes large,
And on hir feet a paire of spores sharpe.
In felawship wel coude she laughe and carpe.
Of remedies of love she knew perchaunce, 475
For she coude of that art the olde daunce.

   A good man was ther of religioun,
And was a povre Persoun of a toun;
But riche he was of holy thoght and werk;
He was also a lerned man, a clerk, 480
That Cristes gospel trewely wolde preche;
His parisshens devoutly wolde he teche.
Benygne he was, and wonder diligent,
And in adversitee ful pacient;
And swich he was y-preved ofte sithes. 485
Ful looth were him to cursen for his tithes,
But rather wolde he yeven, out of doute,
Unto his povre parisshens aboute
Of his offring and eek of his substaunce.
He coude in litel thing han suffisaunce. 490
Wyd was his parisshe, and houses fer asonder,
But he ne lafte nat, for reyn ne thonder,

---

467. E., *muchel*; Hl., Cp., Pt., *moche*.   486. E., *hise*.
474. E., *felaweship*.   490. E., *haue*.
485. E., *preved*; Hl., *i-preved*.

In siknes nor in meschief to visyte
The ferreste in his parisshe, muche and lyte,
495 Upon his feet, and in his hand a staf.
This noble ensample to his sheep he yaf,
That first he wroghte, and afterward he taughte;
Out of the gospel he tho wordes caughte;
And this figure he added eek therto,
500 That if gold ruste what shal yren do?
For if a preest be foul, on whom we truste,
No wonder is a lewed man to ruste;
And shame it is, if a preest take keep,
A [foule] shepherde and a clene sheep.
505 Wel oghte a preest ensample for to yive,
By his clennesse, how that his sheep shold lyve.
He sette nat his benefice to hyre,
And leet his sheep encombred in the myre,
And ran to London, unto seynte Poules,
510 To seken him a chaunterie for soules,
Or with a bretherhed to been withholde;
But dwelte at hoom, and kepte wel his folde,
So that the wolf ne made it nat miscarie;
He was a shepherde and no mercenarie.
515 And though he holy were and vertuous
He was to sinful man nat despitous,
Ne of his speche daungerous ne digne,

---

493. E., *siknesse*.
494. E., *firste*; E., ins. *that* bef. *he*; rest omit.
505. E., *yeue*.
509. E., *seint*; Hl., Cp., *seynte*.
510. E., *chauntrie*; Hl., *chaunterie*.
512. E., *dwelleth*; all others *dwelte*; E., *keepeth*; Ln., *keped*; rest *kepte*.
514. E., *not a*; so all exc. Hl. *no*.
516. E., *nat* after *was*; so all but Hl., *to senful man nought*.

PROLOGUE

But in his teching discreet and benigne;
To drawen folk to hevene by fairnesse,
By good ensample, this was his bisynesse. 520
But it were any persone obstinat,
What so he were, of heigh or lowe estat,
Him wolde he snibben sharply for the nonys.
A bettre preest I trowe that nowher non is.
He wayted after no pompe and reverence, 525
Ne maked him a spyced conscience,
But Cristes lore, and his apostles twelve,
He taughte, but first he folwed it himselve.

With him ther was a Plowman, was his brother,
That hadde y-lad of dong ful many a fother,— 530
A trewe swinkere and a good was he,
Livinge in pees and parfit charitee.
God loved he best with al his hoole herte
At alle tymes, thogh him gamed or smerte,
And thanne his neighebour right as himselve. 535
He wolde thresshe, and therto dyke and delve,
For Cristes sake, for every povre wight,
Withouten hyre, if it lay in his might.
His tythes payed he ful faire and wel,
Bothe of his propre swynk and his catel. 540
In a tabard he rood upon a mere.
    Ther was also a Reve and a Millere,

---
519. E., Pt., Hn., *hevene.*
523. E., *lough*; rest *lowe* or *low*; Pt., *lowle.*
525. E., *wayteth*; rest *-ted, -tid, -tede.*
534. E., *he.*
535. E.,*-bore,* so Hn., Cp., and Ln.; rest *-bour, -bure.*
539. E., *Hise, payde*; Cm., *payede.*

A Somnour and a Pardoner also,
A Maunciple, and myself; ther were namo.

545 The Miller was a stout carl for the nones,
Ful big he was of brawn and eek of bones;
That proved wel, for overal ther he cam,
At wrastling he wolde have alwey the ram.
He was short-sholdred, brood, a thikke knarre,
550 Ther nas no dore that he nolde heve of harre,
Or breke it, at a renning, with his heed.
His berd as any sowe or fox was reed,
And therto brood, as though it were a spade.
Upon the cop right of his nose he hade
555 A werte, and theron stood a tuft of heres,
Reed as the bristles of a sowes eres;
His nose-thirles blake were and wyde.
A swerd and bokeler bar he by his syde;
His mouth as greet was as a greet forneys.
560 He was a janglere and a goliardeys,
And that was most of synne and harlotryes.
Wel coude he stelen corn and tollen thryes;
And yet he hadde a thombe of gold, pardee!
A whyt cote and a blew hood wered he.
565 A baggepipe wel coude he blowe and sowne,
And therwithal he broghte us out of towne.

A gentil Maunciple was ther of a temple,

---

546. E., Cp., *brawn*; Cm., *braun*; Pt., Ln., *braune*.
548. E., *wrastlynge*.
550. E., *ne wolde*; Cp., Hl., *nolde*.
555. E., *toft, herys*.
556. E., *brustles, erys*.   558. All but Cp., *and a*.

Of which achatours mighte take exemple
For to be wyse in byinge of vitaille;
For whether that he payde or took by taille,   570
Algate he wayted so in his achaat,
That he was ay biforn and in good staat.
Now is nat that of God a ful fair grace,
That swich a lewed mannes wit shal pace
The wisdom of an heepe of lerned men?   575
Of maistres hadde he mo than thryës ten,
That were of lawe expert and curious;
Of which ther were a doseyn in that hous,
Worthy to been stywardes of rente and lond
Of any lord that is in Engelond,   580
To make him lyve by his propre good,
In honour dettelees, but he were wood,
Or lyve as scarsly as him list desire·
And able for to helpen al a shire
In any cas that mighte falle or happe;   585
And yit this maunciple sette hir aller cappe.

  The Reve was a sclendre colerik man,
His berd was shave as ny as ever he can.
His heer was by his eres round y-shorn.
His top was dokked lyk a preest biforn.   590
Ful longe were his legges and ful lene,
Y-lyk a staf, ther was no calf y-sene.

---

570. E., *wheither*; so Hn.   578. E., *whiche*; *duszeyne*.
577. E., *weren*.   581. E., *maken*.
582. E., *but if*; Cp., Pt., *but if that*; Cm., *but*.
586. E., *manciple*.
589. E., ins. *ful* after *eres*; so all but Hl., Ln.
590. E., *doked*.

Wel coude he kepe a gerner and a bynne;
Ther was noon auditour coude on him wynne.
595 Wel wiste he, by the droghte and by the reyn,
The yelding of his seed and of his greyn.
His lordes sheep, his neet, his dayerye,
His swyn, his hors, his stoor, and his pultrye,
Was hoolly in this reves governing,
600 And by his covenaunt yaf the rekening,
Sin that his lord was twenty yeer of age;
Ther coude no man bringe him in arrerage.
Ther nas baillif, ne herde, ne other hyne,
That he ne knew his sleighte and his covyne;
605 They were adrad of him as of the deeth.
His woning was ful fair upon an heeth,
With grene treës shadwed was his place.
He coude bettre than his lord purchace.
Ful riche he was astored prively,
610 His lord wel coude he plesen subtilly,
To yeve and lene him of his owne good,
And have a thank, and yet a cote, and hood.
In youthe he lerned hadde a good mister
He was a wel good wrighte, a carpenter.
615 This reve sat upon a ful good stot,
That was al pomely grey, and highte Scot.
A long surcote of pers upon he hade,
And by his syde he bar a rusty blade.
Of Northfolk was this reve, of which I telle,
620 Bisyde a toun men clepen Baldeswelle.

---

594. E., *of*; rest *on*. 604. E., om. *ne*; so Cm.
603. E., *hierde*; *nor*. 611. E. *owene*.
612. E., om. *and* bef. *yet*; *gowne*; rest *cote*.
613. E. *hadde lerned*; so all but Hn., Hl.

PROLOGUE 89

Tukked he was, as is a frere, aboute,
And ever he rood the hindreste of our route.

A Somnour was ther with us in that place,
That hadde a fyr-reed cherubinnes face,
For sawceflem he was, with eyen narwe. 625
As hot he was, and lecherous as a sparwe,
With scalled browes blake, and piled berd;
Of his visage children were aferd.
Ther nas quik-silver, litarge, ne brimstoon,
Boras, ceruce, ne oille of Tartre noon, 630
Ne oynement that wolde clense and byte,
That him mighte helpen of his whelkes whyte,
Ne of the knobbes sittingé on his chekes.
Wel loved he garleek, oynons, and eek lekes,
And for to drinken strong wyn, reed as blood. 635
Thanne wolde he speke, and crye as he were wood.
And whan that he wel dronken hadde the wyn,
Than wolde he speke no word but Latyn.
A fewe termes hadde he, two or thre,
That he had lerned out of som decree; 640
No wonder is, he herde it al the day;
And eek ye knowen wel how that a jay
Can clepen 'Watte,' as well as can the pope.
But whoso coude in other thing him grope,
Thanne hadde he spent al his philosophye; 645
Ay '*Questio quid iuris*' wolde he crye.
He was a gentil harlot and a kynde;

---

623. E., *Somonour*.   628. E., *scaled*.
632. E., *the*; rest *his*.
633. E., *nor*; so Hn., Cp., and Pt., Cm. *ne*.

A bettre felawe sholde men noght fynde.
He wolde suffre for a quart of wyn
650 A good felawe to have his concubyn
A twelf-month, and excuse him atte fulle:
And prively a finch eek coude he pulle.
And if he fond owher a good felawe,
He wolde techen him to have non awe,
655 In swich cas, of the erchedeknes curs,
But if a mannes soule were in his purs;
For in his purs he sholde y-punisshed be.
'Purs is the erchedeknes helle,' seyde he.
But wel I woot he lyed right in dede;
660 Of cursing oghte ech gilty man him drede—
For curs wol slee right as assoilling savith—
And also war him of a *Significavit*.
In daunger hadde he at his owne gyse
The yonge girles of the diocyse,
665 And knew hir counseil, and was al hir reed.
A gerland hadde he set upon his heed,
As greet as it were for an ale-stake;
A bokeler hadde he maad him of a cake.

With him ther rood a gentil Pardoner
670 Of Rouncivale, his freend and his compeer,
That streight was comen fro the court of Rome.
Ful loude he song, 'Com hider, love, to me.'
This somnour bar to him a stif burdoun,

---

655. E., *ercedekenes*; Cm., Cp., *erche-*.
658. E., *Ercedekenes*; Hn., *Ercedeknes*; Cm., Cp., *erche-*.
660. E., om. *him*; Cp., Ln., ins.; Hl., Pt., *to*.
669. E., *was*; rest *rood, rode, rod*.
673. E., *Somonour*.

PROLOGUE

Was never trompe of half so greet a soun.
This pardoner hadde heer as yelow as wex, 675
But smothe it heng, as dooth a strike of flex;
By ounces henge his lokkes that he hadde,
And therwith he his shuldres overspradde;
But thinne it lay, by colpons oon and oon;
But hood, for jolitee, wered he noon, 680
For it was trussed up in his walet.
Him thoughte he rood al of the newe jet;
Dischevele, save his cappe, he rood al bare.
Swiche glaringe eyen hadde he as an hare.
A vernicle hadde he sowed upon his cappe. 685
His walet lay biforn him in his lappe,
Bret-ful of pardoun come from Rome al hoot.
A voys he hadde as smal as hath a goot.
No berd hadde he, ne never sholde have,
As smothe it was as it were late y-shave; 690

. . . . .

But of his craft, fro Berwyk unto Ware,
Ne was ther swich another pardoner.
For in his male he hadde a pilwe-beer,
Which that, he seyde, was our lady veyl: 695
He seyde he hadde a gobet of the seyl
That seynte Peter hadde, whan that he wente
Upon the see, til Jhesu Crist him hente.
He hadde a croys of latoun, ful of stones,
And in a glas he hadde pigges bones. 700
But with thise relikes, whan that he fond

---

680. Hl., *ne wered*; rest om.
686. E., om. *lay*; only in Hl.
687. E., *comen.*

A povre person dwelling upon lond,
Upon a day he gat him more moneye
Than that the person gat in monthes tweye.
705 And thus with feyned flaterye and japes,
He made the person and the peple his apes.
But trewely to tellen atte laste,
He was in chirche a noble ecclesiaste;
Wel coude he rede a lessoun or a storie;
710 But alderbest he song an offertorie;
For wel he wiste, whan that song was songe,
He moste preche, and wel affile his tonge,
To wynne silver, as he ful wel coude;
Therefore he song so meriely and loude.

715 Now have I told you shortly, in a clause,
Thestat, tharray, the nombre, and eek the cause
Why that assembled was this compaignye
In Southwerk, at this gentil hostelrye,
That highte the Tabard, faste by the Belle.
720 But now is tyme to yow for to telle
How that we baren us that ilke night,
Whan we were in that hostelrye alight.
And after wol I telle of our viage,
And al the remenaunt of our pilgrimage.
725 But first I pray yow of your curteisye,
That ye narette it nat my vileinye,
Thogh that I pleynly speke in this matere,
To telle yow hir wordes and hir chere;

---

714. E., *the murierly*; so Hn., Cm.
715. E., Hl., *shortly*; rest *soothly*.
718. E., *as*.
726. E., Hn., Cm., as in text; Cp., Pt., Hl., *ne rette*.

Ne thogh I speke hir wordes proprely.
For this ye knowen also wel as I, 730
Whoso shal telle a tale after a man,
He moot reherce, as ny as evere he can,
Everich a word, if it be in his charge,
Al speke he never so rudeliche and large;
Or elles he moot telle his tale untrewe, 735
Or feyne thing, or finde wordes newe.
He may nat spare, althogh he were his brother;
He moot as wel seye o word as another.
Crist spak himself ful brode in holy writ,
And wel ye woot no vileinye is it. 740
Eek Plato seïth, whoso can him rede,
The wordes mote be cosyn to the dede.
Also I prey yow to foryeve it me,
Al have I nat set folk in hir degree
Here in this tale, as that they sholde stonde; 745
My wit is short, ye may wel understonde.

Greet chere made our hoste us everichon,
And to the soper sette he us anon;
And served us with vitaille at the beste.
Strong was the wyn, and wel to drinke us leste. 750
A semely man our hoste was withalle
For to han been a marshal in an halle.
A large man he was with eyen stepe,
A fairer burgeys was ther noon in Chepe:
Bold of his speche, and wys, and wel y-taught, 755
And of manhod him lakkede right naught.

---

734. E., *or*; Hl., *ne*; rest *and*.
741. Hl., *that can.*   747. E., *chiere*.
752. E., *marchal*; Hl., only, *han beeen*.
756. E., *lakked*: Cm., Cp., *-ede*.

Eek therto he was right a mery man,
And after soper pleyen he bigan,
And spak of mirthe amonges other thinges,
760 Whan that we hadde maad our rekeninges;
And seyde thus: 'Now, lordinges, trewely
Ye been to me right welcome hertely:
For by my trouthe, if that I shal nat lye,
I ne saugh this yeer so mery a compaignye
765 At ones in this herberwe as is now;
Fayn wolde I doon yow mirthe, wiste I how.
And of a mirthe I am right now bithoght,
To doon yow ese, and it shal coste noght.

'Ye goon to Caunterbury; God yow spede,
770 The blisful martir quite yow your mede!
And wel I woot, as ye goon by the weye,
Ye shapen yow to talen and to pleye;
For trewely, confort ne mirthe is noon
To ride by the weye doumb as a stoon;
775 And therfor wol I maken yow disport,
As I seyde erst, and doon yow som confort.
And if yow lyketh alle, by oon assent,
Now for to stonden at my jugement,
And for to werken as I shal yow seye,
780 Tomorwe, whan ye riden by the weye,
Now, by my fader soule, that is deed,
But ye be merye, I wol yeve yow myn heed!
Hold up your hond, withouten more speche.'

---

757. E., *myrie*.
764. E., *saugh nat*; so all but Hl. E., *myrie*.
774. E., *the*; rest *a* exc. Hn., om.
778. Hl., *now for*; rest om. *now*; E., *juggement*.
782. E., *But if*; rest *but*; E., *myrie*.

Our counseil was nat longe for to seche;
Us thoughte it was noght worth to make it wys, 785
And graunted him withouten more avys,
And bad him seye his verdit, as him leste.

   'Lordinges,' quod he, 'now herkneth for the beste;
But tak it nought, I prey yow, in desdeyn;
This is the poynt, to speken short and pleyn, 790
That ech of yow, to shorte with your weye,
In this viage shal telle tales tweye,
To Caunterbury-ward, I mene it so,
And hom-ward he shal tellen othere two,
Of aventures that whilom han bifalle. 795
And which of yow that bereth him beste of alle,
That is to seyn, that telleth in this cas
Tales of best sentence and most solas,
Shal have a soper at oure aller cost
Here in this place, sitting by this post, 800
Whan that we come agayn fro Caunterbury.
And for to make yow the more mery,
I wol myselven gladly with yow ryde,
Right at myn owne cost, and be your gyde.
And who-so wol my jugement withseye 805
Shal paye al that we spenden by the weye.
And if ye vouchesauf that it be so,
Tel me anon, withouten wordes mo,
And I wol erly shape me therfore.'

---

786. E., *wit outen*.
787. E., *voirdit*.
791. Cp., Hl., *your*; rest *our*.
802. E., *mury*.
803. E., *myself*; Hl., *myselven*.
805. E., *wole*; so Hn., Cm.; Cp., *wol*; Pt., and Ln., *wil*. E., *juggement*.

THE CANTERBURY TALES

810 This thing was graunted and oure othes swore
With ful glad herte, and preyden him also
That he wold vouchesauf for to do so,
And that he wolde been our governour,
And of our tales juge and reportour,
815 And sette a soper at a certeyn prys;
And we wol reuled been at his devys,
In heigh and lowe; and thus, by oon assent,
We been acorded to his jugement.
And therupon the wyn was fet anon;
820 We dronken, and to reste wente echon,
Withouten any lenger taryinge.

A-morwe, whan that day bigan to springe,
Up roos oure host, and was oure aller cok,
And gadrede us togidre alle in a flok,
825 And forth we riden, a litel more than pas,
Unto the Watering of Seynt Thomas.
And there oure host bigan his hors areste,
And seyde: 'Lordinges, herkneth if yow leste.
Ye woot your forward, and I it yow recorde.
830 If even-song and morwe-song acorde,
Lat se now who shal telle the firste tale.
As ever mote I drinke wyn or ale,
Who-so be rebel to my jugement
Shal paye for al that by the weye is spent.

---

810. E., *oure*; so Hn., and Cm.; Cp., Pt., *our*.
812. E., *would*; rest *wolde*.
817. E., *lough*.
818. E., *juggement*.
822. E., *gan for*; Hn., Cp., *bigan*; Cm., Pt., Ln., *gan*.
829. E., *youre*, om. *I*; so Hn.; Cm., Cp., Pt., Ln., ins. *I*.
830. E., *ascorde*.
834. E., Hn., Cm., *wey*.

Now draweth cut, er that we ferrer twynne; 835
He which that hath the shortest shal bigynne.
Sir Knight,' quod he, 'my maister and my lord,
Now draweth cut, for that is myn acord.
Cometh neer,' quod he, 'my lady Prioresse;
And ye, sir Clerk, lat be your shamfastnesse, 840
Ne studieth noght; ley hond to, every man.'

   Anon to drawen every wight bigan,
And shortly for to tellen as it was,
Were it by aventure, or sort, or cas,
The sothe is this, the cut fil to the knyght, 845
Of which ful blythe and glad was every wyght;
And telle he moste his tale, as was resoun,
By forward and by composicioun,
As ye han herd; what nedeth wordes mo?
And whan this goode man saugh that it was so, 850
As he that wys was and obedient
To kepe his forward by his free assent,
He seyde: 'Syn I shal bigynne the game,
What, welcome be the cut, a Goddes name!
Now lat us ryde, and herkneth what I seye.' 855

   And with that word we ryden forth our weye;
And he bigan with right a mery chere
His tale anon, and seyde in this manere.

Heere endith the prolog of this book; and heere biginneth the first tale which is the Knyghtes Tale.

---

836. E., *shorteste*.
837. E., *sire*.
840. E., *sire*; *shame-*.
The colophon is from Cm.

848. E., *foreward*.
852. E., *foreward*.
857. E., *myrie*.

THE KNIGHTES TALE

*Iamque domos patrias, Scithice post aspera gentis
Prelia laurigero, etc.*

Whylom, as olde stories tellen us,
Ther was a duk that highte Theseus;
Of Athenes he was lord and governour,
And in his tyme swich a conquerour,
5   That gretter was ther noon under the sonne.
Ful many a riche contree hadde he wonne;
That with his wisdom and his chivalrye
He conquered al the regne of Femenye,
That whylom was y-cleped Scithia;
10   And weddede the queene Ypolita,
And broghte hir hoom with him in his contree
With muchel glorie and greet solempnitee,
And eek hir yonge suster Emelye.
And thus with victorie and with melodye
15   Lete I this noble duk to Athenes ryde,
And al his hoost in armes him bisyde.

And certes, if it nere to long to here,
I wolde han told yow fully the manere
How wonnen was the regne of Femenye
20   By Theseus and by his chivalrye;
And of the grete bataille for the nones

---

10. E., *wedded*; Cp., Hl., *weddede*.
13. E., *faire*; all others *yonge*.
18. E., *wolde you haue toold*; Hn., *wolde haue toold*.

98

THE KNIGHTES TALE

Bitwixen Athenes and Amazones;
And how asseged was Ypolita,
The faire, hardy queene of Scithia;
And of the feste that was at hir weddinge, 25
And of the tempest at hir hoom-cominge;
But al that thing I moot as now forbere.
I have, God woot, a large feeld to ere,
And wayke been the oxen in my plough,
The remenant of the tale is long ynough; 30
I wol nat letten eek noon of this route,
Lat every felawe telle his tale aboute,
And lat see now who shal the soper winne,
And ther I lefte, I wol ageyn biginne.

This duk, of whom I make mencioun, 35
When he was come almost unto the toun,
In al his wele and in his moste pryde,
He was war, as he caste his eye asyde,
Wher that ther kneled in the hye weye
A compaignye of ladies, tweye and tweye, 40
Ech after other, clad in clothes blake;
But swich a cry and swich a wo they make,
That in this world nys creature livinge,
That herde swich another weymentinge;
And of this cry they nolde nevere stenten, 45
Til they the reynes of his brydel henten.

'What folk been ye, that at myn hom-cominge
Perturben so my feste with cryinge?'
Quod Theseus, 'Have ye so greet envye
Of myn honour, that thus compleyne and crye? 50

---

39. E., om. *hye*; rest insert.

Or who hath yow misboden, or offended?
And telleth me if it may been amended;
And why that ye been clothed thus in blak?
 The eldest lady of hem alle spak,
55 Whan she hadde swowned with a deedly chere,
That it was routhe for to seen and here,
And seyde: 'Lord, to whom Fortune hath yiven
Victorie, and as a conquerour to liven,
Noght greveth us your glorie and your honour;
60 But we biseken mercy and socour.
Have mercy on our wo and our distresse.
Som drope of pitee, thurgh thy gentillesse,
Upon us wrecched wommen lat thou falle.
For certes, lord, ther is noon of us alle,
65 That she nath been a duchesse or a quene;
Now be we caitifs, as it is wel sene:
Thanked be Fortune, and hir false wheel,
That noon estat assureth to be weel.
 And certes, lord, to abyden your presence,
70 Here in the temple of the goddesse Clemence
We han ben waitinge al this fourtenight;
Now help us, lord, sith it is in thy might.
 'I wrecche, which that wepe and waille thus,
Was whylom wyf to king Capaneus,
75 That starf at Thebes, cursed be that day!
And alle we, that been in this array,
And maken al this lamentacioun,
We losten alle our housbondes at that toun,

---

54. E., *eldeste*.   65. E., *ne hath*.
57. E., *yeuen*.   66. E., *caytyues*; Cp., Hl., *caytifs*.
73. E., *crie*; rest *waille*, or *weille*.

THE KNIGHTES TALE

Whyl that the seege theraboute lay.
And yet now the olde Creon, weylaway!   80
That lord is now of Thebes the citee,
Fulfild of ire and of iniquitee,
He, for despyt, and for his tirannye,
To do the dede bodies vileinye,
Of alle our lordes, whiche that ben slawe,   85
Hath alle the bodies on an heep y-drawe,
And wol nat suffren hem, by noon assent,
Neither to been y-buried nor y-brent,
But maketh houndes ete hem in despit.'
And with that word, withouten more respit,   90
They fillen gruf, and cryden pitously,
'Have on us wrecched wommen som mercy,
And lat our sorwe sinken in thyn herte.'

  This gentil duk doun from his courser sterte
With herte pitous, whan he herde hem speke.   95
Him thoughte that his herte wolde breke,
Whan he saugh hem so pitous and so mat,
That whylom weren of so greet estat.
And in his armes he hem alle up hente,
And hem conforteth in ful good entente,   100
And swoor his ooth, as he was trewe knight
He wolde doon so ferforthly his might
Upon the tyraunt Creon hem to wreke,
That al the peple of Grece sholde speke
How Creon was of Theseus y-served,   105
As he that hadde his deeth ful wel deserved
And right anoon, withouten more abood,
His baner he desplayeth, and forth rood
To Thebes-ward, and al his host bisyde;

No neer Athenes wolde he go ne ryde,
Ne take his ese fully half a day,
But onward on his wey that nyght he lay
And sente anoon Ypolita the quene,
And Emelye hir yonge suster shene,
Unto the toun of Athenes to dwelle;
And forth he rit; ther is namore to telle.

    The rede statue of Mars with spere and targe
So shyneth in his whyte baner large,
That alle the feeldes gliteren up and doun;
And by his baner born is his penoun
Of gold ful riche, in which ther was y-bete
The Minotaur, which that he slough in Crete.
Thus rit this duk, thus rit this conquerour,
And in his host of chivalrye the flour,
Til that he cam to Thebes, and alighte
Faire in a feeld, ther as he thoughte fighte.
But shortly for to speken of this thing,
With Creon, which that was of Thebes king,
He faught, and slough him manly as a knight
In pleyn bataille, and putte the folk to flight;
And by assaut he wan the citee after,
And rente adoun bothe wal and sparre and rafter:
And to the ladyes he restored agayn
The bones of hir housbondes that were slayn,
To doon obsequies, as was tho the gyse.
But it were al to long for to devyse
The grete clamour and the waymentinge
That the ladyes made at the brenninge
Of the bodies, and the grete honour

---

116. Hn., Cp., *nys*, rest *is*. 134. E. *weren*.

THE KNIGHTES TALE

That Theseus, the noble conquerour, 140
Doth to the ladyes, whan they from him wente;
But shortly for to telle is myn entente.
  Whan that this worthy duk, this Theseus,
Hath Creon slayn, and wonne Thebes thus,
Stille in that feeld he took al night his reste, 145
And dide with al the contree as him leste.
  To ransake in the tas of bodies dede,
Hem for to strepe of harneys and of wede,
The pilours diden bisinesse and cure,
After the bataille and disconfiture. 150
And so bifel that in the tas they founde,
Thurgh-girt with many a grevous, blody wounde,
Two yonge knightes ligging by and by,
Bothe in oon armes, wroght ful richely;
Of whiche two Arcita hight that oon, 155
And that other knight hight Palamon.
Nat fully quike, ne fully dede they were,
But by hir cote-armures and by hir gere,
The heraudes knewe hem best in special,
As they that weren of the blood roial 160
Of Thebes, and of sustren two y-born.
Out of the tas the pilours han hem torn,
And han hem caried softe unto the tente
Of Theseus, and he ful sone hem sente
To Athenës, to dwellen in prisoun 165
Perpetuelly, he nolde no raunsoun.
And whan this worthy duk hath thus y-don,

---

147. E., *taas*; Cp., Pt., Ln., *caas*; so 151, 162.
155–6. E., *highte*; Pt., *hight*.   158. E., *here*.
164. E., *ful soone he hem*; Cm., om. *he*; rest as in text.

He took his host and hoom he rood anon.
With laurer crowned as a conquerour;
170 And there he liveth in joye and in honour
Terme of his lyf; what nedeth wordes mo?
And in a tour, in angwish and in wo,
This Palamon and his felawe Arcite,
For evermore, ther may no gold hem quite.

175 This passeth yeer by yeer, and day by day,
Til it fil ones, in a morwe of May,
That Emelye, that fairer was to sene
Than is the lilie upon his stalke grene,
And fressher than the May with floures newe
180 —For with the rose colour strof hir hewe,
I noot which was the fairer of hem two—
Er it were day, as was hir wone to do,
She was arisen and al redy dight;
For May wol have no slogardye anight;
185 The sesoun priketh every gentil herte,
And maketh him out of his slepe to sterte,
And seith, 'Arys, and do thyn observaunce.'
This maked Emelye have remembraunce
To doon honour to May, and for to ryse.
190 Y-clothed was she fressh, for to devyse;
Hir yelow heer was broyded in a tresse
Bihinde hir bak, a yerde long, I gesse.
And in the gardyn, at the sonne upriste,
She walketh up and doun, and as hir liste

---

171. E., Cm., om. *his*; *lyue*; rest ins. *his*.
181. E., Hl., *fyner*; Cm., *fynere*; Hn., Cp., Pt., *fairer*
184. E., *-drie*; rest *-dye*.
186. E., *hym*; rest *it* or *hit*.
188. Cm., Cp., Pt., Ln., ins. *to* bef. *have*.

THE KNIGHTES TALE

She gadereth floures, party whyte and rede, 195
To make a subtil gerland for hir hede,
And as an aungel hevenisshly she song.
The grete tour, that was so thikke and strong,
Which of the castel was the chief dongeoun,
—Ther as the knightes weren in prisoun, 200
Of which I tolde yow, and tellen shal—
Was evene joynant to the gardyn-wal,
Ther as this Emelye hadde hir pleyinge.
Bright was the sonne, and cleer that morweninge,
And Palamon, this woful prisoner, 205
As was his wone, by leve of his gayler,
Was risen, and romed in a chambre on heigh,
In which he al the noble citee seigh,
And eek the gardyn, ful of braunches grene,
Ther as this fresshe Emelye the shene 210
Was in hir walk, and romed up and doun.
This sorweful prisoner, this Palamoun,
Goth in the chambre roming to and fro,
And to himself compleyning of his wo;
That he was born, ful ofte he seyde, 'alas!' 215
And so bifel, by aventure or cas,
That thurgh a window, thikke of many a barre
Of iren greet, and square as any sparre,
He caste his eye upon Emelya,
And therwithal he bleynte, and cryde 'A!' 220
As though he stongen were unto the herte.
And with that cry Arcite anon up-sterte,

---

196. Cp. and Ln., *sotil*.
197. Hl., Pt., *heuenly*.
213, 214. E., *-ynge*.
219. E., *cast*; Hn., Cm., *caste*.

And seyde, 'Cosyn myn, what eyleth thee,
That art so pale and deedly on to see?
225 Why cridestow? who hath thee doon offence?
For Goddes love, tak al in pacience
Our prisoun, for it may non other be;
Fortune hath yeven us this adversitee.
Som wikke aspect or disposicioun
230 Of Saturne, by sum constellacioun,
Hath yeven us this, although we hadde it sworn;
So stood the heven whan that we were born;
We moste endure it: this is the short and playn.'
    This Palamon answerde, and seyde agayn,
235 'Cosyn, for sothe, of this opinioun
Thou hast a veyn ymaginacioun;
This prison caused me nat for to crye,
But I was hurt right now thurgh-out myn yë
Into myn herte, that wol my bane be.
240 The fairnesse of that lady that I see
Yond in the gardyn romen to and fro,
Is cause of al my crying and my wo.
I noot wher she be womman or goddesse;
But Venus is it, sothly, as I gesse.'
245 And therwithal on kneës doun he fil,
And seyde: 'Venus, if it be thy wil
Yow in this gardyn thus to transfigure,
Bifore me sorweful wrecche creature,
Out of this prisoun help that we may scapen.
250 And if so be my destynee be shapen

---

232. E., *hevene*; Cp., Ln., *heuen*.
233. E., omits *it*; rest insert.
238. E., *eye.*; Cm., Pt., *ÿe*.
243. Cm., *ne wot whether*; Pt., Ln., *where*.

By eterne word to dyen in prisoun,
Of our lynage have som compassioun,
That is so lowe y-broght by tirannye.'
And with that word Arcite gan espye
Wheras this lady romed to and fro, 255
And with that sighte hir beautee hurte him so,
That if that Palamon was wounded sore,
Arcite is hurt as moche as he, or more.
And with a sigh he seyde pitously:
'The fresshe beautee sleeth me sodeynly 260
Of hir that rometh in the yonder place;
And but I have hir mercy and hir grace,
That I may seen hir atte leste weye,
I nam but deed; ther nis namore to seye.'

This Palamon, whan he tho wordes herde, 265
Dispitously he loked, and answerde:
'Whether seistow this in ernest or in pley?'
'Nay,' quod Arcite, 'in ernest, by my fey!
God help me so, me list ful evele pleye.'

This Palamon gan knitte his browes tweye: 270
'It nere,' quod he, 'to thee no greet honour
For to be fals, ne for to be traitour
To me, that am thy cosyn and thy brother
Y-sworn ful depe, and ech of us til other,
That never, for to dyen in the peyne, 275
Til that the deeth departe shal us tweyne,
Neither of us in love to hindren other,
Ne in noon other cas, my leve brother;
But that thou sholdest trewely forthren me

---

276. E., Ln., om. *the*; rest
277. All exc. Hn., *hyndre*.

280   In every cas, as I shal forthren thee.
      This was thyn ooth, and myn also, certeyn;
      I wot right wel thou darst it nat withseyn.
      Thus artow of my counseil, out of doute.
      And now thou woldest falsly been aboute
285   To love my lady, whom I love and serve,
      And ever shal, til that myn herte sterve.
      Now certes, fals Arcite, thou shalt nat so.
      I loved hir first, and tolde thee my wo
      As to my counseil, and my brother sworn
290   To forthre me, as I have told biforn.
      For which thou art y-bounden as a knight
      To helpen me, if it lay in thy might,
      Or elles artow fals, I dar wel seyn.'
      This Arcitë ful proudly spak ageyn,
295   'Thou shalt,' quod he, 'be rather fals than I;
      But thou art fals, I telle thee outrely;
      For *par amour* I loved hir first er thow.
      What wiltow seyn? thou wistest nat yet now
      Whether she be a womman or goddesse.
300   Thyn is affeccioun of holinesse,
      And myn is love as to a creature;
      For which I tolde thee myn aventure
      As to my cosyn, and my brother sworn.
      I pose that thou lovedest hir biforn;
305   Wostow nat wel the olde clerkes sawe,
      That "who shal yeve a lovere any lawe?
      Love is a gretter lawe, by my pan,
      Than may be yeve to any erthly man."

---

280. E., *as I*; rest *and*.   299. E., *wheither*.
296. E., Hn., *And*; rest *But*.   308. E., *of*; rest *to*.

And therfore positif lawe and swich decree
Is broke al-day for love, in ech degree. 310
A man moot nedes love, maugree his heed.
He may nat fleen it, thogh he sholde be deed,
Al be she mayde, or wydwe, or elles wyf.
And eek it is nat likly, al thy lyf,
To stonden in hir grace; namore shal I; 315
For wel thou wost thyselven, verraily,
That thou and I be dampned to prisoun
Perpetuelly; us gayneth no raunsoun.
We stryve, as dide the houndes for the boon,
They foughte al day, and yet hir part was noon; 320
Ther cam a kyte, whyl they were so wrothe,
And bar awey the boon bitwixe hem bothe.
And therfore at the kinges court, my brother,
Éch man for himself, ther is noon other.
Love if thee list, for I love and ay shal; 325
And soothly, leve brother, this is al:
Here in this prisoun mote we endure,
And everich of us take his aventure.'

   Greet was the stryf and long bitwixe hem tweye,
If that I hadde leyser for to seye; 330
But to theffect. It happed on a day,
—To telle it yow as shortly as I may—
A worthy duk that highte Perotheus,
That felawe was unto duk Theseus
Sin thilke day that they were children lite, 335
Was come to Athenes, his felawe to visite,

---

  310. E., Cm., *broken*; rest *broke*.   334. E., *to*; Hl., *to the*; rest *unto*.
  312. E., *flee*; rest *fleen*.
  319. E., Cp., Pt., Ln., *stryuen*; rest *stryue*.

And for to pleye, as he was wont to do,
For in this world he loved no man so:
And he loved him as tendrely agayn.
340 So wel they loved, as olde bokes sayn
That whan that oon was deed, soothly to telle,
His felawe wente and soughte him doun in helle,—
But of that story list me nat to write.
Duk Perotheüs loved wel Arcite,
345 And hadde him knowe at Thebes yeer by yere;
And finally, at requeste and preyere
Of Perotheus, withoute any raunsoun,
Duk Theseus him leet out of prisoun,
Frely to goon wher that him liste over-al,
350 In swich a gyse, as I you tellen shal.
This was the forward, pleynly for tendite,
Bitwixen Theseus and him Arcite:
That if so were, that Arcite were y-founde
Evere in his lyf, by day or night, o stounde,
355 In any contree of this Theseus,
And he were caught, it was acorded thus,
That with a swerd he sholde lese his heed;
Ther nas noon other remedye ne reed,
But taketh his leve, and homward he him spedde:
360 Lat him be war, his nekke lith to wedde!

How greet a sorwe suffreth now Arcite!
The deeth he feleth thurgh his herte smyte;
He wepeth, wayleth, cryeth pitously;
To sleen himself he wayteth prively.
365 He seyde, 'Allas that day that I was born!

---

339. E., *als*.
340. E., *louede*.
347. E. *withouten;* He, Cp, Pt, *withoute*.
365. E. *he*; rest *I*.

Now is my prisoun worse than biforn;
Now is me shape eternally to dwelle
Nóght in purgatorie, but in helle.
Allas! that ever knew I Perotheus!
For elles hadde I dwelled with Theseus   370
Y-fetered in his prisoun evermo.
Than hadde I been in blisse, and nat in wo.
Only the sighte of hir whom that I serve,
Though that I never hir grace may deserve,
Wolde han suffised right ynough for me.   375
O dere cosyn Palamon,' quod he,
'Thyn is the victorie of this aventure,
Ful blisfully in prison maistow dure.
In prison? certes nay, but in paradys!
Wel hath Fortune y-turned thee the dys,   380
That hast the sight of hir, and I thabsence.
For possible is, syn thou hast hir presence,
And art a knyght, a worthy and an able,
That by som cas, syn Fortune is chaungeable,
Thou maist to thy desyr somtyme atteyne.   385
But I, that am exiled, and bareyne
Of alle grace, and in so greet despeir,
That ther nis erthe, water, fyr, ne eir,
Ne creature, that of hem maked is,
That may me helpe or doon confort in this,—   390
Wel oughte I sterve in wanhope and distresse;
Farwel my lyf, my lust and my gladnesse.

---

368. E., ins. *my* bef. *purgatorie*; rest om.
381. E., Hn., *sighte*; rest *sight*.
384. E., om. *by*; rest ins.
390. E., *heele*; rest *helpe, helpyn*.

'Allas, why pleynen folk so in commune
Of purveiaunce of God, or of Fortune,
That yeveth hem ful ofte in many a gyse
Wel bettre than they can hemself devyse?
Som man desyreth for to han richesse,
That cause is of his mordre or greet siknesse.
And som man wolde out of his prison fayn,
That in his hous is of his meynee slayn.
Infinite harmes been in this matere;
We witen nat what thing we prayen here.
We faren as he that dronke is as a mous;
A dronke man wot wel he hath an hous,
But he noot which the righte wey is thider;
And to a dronke man the wey is slider;
And certes in this world so faren we;
We seken faste after felicitee,
But we goon wrong ful often, trewely.
Thus may we seyen alle, and namely I,
That wende and hadde a greet opinioun,
That if I mighte escapen from prisoun,
Than hadde I been in joye and perfit hele,
Ther now I am exyled fro my wele.
Syn that I may nat seen yow, Emelye,
I nam but deed; ther nis no remedye.'

Upon that other syde Palamon,
Whan that he wiste Arcite was agon,
Swich sorwe he maketh, that the grete tour

---

397. E., Hn., *moerdre*.
402. E., om. *thyng*.
404. E., Cm., *wel that he*.
410. All have *seyn*, exc. Hl., *seyen*.
414. E., *that*; rest *ther(e)*.

THE KNIGHTES TALE

Resouneth of his youling and clamour. 420
The pure fettres on his shines grete
Weren of his bittre salte teres wete.
'Allas!' quod he, 'Arcita, cosyn myn,
Of al our stryf, God woot, the fruyt is thyn.
Thow walkest now in Thebes at thy large, 425
And of my wo thou yevest litel charge.
Thou mayst, syn thou hast wisdom and manhede,
Assemblen alle the folk of our kynrede,
And make a werre so sharpe on this citee,
That by som aventure, or som tretee, 430
Thou mayst have hir to lady and to wyf,
For whom that I most nedes lese my lyf.
For, as by wey of possibilitee,
Sith thou art at thy large, of prison free,
And art a lord, greet is thyn avauntage, 435
More than is myn, that sterve here in a cage.
For I mot wepe and wayle whyl I live,
With al the wo that prison may me yive,
And eek with peyne that love me yiveth also,
That doubleth al my torment and my wo.' 440
Therwith the fyr of jelousye up-sterte
Withinne his brest, and hente him by the herte
So woodly, that he lyk was to biholde
The box-tree, or the asshen dede and colde.
Than seyde he: 'O cruel goddes, that governe 445
This world with binding of your word eterne,
And wryten in the table of athamaunt

---

420. E., *resouned*; rest *-eth*.   441. E., Hn., *jalousie*.
438. E., *yeue*.   445. E., *thanne*; Hl., *tho*.
439. E., *yeueth*.   447. E., *atthamaunt*.

Your parlement, and your eterne graunt,
What is mankinde more unto yow holde
450 Than is the sheep that rouketh in the folde?
For slayn is man right as another beest,
And dwelleth eek in prison and arreest,
And hath siknesse and greet adversitee,
And ofte tymes giltelees, pardee.

455 'What governaunce is in this prescience,
That giltelees tormenteth innocence?
And yet encreseth this al my penaunce,
That man is bounden to his observaunce,
For Goddes sake, to letten of his wille,
460 Ther as a beest may al his lust fulfille.
And whan a beest is deed he hath no peyne;
But man after his deeth moot wepe and pleyne,
Though in this world he have care and wo:
Withouten doute it may stonden so.
465 The answere of this I lete to divynis,
But wel I woot that in this world gret pyne is.
Allas, I se a serpent or a theef,
That many a trewe man hath doon mescheef.
Goon at his large, and wher him list may turne.
470 But I moot been in prisoun thurgh Saturne,
And eek thurgh Juno, jalous and eek wood,
That hath destroyed wel ny al the blood
Of Thebes, with his waste walles wyde.
And Venus sleeth me on that other syde

---

451. E., *beest*; Cm., Hl., *beste*.
452. E., *arreest*; Cm., *areste*.
454. E., *giltlees*; Cm., Cp., Hl., *gilteles*; so 456.
462. E., *after his deeth man*; Cp., *the man mot*; Hn., *man after his deeth most*; Cm., *man aftyr his ded hym muste*.

THE KNIGHTES TALE

For jalousye, and fere of him Arcite.' 475
  Now wol I stinte of Palamon a lite,
And lete him in his prisoun stille dwelle,
And of Arcita forth I wol yow telle.
The somer passeth, and the nightes longe
Encresen double wyse the peynes stronge 480
Bothe of the lovere and the prisoner.
I noot which hath the wofuller mester.
For shortly for to seyn, this Palamoun
Perpetuelly is dampned to prisoun,
In cheynes and in fettres to been deed; 485
And Arcite is exyled upon his heed
For evermo as out of that contree,
Ne nevermo he shal his lady see.
  Yow loveres axe I now this questioun,
Who hath the worse, Arcite or Palamoun? 490
That oon may seen his lady day by day,
But in prisoun he moot dwelle alway.
That other wher him list may ride or go,
But seen his lady shal he nevermo.
Now demeth as yow liste, ye that can, 495
For I wol telle forth as I bigan.

Explicit prima Pars. Sequitur pars secunda.

Part II

  Whan that Arcite to Thebes comen was,
Ful ofte a day he swelte and seyde 'Allas,'
For seen his lady shal he nevermo.

---

479. E., *sonne*; rest *somer*.
489. E., *Now loveres*; rest *Yow*.

500 And shortly to concluden al his wo,
So muche sorwe hadde never creature
That is, or shal, whyl that the world may dure.
His sleep, his mete, his drinke is him biraft,
That lene he wex and drye as is a shaft.
505 His eyen holwe, and grisly to biholde;
His hewe falwe, and pale as asshen colde,
And solitarie he was, and ever allone,
And wailling al the night, making his mone.
And if he herde song or instrument,
510 Than wolde he wepe, he mighte nat be stent;
So feble eek were his spirits, and so lowe,
And chaunged so, that no man coude knowe
His speche nor his voys, though men it herde.
And in his gere for al the world he ferde
515 Nat only lyk the loveres maladye
Of Hereos, but rather lyk manye
Engendred of humour malencolik,
Biforen, in his celle fantastik.
And shortly, turned was al up-so-doun
520 Bothe habit and eek disposicioun
Of him, this woful lovere daun Arcite.
What sholde I alday of his wo endite?
Whan he endured hadde a yeer or two
This cruel torment and this peyne and wo,
525 At Thebes, in his contree, as I seyde,

---

504. E., Pt., *wexeth*; rest *wex, weex*.
506. E., Hn., *falow*; Pt., Ln., *falowe*; Cm., Pt., *falwe*.
508. E., *makynge*.
511. E., *spiritz*.
515. E., *loveris*.
518. E., *Biforn his owene*, so Cm., rest om. *owene*.

THE KNIGHTES TALE

Upon a night, in sleep as he him leyde,
Him thoughte how that the winged god Mercurie
Biforn him stood and bad him to be murie.
His slepy yerde in hond he bar uprighte;
An hat he werede upon his heres brighte.   530
Arrayed was this god, as he took keep,
As he was whan that Argus took his sleep;
And seyde him thus: 'To Athenes shaltow wende;
Ther is thee shapen of thy wo an ende.'
And with that word Arcite wook and sterte.   535
'Now trewely, how sore that me smerte,'
Quod he, 'to Athenes right now wol I fare;
Ne for the drede of deeth shal I nat spare
To see my lady, that I love and serve;
In hir presence I recche nat to sterve.'   540
And with that word he caughte a greet mirour,
And saugh that chaunged was al his colour,
And saugh his visage al in another kinde.
And right anon it ran him in his minde,
That, sith his face was so disfigured   545
Of maladye the which he hadde endured,
He mighte wel, if that he bar him lowe,
Live in Athenes evermore unknowe,
And seen his lady wel ny day by day.
And right anon he chaungede his array,   550
And cladde him as a povre laborer,
And al allone, save oonly a squyer,
That knew his privetee and al his cas,
Which was disgised povrely, as he was,

---

530. E., *up*; *heris*.   531. E., *I*; rest *he*.
550. E., *chaunged*, so Hn., Cp., Pt., Ln.

118   THE CANTERBURY TALES

555 To Athenes is he goon the nexte way.
And to the court he wente upon a day,
And at the gate he profreth his servyse,
To drugge and drawe, what so men wol devyse.
And shortly of this matere for to seyn,
560 He fil in office with a chamberleyn,
The which that dwelling was with Emelye.
For he was wys, and coude soone espye
Of every servaunt which that serveth here.
Wel coude he hewen wode, and water bere,
565 For he was yong and mighty for the nones,
And therto he was strong and big of bones
To doon that any wight can him devyse.
A yeer or two he was in this servyse,
Page of the chambre of Emelye the brighte;
570 And Philostrate he seyde that he highte.
But half so wel biloved a man as he
Ne was ther never in court of his degree;
He was so gentil of condicioun,
That thurghout al the court was his renoun.
575 They seyden that it were a charitee
That Theseus wolde enhauncen his degree,
And putten him in worshipful servyse,
Ther as he mighte his vertu excercyse.
And thus, withinne a whyle, his name is spronge,
580 Bothe of his dedes and his goode tonge,
That Theseus hath taken him so neer
That of his chambre he made him a squyer,
And yaf him gold to mayntene his degree;

---

566. E., Cm., *long*; rest *strong(e)*.
573. E., Hl., ins. *his* after *of*; rest om.

THE KNIGHTES TALE

And eek men broghte him out of his contree
From yeer to yeer ful prively his rente; 585
But honestly and slyly he it spente,
That no man wondred how that he it hadde.
And thre yeer in this wyse his lyf he ladde,
And bar him so in pees and eek in werre,
Ther was no man that Theseus hath derre. 590
And in this blisse lete I now Arcite,
And speke I wol of Palamon a lite.

In derknesse and horrible and strong prisoun
This seven yeer hath seten Palamoun,
Forpyned, what for wo and for distresse; 595
Who feeleth double soor and hevynesse
But Palamon? that love destreyneth so,
That wood out of his wit he goth for wo;
And eek therto he is a prisoner
Perpetuelly, noght only for a yeer. 600
Who coude ryme in Englissh proprely
His martirdom? for sothe, it am nat I;
Therfore I passe as lightly as I may.

It fel that in the seventhe yeer, in May,
The thridde night,—as olde bookes seyn, 605
That al this storie tellen more pleyn,—
Were it by aventure or destinee,
As, whan a thing is shapen, it shal be,—
That, sone after the midnight, Palamoun,
By helping of a freend, brak his prisoun, 610
And fleeth the citee, faste as he may go,
For he had yive his gayler drinke so

---
584. E., Hn., Cp., *gaf*.   592. E., *wole*.
590. Pt., *ther is*; rest *was*.   596. E., om. *and*.
612. E., *yeue*.

Of a clarree, maad of a certeyn wyn,
With nercotikes, and opie of Thebes fyn,
615 That al that night, thogh that men wolde him shake,
The gayler sleep, he mighte nat awake;
And thus he fleeth as faste as ever he may.
The night was short, and faste by the day,
That nedes-cost he moste himselven hyde,
620 And til a grove, faste ther bisyde,
With dredful foot than stalketh Palamoun.
For shortly, this was his opinioun,
That in that grove he wolde him hyde al day,
And in the night than wolde he take his way
625 To Thebes-ward, his frendes for to preye
On Theseus to helpe him to werreye;
And, shortly, outher he wolde lese his lyf,
Or winnen Emelye unto his wyf;
This is theffect and his entente pleyn.

630 Now wol I turne unto Arcite ageyn,
That litel wiste how ny that was his care,
Til that fortune had broght him in the snare.

The bisy larke, messager of day,
Salueth in hir song the morwe gray;
635 And firy Phebus riseth up so brighte,
That al the orient laugheth of the lighte,
And with his stremes dryeth in the greves
The silver dropes hanging on the leves.
And Arcite, that is in the court roial
640 With Theseus, his squyer principal,

---
614. E., *Of*; rest *With*.
619. E., *moot*; rest *moste, muste, must*.
621. E., *dredeful . . . thanne*.
630. E., *to*, so Hn.; rest *unto*, exc. Ln., *nowwhiles turne we*.

Is risen, and loketh on the myrie day;
And, for to doon his observaunce to May,
Remembring on the poynt of his desyr,
He on a courser, stertling as the fyr,
Is riden into the feeldes, him to pleye,   645
Out of the court, were it a myle or tweye;
And to the grove of which that I yow tolde,
By aventure his wey he gan to holde,
To maken him a gerland of the greves,
Were it of wodebinde or hawethorn leves,   650
And loude he song ageyn the sonne shene:
'May, with alle thy floures and thy grene,
Welcome be thou, faire fresshe May,
I hope that I som grene gete may.'
And from his courser with a lusty herte   655
Into the grove ful hastily he sterte,
And in a path he rometh up and doun,
Ther as by aventure this Palamoun
Was in a bussh, that no man mighte him see,
For sore afered of his deeth was he.   660
Nothing ne knew he that it was Arcite:
God wot he wolde have trowed it ful lite.
But sooth is seyd, gon sithen many yeres,
That feeld hath eyen, and the wode hath eres.
It is ful fair a man to bere him evene,   665
For alday meeteth men at unset stevene.
Ful litel wot Arcite of his felawe,

---

 643. E., *Remembrynge*.
 644. E., *startlynge*.
 654. E., *In hope*; so Hn., Cm.; rest *I*.
 660. E., *aferd*; ins. *thanne* bef. *was*.
 663. E., Hn., Cp., *go*; rest *gon, goon*.

That was so ny to herknen al his sawe,
For in the bussh he sitteth now ful stille.
670 Whan that Arcite hadde romed al his fille,
And songen al the roundel lustily,
Into a studie he fil sodeynly,
As doon thise loveres in hir queynte geres,
Now in the croppe, now doun in the breres,
675 Now up, now doun, as boket in a welle.
Right as the Friday, sothly for to telle,
Nów it shyneth, now it reyneth faste,
Right so can gery Venus overcaste
The hertes of hir folk; right as hir day
680 Is gerful, right so chaungeth she array.
Selde is the Friday al the wyke ylike.
Whan that Arcite had songe, he gan to sike,
And sette him doun withouten any more:
'Allas!' quod he, 'that day that I was bore!
685 How longe, Juno, thurgh thy crueltee,
Woltow werreyen Thebes the citee?
Allas! y-brought is to confusioun
The blood roial of Cadme and Amphioun,—
Of Cadmus, which that was the firste man
690 That Thebes bulte, or first the toun bigan,
And of the citee first was crouned king,
Of his lynage am I, and his ofspring
By verray ligne, as of the stok roial;
And now I am so caitif and so thral,
695 That he that is my mortal enemy,

---

672. E., *fil al*; rest om. *al*.
674. E., *crope*.
678. E. *geery*.
680. E., *gereful*.
681. E., *wowke*; Hl., *wyke*.

THE KNIGHTES TALE

I serve him as his squyer povrely.
And yet doth Juno me wel more shame,
For I dar noght biknowe myn owne name,
But ther as I was wont to highte Arcite,
Now highte I Philostrate, noght worth a myte.   700
Allas thou felle Mars! allas Juno!
Thus hath your ire our kinrede al fordo,
Save only me, and wrecched Palamoun,
That Theseus martireth in prisoun.
And over al this, to sleen me utterly,   705
Love hath his fyry dart so brenningly
Y-stiked thurgh my trewe careful herte,
That shapen was my deeth erst than my sherte.
Ye sleen me with your eyen, Emelye;
Ye been the cause wherfor that I dye.   710
Of al the remenant of myn other care
Ne sette I nat the mountaunce of a tare,
So that I coude doon aught to your plesaunce.'
And with that word he fil doun in a traunce
A longe tyme; and afterward he upsterte.   715

   This Palamoun, that thoughte that thurgh his herte
He felte a cold swerd sodeynliche glyde,
For ire he quook, no lenger wolde he byde.
And whan that he had herd Arcites tale,
As he were wood, with face deed and pale,   720
He sterte him up out of the buskes thikke,
And seyde, 'Arcite, false traitour wikke,

---

698. E., *owene*; Cp., Pt., Ln., *owne*.
702. All *lynage* exc. E., *kynrede*.
705. E., Hn., *outrely*; rest *utterly, uttyrly*.
712. E., *montance*.
715. E., *after*; rest *afterward*.   721. E., *stirte*.

Now artow hent, that lovest my lady so,
For whom that I have al this peyne and wo,
725 And art my blood, and to my counseil sworn,
As I ful ofte have told thee heer-biforn,
And hast by-japed heer duk Theseus,
And falsly chaunged hast thy name thus;
I wol be deed, or elles thou shalt dye.
730 Thou shalt nat love my lady Emelye,
But I wol love hir only and namo;
For I am Palamoun, thy mortal fo.
And though that I no wepne have in this place,
But out of prison am astert by grace,
735 I drede noght that outher thou shalt dye,
Or thou ne shalt nat loven Emelye.
Chees which thou wolt, for thou shalt nat asterte.'
 This Arcite, with ful despitous herte,
Whan he him knew, and hadde his tale herd,
740 As fiers as leoun pulled out a swerd,
And seyde thus: 'By God that sit above,
Nere it that thou art sik and wood for love,
And eek that thou no wepne hast in this place,
Thou sholdest nevere out of this grove pace,
745 That thou ne sholdest dyen of myn hond.
For I defye the seurtee and the bond
Which that thou seist that I have maad to thee.
What, verray fool, think wel that love is free!

---

723. E., Hn., *artow*; rest *art thou*.
726. E., Cm., *seyd*; rest *told*.
733. E., *wepene*.
737. Hl., *for*; rest *or*.
740. E., Hn., *his*; rest *a*.
746. E., *seurtee*.

THE KNIGHTES TALE

And I wol love hir, maugre al thy might!
But, for as muche as thou art a worthy knyght, 750
And wilnest to darreyne hir by bataille,
Have heer my trouthe, tomorwe I wol nat faile,
Withouten witing of any other wight,
That heer I wol be founden as a knight,
And bringen harneys right ynough for thee; 755
And chees the beste, and leve the worste for me.
And mete and drinke this night wol I bringe
Ynough for thee, and clothes for thy beddinge.
And, if so be that thou my lady winne,
And sle me in this wode ther I am inne, 760
Thou mayst wel have thy lady, as for me.'
This Palamon answerde: 'I graunte it thee.'
And thus they been departed til amorwe,
When ech of hem had levd his feith to borwe.

O Cupide, out of alle charitee! 765
O regne, that wolt no felawe have with thee!
Ful sooth is seyd, that love ne lordshipe
Wol noght, his thankes, have no felaweshipe;
Wel finden that Arcite and Palamoun.

Arcite is riden anon unto the toun, 770
And on the morwe, er it were dayes light,
Ful prively two harneys hath he dight,
Bothe suffisaunt and mete to darreyne
The bataille in the feeld bitwix hem tweyne.
And on his hors, allone as he was born, 775

---

749. E., *mawgree*.
750. E., Cm., Cp., om. second *as*; rest ins.
751. E., *hire*.
756. E., *chese*; Hn., Hl., Cm., *ches, chees*.
768. E., *hir*; Cm., *hese*; rest *his*.

He carieth al the harneys him biforn;
And in the grove, at tyme and place y-set,
This Arcite and this Palamon ben met.
Tho chaungen gan the colour in hir face;
⁷⁸⁰ Right as the hunters in the regne of Trace,
That stondeth at the gappe with a spere,
Whan hunted is the leoun or the bere,
And hereth him come russhing in the greves,
And breketh bothe bowes and the leves,
⁷⁸⁵ And thinketh, 'Heer cometh my mortel enemy,
Withoute faile, he moot be deed, or I;
For outher I moot sleen him at the gappe,
Or he moot sleen me, if that me mishappe:'
So ferden they, in chaunging of hir hewe,
⁷⁹⁰ As fer as everich of hem other knewe.
Ther nas no 'Good day,' ne no saluing;
But streight withouten word or rehersing,
Everich of hem heelp for to armen other,
As frendly as he were his owene brother;
⁷⁹⁵ And after that, with sharpe speres stronge
They foynen ech at other wonder longe.
Thou mightest wene that this Palamoun
In his fighting were as a wood leoun;
And as a cruel tigre was Arcite:
⁸⁰⁰ As wilde bores gonne they to smyte,
That frothen whyte as foom for ire wood.
Up to the ancle foghte they in hir blood.
And in this wyse I lete hem fighting dwelle;

---

776. E., *the*; Hn., *this*; rest *his*. 794. E., *freenly . . . owene*.
779. All have *To*; exc. Hl., *Tho*. 798. Hl., ins. *as* bef. *a*; rest om.
780. All have *hunters, hunterys*. 801. E., *whit*.
782. E., *and*; rest *or*.

And forth I wol of Theseus yow telle.
  The Destinee, Ministre General,   805
That executeth in the world over-al
The purveiaunce, that God hath seyn biforn,
So strong it is, that though the world had sworn
The contrarie of a thing by ye or nay,
Yet somtyme it shall fallen on a day   810
That falleth nat eft withinne a thousand yere.
For certeynly our appetites here,
Be it of werre, or pees, or hate, or love,
Al is this reuled by the sighte above.
This mene I now by mighty Theseus,   815
That for to hunten is so desirous,
And namely at the grete hert in May,
That in his bed ther daweth him no day,
That he nis clad, and redy for to ryde
With hunte and horn, and houndes him bisyde.   820
For in his hunting hath he swich delit,
That it is al his joye and appetit
To been himself the grete hertes bane;
For after Mars he serveth now Diane.
  Cleer was the day, as I have told er this,   825
And Theseus, with alle joye and blis,
With his Ypolita, the faire quene,
And Emelyë, clothed al in grene,
On hunting be they riden roially.
And to the grove, that stood ful faste by,   830
In which ther was an hert, as men him tolde,
Duk Theseus the streighte wey hath holde.
And to the launde he rideth him ful right,

---

804. E., *wole*.

128   THE CANTERBURY TALES

     For thider was the hert wont have his flight,
835 And over a brook, and so forth on his weye.
     This duk wol han a cours at him or tweye,
     With houndes, swiche as that him list comaunde.
        And whan this duk was come unto the launde,
     Under the sonne he loketh, and anon
840 He was war of Arcite and Palamon,
     That foughten breme, as it were bores two;
     The brighte swerdes wenten to and fro
     So hidously, that with the leeste strook
     It semed as it wolde felle an ook;
845 But what they were, nothing he ne woot.
     This duk his courser with his spores smoot,
     And at a stert he was bitwix hem two,
     And pulled out a swerd and cride, 'Ho!
     Namore, up peyne of lesing of your heed.
850 By mighty Mars, he shal anon be deed,
     That smyteth any strook, that I may seen!
     But telleth me what myster men ye been,
     That been so hardy for to fighten here
     Withouten juge or other officere,
855 As it were in a listes roially?'
        This Palamon answerde hastily
     And seyde: 'Sire, what nedeth wordes mo?
     We have the deeth deserved bothe two.
     Two woful wrecches been we, two caytyves,

---

  835. E., *in*; rest *on*.
  837. E., Cm., Ln., om. *that*; rest ins.
  844. E., *fille*; rest *felle(n)*.
  848. E., *cride*; Hn., Cp., Pt., *cryed*.
  849. E., Hn., Ln., *upon*; rest *up*.
  852. E., *mystiers*; rest *myster, mester*.
  858. E., Hn., *diserved*.

THE KNIGHTES TALE

That been encombred of oure owene lyves; 860
And as thou art a rightful lord and juge,
Ne yeve us neither mercy ne refuge,
But sle me first, for seynte charitee,
But sle my felawe eek as wel as me;
Or sle him first; for, though thou knowe it lite, 865
This is thy mortal fo, this is Arcite,
That fro thy lond is banisshed on his heed,
For which he hath deserved to be deed.
For this is he that cam unto thy gate,
And seyde, that he highte Philostrate. 870
Thus hath he japed thee ful many a yeer,
And thou hast maked him thy chief squyer;
And this is he that loveth Emelye.
For sith the day is come that I shal dye,
I make pleynly my confessioun, 875
That I am thilke woful Palamoun,
That hath thy prisoun broken wikkedly.
I am thy mortal foo, and it am I
That loveth so hote Emelye the brighte,
That I wol dye present in hir sighte. 880
Therfore I axe deeth and my juwyse;
But sle my felawe in the same wyse,
For bothe han we deserved to be slayn.'

   This worthy duk answerde anon agayn,
And seide, 'This is a short conclusioun: 885
Youre owne mouth, by your confessioun,
Hath dampned you, and I wol it recorde,

---

860. E., *oure.*
865. Hl., Hn., *knowe,* rest *knowest.*
886. E., *owene.*

It nedeth noght to pyne yow with the corde.
Ye shul be deed, by mighty Mars the rede!'
890 The quene anon, for verray wommanhede
Gan for to wepe, and so dide Emelye,
And alle the ladies in the companye,
Gret pitee was it, as it thoughte hem alle,
That ever swich a chaunce sholde falle;
895 For gentil men they were, of greet estat,
And nothing but for love was this debat,—
And sawe hir blody woundes, wyde and sore;
And alle cryden, bothe lasse and more,
'Have mercy, lord, upon us wommen alle!'
900 And on hir bare knees adoun they falle,
And wolde have kist his feet ther as he stood,
Til at the laste aslaked was his mood;
For pitee renneth soone in gentil herte.
And though he firste for ire quook and sterte,
905 He hath considered shortly, in a clause,
The trespas of hem bothe, and eek the cause;
And although that his ire hir gilt accused,
Yet in his resoun he hem bothe excused;
And thus he thoghte wel, that every man
910 Wol helpe himself in love, if that he can,
And eek delivere himself out of prisoun;
And eek his herte had compassioun
Of wommen, for they wepen ever in oon;
And in his gentil herte he thoghte anoon,
915 And softe unto himself he seyde, 'Fy

---

889. E., *shal*; Hn., Pt., *shul*; Cm., Hl., *schal*.
898. E., *crieden*.
909. Hn., Cm., Cp., *As*; rest *And*.
912. Hl., Pt., Ln., *had*; rest *hadde*.

Upon a lord that wol have no mercy,
But been a leoun, bothe in word and dede,
To hem that been in repentaunce and drede,
As wel as to a proud despitous man,
That wol maynteyne that he first bigan. 920
That lord hath litel of discrecioun,
That in swich cas can no divisioun,
But weyeth pride and humblesse after oon.'
And shortly, whan his ire is thus agoon,
He gan to loken up with eyen lighte, 925
And spak thise same wordes al on highte:—
'The god of love, a! *benedicite*,
How mighty and how greet a lord is he!
Ayeins his might ther gayneth none obstacles,
He may be cleped a god for his miracles; 930
For he can maken at his owne gyse
Of everich herte, as that him list devyse.
Lo heer, this Arcite and this Palamoun,
That quitly weren out of my prisoun,
And mighte han lived in Thebes roially, 935
And witen I am hir mortal enemy,
And that hir deth lyth in my might also,
And yet hath love, maugree hir eyen two,
Y-broght hem hyder, bothe for to dye!
Now loketh, is nat that an heigh folye? 940
Who may been a fool, but if he love?
Bihold, for Goddes sake that sit above,
Se how they blede! be they noght wel arrayed?

---

931. E., *owene*.
939. E., *Broght*; Hl., *I-brought*.
941. Hl., *if that*; rest *but-if*.

132 THE CANTERBURY TALES

Thus hath hir lord, the god of love, y-payed
945 Hir wages and hir fees for hir servyse!
And yet they wenen for to been ful wyse
That serven love, for aught that may bifalle!
But this is yet the beste game of alle,
That she, for whom they han this jolitee,
950 Can hem therfor as muche thank as me;
She woot namore of al this hote fare,
By God, than woot a cokkow or an hare!
But al moot been assayed, hoot and cold;
A man moot been a fool, or yong or old;
955 I woot it by myself ful yore agoon:
For in my tyme a servant was I oon.
And therfore, sin I knowe of loves peyne,
And woot how sore it can a man distreyne,
As he that hath ben caught ofte in his las,
960 I yow foryeve al hoolly this trespas,
At requeste of the quene that kneleth here,
And eek of Emelye, my suster dere.
And ye shul bothe anon unto me swere,
That nevermo ye shul my contree dere,
965 Ne make werre upon me night ne day,
But been my freendes in al that ye may;
I yow foryeve this trespas every deel.'
And they him swore his axing fayre and weel,
And him of lordshipe and of mercy preyde,
970 And he hem graunteth grace, and thus he seyde:
  'To speke of roial lynage and richesse,
Though that she were a quene or a princesse,

---

950. E., -fore.   952. E. Hn., *of*; rest *or*.
968. E., Cp., Hn., Cm., *sworen, sworyn*, rest *swore*.

THE KNIGHTES TALE

Ech of yow bothe is worthy, doutelees,
To wedden whan tyme is, but nathelees,
—I speke as for my suster Emelye, 975
For whom ye have this stryf and jelousye,—
Ye woot yourself she may not wedden two
At ones, though ye fighten evermo,—
That oon of yow, al be him looth or leef,
He moot go pypen in an ivy leef; 980
This is to seyn, she may nat now han bothe,
Al be ye never so jelous, ne so wrothe.
And for-thy, I yow putte in this degree,
That ech of yow shal have his destinee
As him is shape, and herkneth in what wyse; 985
Lo, heer your ende of that I shal devyse.

'My wil is this, for plat conclusioun,
Withouten any replicacioun,
If that yow lyketh, tak it for the beste,
That everich of yow shal goon wher him leste 990
Frely, withouten raunson or daunger;
And this day fifty wykes, fer ne ner,
Everich of yow shal bringe an hundred knyghtes,
Armed for listes up at alle rightes,
Al redy to darreyne hir by bataille. 995
And this bihote I yow withouten faille
Upon my trouthe and as I am a knight,
That whether of yow bothe that hath might,
This is to seyn, that whether he or thou

---

974. E., om. *but* and repeats *doutelees*, by mistake.
976. E., *Ialousye*.
980. E., om. *go*; rest ins.
982. E., *ialous*.
998, 999. E., *wheither*.

THE CANTERBURY TALES

1000 May with his hundred, as I spak of now,
Sleen his contrarie, or out of listes dryve,—
Than shal I yeve Emelya to wyve
To whom that fortune yeveth so fair a grace.
The listes shal I maken in this place,
1005 And God so wisly on my soule rewe,
As I shal even juge been and trewe.
Ye shul non other ende with me maken,
That oon of yow ne shal be deed or taken.
And if yow thinketh this is wel y-sayd,
1010 Seyth your avys, and holdeth yow apayd.
This is your ende and your conclusioun.'

Who loketh lightly now but Palamoun?
Who springeth up for joye but Arcite?
Who couthe telle, or who couthe it endite,
1015 The joye that is maked in the place
Whan Theseus hath doon so fair a grace?
But doun on knees wente every maner wight,
And thanked him with al hir herte and might,
And namely the Thebans ofte sythe.
1020 And thus with good hope and with herte blythe
They take hir leve, and homward gonne they ryde
To Thebes, with his olde walles wyde.

Explicit secunda pars.   Sequitur pars tercia.

1002. E., Hn., *Thanne*; Cm., Pt., *Than*; Cp., Ln., *That*; Hl., *Him*.
1004. E., *Tho*; rest *The*.
1014. E., Cm., om. *it*; rest ins.
1018. E., *thonken*, so Hn.; rest *-ed(e)*.
1019. E., *often*; Pt., *mony*.
1021. E., *taken*.

Part III

I trowe men wolde deme it necligence,
If I foryete to tellen the dispence
Of Theseus, that goth so bisily   1025
To maken up the listes roially;
That swich a noble theatre as it was,
I dar wel seyn that in this world ther nas.
The circuit a myle was aboute,
Walled of stoon, and diched al withoute.   1030
Round was the shap, in maner of compas,
Ful of degrees, the heighte of sixty pas,
That, whan a man was set on o degree,
He lette nat his felawe for to see.

Estward ther stood a gate of marbel whit, 1035
Westward, right swich another in the opposit.
And shortly to concluden, swich a place
Was noon in erthe, as in so litel space;
For in the lond ther nas no crafty man,
That geometrie or ars-metrik can,   1040
Ne purtreyour, ne kerver of ymages,
That Theseus ne yaf him mete and wages
The theatre for to maken and devyse.
And for to doon his ryte and sacrifyse,
He estward hath upon the gate above,   1045
In worship of Venus, goddesse of love,
Doon make an auter and an oratorie;

1028. E., om. *that*, as all exc. Hl.
1034. E., *lette*; Hn., *letted*; Cp., =*ede*; Cm., =*tyth*.
1035. E., *marbul*.
1039. E., Hn., *was*; rest *nas*.
1041. E., *portreitour*.
1042. E., Hn., Ln. om. *him*; rest ins.

And westward, in the mynde and in memorie
Of Mars, he maked hath right swich another,
1050 That coste largely of gold a fother.
And northward, in a touret on the wal,
Of alabastre whyt and reed coral
An oratorie riche for to see,
In worship of Diane of chastitee,
1055 Hath Theseus don wroght in noble wyse.
But yet hadde I foryeten to devyse
The noble kerving, and the portreitures,
The shap, the contenaunce, and the figures,
That weren in thise oratories thre.
1060   First in the temple of Venus maystow se
Wroght on the wal, ful pitous to biholde,
The broken slepes, and the sykes colde;
The sacred teeres, and the waymentinge;
The fyry strokes of the desiringe,
1065 That loves servaunts in this lyf enduren;
The othes, that hir covenants assuren;
Plesaunce and Hope, Desyr, Foolhardinesse,
Beautee and Youthe, Bauderie, Richesse,
Charmes and Force, Lesinges, Flaterye,
1070 Dispense, Bisinesse, and Jelousye,
That wered of yelwe goldes a gerland,
And a cokkow sitting on hir hand;
Féstes, instruments, caroles, daunces,
Lust and Array, and alle the circumstaunces

1048. E., *And on the westward in memorie*; so Hn., Cm., Cp., Ln.; Hl., as in text.
1064. E., *and*; rest *of*.
1065. E., *servauntz*.
1066. E., *covenauntz*.
1070. E., *Ialousye*.
1071. E., *yelewe*.
1072. E., *sittynge*.
1073. E., *instrumentz*.

THE KNIGHTES TALE

Of love, whiche that I rekne and rekne shal,   1075
By ordre weren peynted on the wal,
And mo than I can make of mencioun.
For soothly, al the mount of Citheroun,
Ther Venus hath hir principal dwellinge,
Was shewed on the wal in portreyinge,   1080
With al the gardin, and the lustinesse.
Nat was foryeten the porter Ydelnesse,
Ne Narcisus the faire of yore agon,
Ne yet the folye of king Salamon,
Ne yet the grete strengthe of Hercules,   1085
Thenchauntements of Medea and Circes,
Ne of Turnus, with the hardy fiers corage,
The riche Cresus, caytif in servage.
Thus may ye seen that Wisdom ne Richesse,
Beautee ne Sleighte, Strengthe ne Hardinesse,   1090
Ne may with Venus holde champartye;
For as hir list the world than may she gye.
Lo, alle thise folk so caught were in hir las,
Til they for wo ful ofte seyde 'Allas!'
Suffiseth heer ensamples oon or two,   1095
And though I coude rekne a thousand mo.

    The statue of Venus, glorious for to se,
Was naked, fleting in the large see,
And fro the navel doun al covered was

1075. E., *I rekned have and rekne shal*; Cm., *reken and rekne shal*; Hn., *rekned*.
1084. E., *And*, so Cm.; rest *Ne*.
1085. E., *And eek*; Hl., *Ne eek*; Hn., *Ne yet*; E., *Ercules*.
1086. E., *enchauntementz*.
1090. E., Hn., Pt., om. second *ne*; rest ins.
1095. E., *heere*.   1098. E., *fletynge*.
1096. E., **rekene**.   1099. E., *navele*.

1100 With wawes grene, and brighte as any glas.
A citole in hir right hand hadde she,
And on hir heed, ful semely for to se,
A rose gerland, fressh and wel smellinge;
Above hir heed hir dowves flikeringe.
1105 Biforn hir stood hir sone Cupido,
Upon his shuldres winges hadde he two;
And blind he was, as it is ofte sene;
A bowe he bar and arwes brighte and kene.

Why sholde I noght as wel eek telle yow al
1110 The portreiture, that was upon the wal
Within the temple of mighty Mars the rede?
Al peynted was the wal in lengthe and brede,
Lyk to the estres of the grisly place,
That highte the grete temple of Mars in Trace,
1115 In thilke colde frosty regioun,
Ther as Mars hath his sovereyn mansioun.

First on the wal was peynted a forest,
In which ther dwelleth neither man ne best,
With knotty, knarry, bareyn trees olde
1120 Of stubbes sharpe and hidous to biholde,
In which ther ran a rumbel and a swough,
As though a storm sholde bresten every bough;
And downward from an hille, under a bente,
Ther stood the temple of Mars armipotente,
1125 Wroght al of burned steel, of which thentree
Was long and streit, and gastly for to see.

1107. E., *was* after *it*; rest *is*.   1125. E., Hn., *the entree*
1119. E., *bareyne*.
1120. E., *hidouse*.
1121. E., Pt., *And*; rest *In*. All have *rombel, rumbel*, exc. Hl. *swymbul*.

THE KNIGHTES TALE

And ther-out cam a rage and such a veze,
That it made al the gates for to rese.
The northren light in at the dores shoon,
For windowe on the wal ne was ther noon, 1130
Thurgh which men mighten any light discerne.
The dores were alle of adamant eterne,
Y-clenched overthwart and endelong
With iren tough, and, for to make it strong,
Every piler, the temple to sustene, 1135
Was tonne-greet, of iren bright and shene.
   Ther saugh I first the derke ymagining
Of Felonye, and al the compassing;
The cruel Ire, reed as any glede;
The pykepurs, and eek the pale Drede; 1140
The smyler with the knyf under the cloke;
The shepne brenning with the blake smoke;
The tresoun of the mordring in the bedde;
The Open Werre, with woundes al bi-bledde;
Contek, with blody knyf and sharp manace; 1145
Al ful of chirking was that sory place.
The sleëre of himself yet saugh I ther,
His herte-blood hath bathed al his heer;
The nayl y-driven in the shode a-night;
The colde Deeth, with mouth gaping upright. 1150
Amiddes of the temple sat Meschaunce,

1127. E., Hn., Ln., *veze*; Cp., *vese*; Hl., *prise*.
1128. E., Hn., Cm., *gate*; rest *gates*.
1132. E., Hn., Pt., *dore was*; rest pl.
1137. E., *dirke*.
1138. E., Cm., om. *al*; rest ins.
1139. Hl., Ln., *as reed as*; rest om. first *as*.
1140. E., Cm., om. *eek*; rest ins.

With disconfort and sory contenaunce.
Yet saugh I Woodnesse laughing in his rage,
Armed Compleynt, Outhees, and fiers Outrage.
1155 The careyne in the bussh, with throte y-corve;
A thousand slayn, and nat of qualm y-storve;
The tiraunt, with the prey by force y-raft;
The toun destroyed, ther was no-thing laft.
Yet saugh I brent the shippes hoppesteres;
1160 The hunte strangled with the wilde beres:
The sowe freten the child right in the cradel;
The cook y-scalded, for al his longe ladel.
Noght was foryeten by the infortune of Marte;
The carter over-riden with his carte,
1165 Under the wheel ful lowe he lay adoun.
Ther were also, of Martes divisioun,
The barbour, and the bocher, and the smith
That forgeth sharpe swerdes on his stith.
And al above, depeynted in a tour,
1170 Saw I Conquest sitting in greet honour,
With the sharpe swerde over his heed
Hánging by a sotil twynes threed
Depeynted was the slaughtre of Julius,
Of grete Nero, and of Antonius;
1175 Al be that thilke tyme they were unborn,
Yet was hir deeth depeynted ther-biforn,

1155. E., Cp., Ln., *busk*; Hn., Pt., *bussh*.
1156. E., ins. *oon* after *nat*; rest om
1157. E., *pray*.
1167. E., Cm., *laborer*; rest *barbour*.
1171. E., Pt., Ln., *swerde*; rest *swerd*.
1172. E., *-ynge . . . soutil twynes*; Pt., Cp., Cm., *twyned(e)*; Ln. *twine*.

THE KNIGHTES TALE

By manasinge of Mars, right by figure;
So was it shewed in that portreiture
As is depeynted in the sterres above
Who shal be slayn or elles deed for love. 1180
Suffiseth oon ensample in stories olde,
I may not rekne hem alle thogh I wolde.

   The statue of Mars upon a carte stood,
Armed, and loked grim as he were wood;
And over his heed ther shynen two figures 1185
Of sterres, that been cleped in scriptures,
That oon Puella, that other Rubeus.
This god of armes was arrayed thus:
A wolf ther stood biforn him at his feet
With eyen rede, and of a man he eet; 1190
With sotil pencel depeynted was this storie,
In redoutinge of Mars and of his glorie.

   Now to the temple of Diane the chaste
As shortly as I can I wol me haste,
To telle yow al the descripcioun. 1195
Depeynted been the walles up and doun
Of hunting and of shamfast chastitee.
Ther saugh I how woful Calistopee,
Whan that Diane agreved was with here,
Was turned from a womman to a bere, 1200
And after was she maad the lode-sterre;
Thus was it peynted, I can say no ferre,
Hir sone is eek a sterre, as men may see.

1179. E., Pt., *certres*; Cm., Cp., Ln., Hn., *sertres*; Hl., *sterres*.
1182. E., *rekene*.
1191. E., *sontil*; all have *was depeynted*.
1197. E., *shamefast*.
1202. E., *peynted*; so all. All exc. Hl., ins. *yow* bef. *no*.

142 THE CANTERBURY TALES

<blockquote>

Ther saugh I Dane, y-turned til a tree,—
1205 I mene nat the goddesse Diane,
But Penneus doughter, which that highte Dane.
Ther saugh I Attheon an hert y-maked,
For vengeaunce that he saugh Diane al naked;
I saugh how that his houndes have him caught,
1210 And freten him, for that they knewe him naught.
Yet peynted was a litel forther-moor,
How Atthalante hunted the wilde boor,
And Meleagre,—and many another mo,—
For which Diane wroughte him care and wo.
1215 Ther saugh I many another wonder storie,
The whiche me list nat drawen to memorie.
This goddesse on an hert ful hye seet,
With smale houndes al aboute hir feet;
And undernethe hir feet she hadde a mone,
1220 Wexing it was, and sholde wanie sone.
In gaude grene hir statue clothed was,
With bowe in honde and arwes in a cas.
Hir eyen caste she ful lowe adoun,
Ther Pluto hath his derke regioun.
1225 A womman travailing was hir biforn,
But, for hir child so longe was unborn,
Ful pitously Lucina gan she calle,
And seyde, 'Help, for thou mayst best of alle.'
Wel coude he peynten lifly that it wroghte,
With many a florin he the hewes boghte.   1230

</blockquote>

1204. E., Hn., Cm., *y-turned*; rest *turned*.
1211. E., om. *was*; rest ins.
1213. E., Hn., Cm., *Meleagree*.
1217. E., ins. *wel* bef. *hye*; so Cp., Pt.
1229. E., Hn., Cm., Pt., *koude*; rest *couthe*.

THE KNIGHTES TALE

Now been thise listes maad, and Theseus,
That at his grete cost arrayed thus
The temples and the theatre every del,
Whan it was doon, him liked wonder wel.
But stinte I wol of Theseus a lyte, 1235
And speke of Palamon and of Arcite.

The day approcheth of hir retourninge,
That everich sholde an hundred knightes bringe,
The bataille to darreyne, as I yow tolde;
And til Athenes, hir covenant for to holde, 1240
Hath everich of hem broght an hundred knightes
Wel armed for the werre at alle rightes.
And sikerly, ther trowed many a man
That nevere, sithen that the world bigan,
As for to speke of knighthod of hir hond, 1245
As fer as God hath maked see or lond,
Nas, of so fewe, so noble a compaignye.
For every wight that lovede chivalrye,
And wolde, his thankes, han a passant name,
Hath preyed that he mighte ben of that game; 1250
And wel was him that therto chosen was.
For if ther fille tomorwe swich a cas,
Ye knowen wel, that every lusty knight,
That loveth paramours, and hath his might,
Were it in Engelond, or elleswhere, 1255
They wolde, hir thankes, wilnen to be there.
To fighte for a lady, *benedicite!*

1231. E., *the*; rest *thise, these*.
1235. E., *wole*.
1240. E., *covenantz*.
1250. E., *preyd*; Hn., *prayd*; Hl., Cm., *preyed*.

It were a lusty sighte for to see.
And right so ferden they with Palamon.
1260 With him ther wenten knightes many oon;
Som wol ben armed in an habergeoun,
And in a brest-plat and a light gipoun;
And somme woln have a peyre plates large;
And somme woln have a Pruce sheld or a targe;
1265 Somme woln been armed on hir legges weel,
And have an ax, and somme a mace of steel,—
Ther nis no newe gyse, that it nas old.
Armed were they, as I have you told,
Éverich after his opinioun.

1270 Ther maistow seen coming with Palamoun
Lygurge himself, the grete king of Trace;
Blak was his berd, and manly was his face.
The cercles of his eyen in his heed,
They gloweden bitwixe yelow and reed;
1275 And lyk a griffon loked he aboute,
With kempe heeres on his browes stoute;
His limes grete, his brawnes harde and stronge,
His shuldres brode, his armes rounde and longe.
And as the gyse was in his contree,
1280 Ful hye upon a char of gold stood he,
With foure white boles in the trays.
In-stede of cote-armure over his harnays,
With nayles yelwe, and brighte as any gold,
He hadde a beres skyn, col-blak, for-old.

1262. E., *And in brist-*; Hl., *In a*; Hn., Cm., Cp., Ln., *And in a*; Pt., *And a*.
1264. E., *shield*.
1265. E., *woln*.
1270. E., *comynge*.
1274. E., *betwixen*.
1275. E., *grifphon*.
1283. E., *yelewe*; Hn., Cm., *yelwe*.

THE KNIGHTES TALE

His longe heer was kembd bihinde his bak, 1285
As any ravenes fethere it shoon for-blak.
A wrethe of gold arm-greet, of huge wighte,
Upon his heed, set ful of stones brighte,
Of fyne rubies and of dyamaunts.
Aboute his char ther wenten white alaunts, 1290
Twenty and mo, as grete as any steer,
To hunten at the leoun or the deer,
And folwed him with mosel faste y-bounde,
Colered of golde, and torets fyled rounde.
An hundred lordes hadde he in his route, 1295
Armed ful wel, with hertes sterne and stoute.

With Arcita, in stories as men finde,
The grete Emetreus, the king of Inde,
Upon a stede bay, trapped in steel,
Covered in cloth of gold diapred wel, 1300
Cam riding lyk the god of armes, Mars.
His cote-armure was of cloth of Tars,
Couched with perles white and rounde and grete.
His sadel was of brend gold, newe y-bete;
A mantelet upon his shuldre hanginge 1305
Bret-ful of rubies reede, as fyr sparklinge.
His crispe heer lyk ringes was y-ronne,
And that was yelow, and glitered as the sonne.
His nose was heigh, his eyen bright citryn,

1289. *dyamauntz.*
1290. *alauntz.*
1294. E., Hl., *colerd*; Hn., *colered*; Pt., Ln., *colers.*
1294. *tourettes.*
1296. E., *stierne.*
1297. E, Pt., *Arcite*; rest *Arcita.*
1305. E., Cm., Pt., *mantel*; rest *mantelet.*
1306. E., *Brat-ful.*

1310 His lippes rounde, his colour was sangwyn,
A fewe fraknes in his face y-spreynd,
Betwixen yelow and somdel blak y-meynd,
And as a leoun he his loking caste.
Of fyve and twenty yeer his age I caste.
1315 His berd was wel bigonne for to springe;
His voys was as a trompe thunderinge.
Upon his heed he wered, of laurer grene,
A gerland fresh and lusty for to sene.
Upon his hand he bar, for his deduyt,
1320 An egle tame, as any lilye whyt.
An hundred lordes hadde he with him there,
Al armed, sauf hir heddes, in al hir gere,
Ful richely in alle maner thinges.
For trusteth wel, that dukes, erles, kinges,
1325 Were gadered in this noble compaignye,
For love, and for encrees of chivalrye.
Aboute this king ther ran on every part
Ful many a tame leoun and leopart.
And in this wise thise lordes, alle and some,
1330 Been on the Sonday to the citee come
Aboute pryme, and in the toun alight.

This Theseus, this duk, this worthy knight,
Whan he had broght hem into his citee,
And inned hem, everich in his degree,
1335 He festeth hem, and doth so greet labour
To esen hem, and doon hem al honour,
That yet men weneth that no mannes wit

1311. E., *frakenes*.
1316. E., *thondrynge*.
1328. E., *leopard*.
1334. E., *in*; Pt., *after*; rest *at*.
1337. E.. *maner*; rest *maneres*.

Of noon estat ne coude amenden it.
The minstralcye, the service at the feste,
The grete yiftes to the moste and leste, 1340
The riche array of Theseus paleys,
Ne who sat first ne last upon the deys,
What ladies fairest been or best daunsinge,
Or which of hem can dauncen best and singe,
Ne who most felingly speketh of love: 1345
What haukes sitten on the perche above,
What houndes liggen on the floor adoun:
Of al this make I now no mencioun;
But al theffect, that thinketh me the beste;
Now comth the poynt, and herkneth if yow leste. 1350

The Sonday night, er day bigan to springe,
When Palamon the larke herde singe,
Although it nere nat day by houres two,
Yet song the larke, and Palamon also.
With holy herte, and with an heigh corage 1355
He roos, to wenden on his pilgrimage
Unto the blisful Citherea benigne,
I mene Venus, honurable and digne.
And in hir houre he walketh forth a pas
Unto the listes, ther hir temple was, 1360
And doun he kneleth, and with humble chere
And herte soor, he seyde as ye shul here.

'Faireste of faire, o lady myn Venus,

1340. E., *meeste.*
1347. E., Cm., *in*; rest *on.*
1350. E., *cometh*; so all but Hl., *comth.*
1354. E., *also*; Hn., Cp., Pt., Ln., *right tho.*
1361. E., *with ful* (om. *and*); rest *and with.*
1362. E., *and seyde in this manere*; rest as text.

Doughter to Jove, and spouse of Vulcanus,
1365 Thou gladere of the mount of Citheroun.
For thilke love thou haddest to Adoun,
Have pitee of my bittre teeres smerte,
And tak myn humble preyere at thyn herte.
Allas! I ne have no langage to telle
1370 Theffectes ne the torments of myn helle;
Myn herte may myne harmes nat biwreye;
I am so confus, that I can noght seye.
But mercy, lady bright, that knowest wele
My thought, and seest what harmes that I fele,
1375 Considere al this, and rewe upon my sore,
As wisly as I shal for evermore,
Emforth my might, thy trewe servant be,
And holden werre alwey with chastitee;
That make I myn avow, so ye me helpe.
1380 I kepe noght of armes for to yelpe.
Ne I ne axe nat tomorwe to have victorie,
Ne renoun in this cas, ne veyne glorie
Of pris of armes blowen up and doun,
But I wolde have fully possessioun
1385 Of Emelye, and dye in thy servyse;
Find thou the maner how, and in what wyse.
I recche nat, but it may bettre be,
To have victorie of hem, or they of me,
So that I have my lady in myne armes.
1390 For though so be that Mars is god of armes,
Your vertu is so greet in hevene above
That, if yow list, I shal wel have my love.
Thy temple wol I worshipe evermo,

1368. Hl., *to thyn herte.*   1370. E., *tormentz.*

THE KNIGHTES TALE

And on thyn auter, wher I ryde or go,
I wol doon sacrifice, and fyres bete.   1395
And if ye wol nat so, my lady swete,
Than preye I thee, tomorwe with a spere
That Arcita me thurgh the herte bere.
Than rekke I noght, whan I have lost my lyf,
Though that Arcita winne hir to his wyf.   1400
This is theffect and ende of my preyere,
Yif me my love, thou blisful lady dere.'

  Whan the orisoun was doon of Palamon,
His sacrifice he dide, and that anon
Ful pitously, with alle circumstaunces,   1405
Al telle I noght as now his observaunces.
But atte laste the statue of Venus shook,
And made a signe, wherby that he took
That his preyere accepted was that day.
For thogh the signe shewed a delay,   1410
Yet wiste he wel that graunted was his bone;
And with glad herte he wente him hoom ful sone.

  The thridde houre inequal that Palamon
Bigan to Venus temple for to gon,
Up roos the sonne and up roos Emelye.   1415
And to the temple of Diane gan hye.
Hir maydens that she thider with hir ladde
Ful redily with hem the fyr they hadde,
Thencens, the clothes, and the remenant al
That to the sacrifice longen shal;   1420

1403. Hl., *thorisoun*; rest as text.
1405. E., Cm., *-staunce*; rest pl.
1406. E., Cm., *-vaunce*; rest pl.
1416. Pt., Hl., ins. *she* bef. *gan*.
1418. E., *ladde*, rest *hadde*.

THE CANTERBURY TALES

The hornes fulle of meth, as was the gyse,—
Ther lakked noght to doon hir sacrifyse.
Smoking the temple, ful of clothes faire,
This Emelye with herte debonaire
1425 Hir body wessh with water of a welle;
But how she dide hir ryte I dar nat telle,
But it be any thing in general;
And yet it were a game to heren al,
To him that meneth wel, it were no charge,—
1430 But it is good a man ben at his large.
Hir brighte heer was kempd, untressed al;
A coroune of a grene ook cerial
Upon hir heed was set ful fair and mete.
Two fyres on the auter gan she bete,
1435 And dide hir thinges, as men may biholde
In Stace of Thebes, and thise bokes olde.
Whan kindled was the fyr, with pitous chere
Unto Diane she spak as ye may here.
'O chaste goddesse of the wodes grene,
1440 To whom bothe hevene and erthe and see is sene,
Quene of the regne of Pluto derk and lowe,
Goddesse of maydens, that myn herte hast knowe
Ful many a yeer, and woost what I desire,
As keep me fro thy vengeaunce and thyn ire,
1445 That Attheon aboghte cruelly.
Chaste goddesse, wel wostow that I
Desire to been a mayden al my lyf,
Ne never wol I be no love ne wyf.

1421. E., Pt., *meth.*; Cm., *mete.*; Cp., Ln., *methe.*; Hn., *mede.*
1423. E., *-ynge.*
1431. E., *kempd*; Hn., Ln., *kembed*; rest *kempt(e).*

THE KNIGHTES TALE 151

I am, thou woost, yet of thy compaignye,
A mayde, and love hunting and venerye, 1450
And for to walken in the wodes wilde,
And noght to been a wyf, and be with childe.
Nought wol I knowe compaignye of man.
Now help me, lady, sith ye may and can,
For tho thre formes that thou hast in thee. 1455
And Palamon, that hath swich love to me,
And eek Arcite, that loveth me so sore,
This grace I preye thee withoute more,
As sende love and pees bitwixe hem two;
And fro me turne awey hir hertes so, 1460
That al hir hote love, and hir desyr,
And al hir bisy torment, and hir fyr
Be queynt, or turned in another place;
And if so be thou wolt do me no grace,
Or if my destinee be shapen so, 1465
That I shal nedes have oon of hem two,
As sende me him that most desireth me.
Bihold, goddesse of clene chastitee,
The bittre teres that on my chekes falle.
Syn thou art mayde, and kepere of us alle, 1470
My maydenhede thou kepe and wel conserve,
And whyl I live a mayde, I wol thee serve.'

   The fyres brenne upon the auter clere,
Whyl Emelye was thus in hir preyere;
But sodeinly she saugh a sighte queynte, 1475
For right anon oon of the fyres queynte,

1453. E., Hl., ins. *the* after *knowe*.
1459. Hn., *As*; rest *And*.
1465. E., *And*; rest *Or*.

THE CANTERBURY TALES

And quiked agayn, and after that anon
That other fyr was queynt, and al agon;
And as it queynte it made a whistelinge,
1480 As doon thise wete brondes in hir brenninge,
And at the brondes ende out-ran anoon
As it were blody dropes many oon;
For which so sore agast was Emelye,
That she was wel ny mad, and gan to crye,
1485 For she ne wiste what it signifyed;
But only for the fere thus hath she cryed,
And weep that it was pitee for to here.
And ther-with-al Diane gan appere,
With bowe in hond, right as an hunteresse,
1490 And seyde: 'Doghter, stint thyn hevinesse.
Among the goddes hye it is affermed,
And by eterne word write and confermed,
Thou shalt ben wedded unto oon of tho
That han for thee so muchel care and wo;
1495 But unto which of hem I may nat telle.
Farwel, for I ne may no lenger dwelle.
The fyres which that on myn auter brenne
Shul thee declaren, er that thou go henne,
Thyn aventure of love, as in this cas.'
1500 And with that word the arwes in the cas
Of the goddesse clateren faste and ringe,
And forth she wente and made a vanisshinge;
For which this Emelye astoned was,
And seyde, 'What amounteth this, allas!

1479. E., *whistlynge*.
1486. Pt., Hl., om. *hath*.
1492. Pt., *writt*; Hl., *write*; rest *writen*.
1498. E., Cp., *declare*; rest *declaren*.

THE KNIGHTES TALE 153

I putte me in thy proteccioun,   1505
Diane, and in thy disposicioun.'
And hoom she goth anon the nexte weye.
This is theffect, ther is namore to seye.

   The nexte houre of Mars folwinge this,
Arcite unto the temple walked is   1510
Of fierse Mars, to doon his sacrifise,
With alle the rytes of his payen wise.
With pitous herte and heigh devocioun,
Right thus to Mars he seyde his orisoun:

   'O stronge god, that in the regnes colde   1515
Of Trace honoured art and lord y-holde,
And hast in every regne and every lond
Of armes al the brydel in thyn hond,
And hem fortunest as thee list devyse,
Accept of me my pitous sacrifise.   1520
If so be that my youthe may deserve,
And that my might be worthy for to serve
Thy godhede, that I may ben oon of thyne,
Than preye I thee to rewe upon my pyne.
For thilke peyne, and thilke hote fyr,   1525
In which thou whilom brendest for desyr,—

. . . .

For thilke sorwe that was in thyn herte,
Have routhe as wel upon my peynes smerte.
I am yong and unkonning, as thou wost,   1535
And, as I trowe, with love offended most,
That ever was any lyves creature;
For she, that doth me al this wo endure,
Ne reccheth never wher I sinke or flete.

1524. E., Hn., Cm., *Thanne.*

1540 And wel I woot, er she me mercy hete,
I moot with strengthe winne hir in the place;
And wel I woot withouten help or grace
Of thee, ne may my strengthe noght availle.
Than help me, lord, tomorwe in my bataille,
1545 For thilke fyr that whilom brente thee
As wel as thilke fyr now brenneth me;
And do that I tomorwe have victorie.
Myn be the travaille, and thyn be the glorie.
Thy soverein temple wol I most honouren
1550 Of any place, and alwey most labouren
In thy plesaunce and in thy craftes stronge,
And in thy temple I wol my baner honge,
And alle the armes of my compaignye;
And evermo, unto that day I dye,
1555 Eterne fyr I wol biforn thee fynde.
And eek to this avow I wol me bynde:
My berd, myn heer that hongeth long adoun,
That never yet ne felte offensioun
Of rasour nor of shere, I wol thee yive,
1560 And ben thy trewe servant whil I live.
Now lord, have routhe upon my sorwes sore,
Yif me the victorie, I aske thee namore.'
The preyere stinte of Arcita the stronge,
The ringes on the temple dore that honge,
1565 And eek the dores, clatereden ful faste,
Of which Arcita somwhat him agaste.
The fyres brende upon the auter brighte,
That it gan al the temple for to lighte;

1562. Hl., *thy*; rest *the*.   1563. E., Hn., *preyere*.
1567. E., Cp., *brenden*; Pt., *brennen*; rest *brende, brente*.

THE KNIGHTES TALE

And swete smel the ground anon up-yaf,
And Arcita anon his hand up-haf,   1570
And more encens into the fyr he caste,
With othere rytes mo; and atte laste
The statue of Mars bigan his hauberk ringe.
And with that soun he herde a murmuringe
Ful lowe and dim, that sayde thus, 'Victorie.'   1575
For which he yaf to Mars honour and glorie.
And thus with joye and hope wel to fare,
Arcite anon unto his inne is fare,
As fayn as fowel is of the brighte sonne.

   And right anon swich stryf ther is bigonne   1580
For thilke graunting, in the hevene above,
Bitwixe Venus, the goddesse of love,
And Mars, the sterne god armipotente,
That Jupiter was bisy it to stente;
Til that the pale Saturnus the colde,   1585
That knew so manye of aventures olde,
Fond in his olde experience an art,
That he ful sone hath plesed every part.
As sooth is sayd, elde hath greet avantage,
In elde is bothe wisdom and usage;   1590
Men may the olde at-renne, and noght at-rede.
Saturne anon, to stinten stryf and drede,
Al be it that it is agayn his kynde,
Of al this stryf he gan remedie fynde.

   'My dere doughter Venus,' quod Saturne,   1595
'My cours, that hath so wyde for to turne,

1575. E., Hn., *and* bef. *sayde*; rest *that*.
1578. E., Hn., Cm., *In.*   1587. E., Pt., *and art.*
1583. E., *stierne.*   1591. Pt., Hl., *but*, rest *and*.

Hath more power than wot any man.
Myn is the drenching in the see so wan;
Myn is the prison in the derke cote;
1600 Myn is the strangling and hanging by the throte;
The murmure and the cherles rebelling,
The groyning and the pryve empoysoning:
I do vengeance and pleyn correccioun,
Whyl I dwelle in the signe of the leoun.
1605 Myn is the ruine of the hye halles,
The falling of the toures and of the walles
Upon the mynour or the carpenter.
I slow Sampsoun shaking the piler;
And myne be the maladyes colde,
1610 The derke tresons and the castes olde;
My looking is the fader of pestilence.
Now weep namore, I shal doon diligence
That Palamon, that is thyn owne knight,
Shal have his lady, as thou hast him hight.
1615 Though Mars shal helpe his knight, yet nathelees
Bitwixe yow ther moot be som tyme pees,
Al be ye noght of o compleccioun,
That causeth al day swich divisioun.
I am thyn ayel, redy at thy wille;
1620 Weep thou namore, I wol thy lust fulfille.'
   Now wol I stinten of the goddes above,
Of Mars, and of Venus, goddesse of love,
And telle yow, as pleynly as I can,
The grete effect, for which that I bigan.

Explicit tercia pars.   Sequitur pars quarta.

1604. E., om. *the* bef. *signe*; rest ins.   1613. E., *owene*.
1608. Hl., alone ins. *in* bef. *shaking*.

Part IV

Greet was the feste in Athenes that day,   1625
And eek the lusty seson of that May
Made every wight to been in swich plesaunce,
That al that Monday justen they and daunce,
And spenden it in Venus heigh servyse.
But by the cause that they sholde ryse   1630
Érly, for to seen the grete fight,
Unto hir reste wenten they at night.
And on the morwe, whan that day gan springe,
Of hors and harneys noyse and clateringe
Ther was in hostelryes al aboute;   1635
And to the paleys rood ther many a route
Of lordes, upon stedes and palfreys.
Ther maystow seen devising of herneys
So uncouth and so riche, and wroght so weel
Of goldsmithrie, of browding, and of steel;   1640
The sheeldes brighte, testers, and trappures;
Gold-hewen helmes, hauberks, cote-armures;
Lordes in paraments on hir courseres,
Knightes of retenue, and eek squyeres
Nailinge the speres, and helmes bokelinge,   1645
Gigginge of sheeldes, with layneres lacinge;
Ther as need is, they weren no-thing ydel;
The fomy stedes on the golden brydel
Gnawinge, and faste the armurers also
With fyle and hamer prikinge to and fro;   1650
Yemen on fote, and communes many oon

1629. E., *spenten*; rest *spenden*.   1642. E., *hauberkes*.
1635. E., *in the*; rest om. *the*.   1643. E., *paramentz*.
1641. E., *testeres*.

With shorte staves, thikke as they may goon;
Pypes, trompes, nakers, clariounes,
That in the bataille blowen blody sounes;
1655 The paleys ful of peples up and doun,
Heer thre, ther ten, holding hir questioun,
Divyninge of thise Theban knightes two.
Somme seyden thus, somme seyde it shal be so;
Somme helden with him with the blake berd,
1660 Somme with the balled, somme with the thikke herd;
Somme sayde, he looked grim and he wolde fighte;
He hath a sparth of twenty pound of wighte.
Thus was the halle ful of divyninge,
Longe after that the sonne gan to springe.
1665 The grete Theseus, that of his sleep awaked
With minstralcye and noyse that was maked,
Held yet the chambre of his paleys riche,
Til that the Theban knightes, bothe y-liche
Honoured, were into the paleys fet.
1670 Duk Theseus was at a window set,
Arrayed right as he were a god in trone.
The peple presseth thider-ward ful sone
Him for to seen, and doon heigh reverence,
And eek to herkne his hest and his sentence.
1675 An heraud on a scaffold made an 'Ho!'
Til al the noyse of peple was y-do;
And whan he saugh the peple of noyse al stille,
Tho shewed he the mighty dukes wille.

1653. E., *nakerers*; Cm., *nakerys*; rest *nakers*.
1661. E., *grymme*.
1675. E., *oo*.
1676. Some MSS. ins. *the* bef. *peple*; E., om.
1677. E., Cm., *noyse of peple*; rest as text.

THE KNIGHTES TALE

'The lord hath of his heigh discrecioun
Considered that it were destruccioun
To gentil blood to fighten in the gyse
Of mortal bataille now in this emprise;
Wherfore, to shapen that they shul nat dye,
He wol his firste purpos modifye.
No man therfore, up peyne of los of lyf,
No maner shot, ne pollax, ne short knyf
Into the listes sende, or thider bringe;
Ne short swerd for to stoke, with poynt bytinge,
No man ne drawe, ne bere by his syde.
Ne no man shal unto his felawe ryde
But o cours, with a sharp y-grounde spere;
Foyne, if him list, on fote, himself to were.
And he that is at meschief shal be take,
And noght slayn, but be broght unto the stake
That shal ben ordeyned on either syde;
But thider he shal by force, and ther abyde.
And if so falle, the chieftayn be take
On either side, or elles sleen his make,
No lenger shal the turneyinge laste.
God spede yow; goth forth, and ley on faste.
With long swerd and with maces fight your fille.
Goth now your wey; this is the lordes wille.'

    The voys of peple touchede the hevene,

1679. E., *heih*.
1686. E., om. first *ne*; rest ins.
1687. E., Cm., Ln., *ne*; rest *or*.
1698. E., *outher*.
1697. E., *be*; rest *falle*.
1701. All exc. Hl., have *fighteth, fihten*.
1703. Cm., Cp., *touchede*; rest *touched*.

So loude cryden they with mery stevene:
1705 'God save swich a lord, that is so good,
He wilneth no destruccioun of blood!'
　　Up goon the trompes and the melodye.
And to the listes rit the compaignye
By ordinaunce, thurghout the citee large,
1710 Hanged with cloth of gold, and nat with sarge.
Ful lyk a lord this noble duk gan ryde,
Thise two Thebanes upon either syde;
And after rood the quene and Emelye,
And after that another compaignye,
1715 Of oon and other, after hir degree.
And thus they passen thurghout the citee,
And to the listes come they by tyme.
It nas not of the day yet fully pryme,
Whan set was Theseus ful riche and hye.
1720 Ypolita the quene and Emelye,
And other ladies in degrees aboute.
Unto the seetes presseth al the route;
And westward, thurgh the gates under Marte,
Arcite, and eek the hundred of his parte,
1725 With baner reed is entred right anon;
And in that selve moment Palamon
Is under Venus, estward in the place,
With baner whyt, and hardy chere and face.
In al the world, to seken up and doun,
1730 So evene withouten variacioun,

1704. All *cride* exc. Cm., *cryedyn*; E., *murie*.
1712. E., *Thebans*; Cp., Pt., Ln., *Thebanes*.
1721. E., *othere*.
1728. E., *chiere*.

THE KNIGHTES TALE

Ther nere swiche compaignyes tweye.
For ther nas noon so wys that coude seye,
That any hadde of other avauntage
Of worthinesse, ne of estaat, ne age,
So evene were they chosen, for to gesse;   1735
And in two renges faire they hem dresse.
Whan that hir names rad were everichoon,
That in hir nombre gyle were ther noon,
Tho were the gates shet, and cried was loude:
'Do now your devoir, yonge knightes proude!'   1740
   The heraudes lefte hir priking up and doun;
Now ringen trompes loude and clarioun;
Ther is namore to seyn, but west and est
In goon the speres ful sadly in arest;
In goth the sharpe spore into the syde.   1745
Ther seen men who can juste and who can ryde;
Ther shiveren shaftes upon sheeldes thikke;
He feeleth thurgh the herte-spoon the prikke.
Up springen speres twenty foot on highte;
Out goon the swerdes as the silver brighte;   1750
The helmes they to-hewen and to-shrede;
Out brest the blood with sterne stremes rede;
With mighty maces the bones they to-breste.
He, thurgh the thikkeste of the throng gan threste;
Ther, stomblen steedes stronge, and doun goth al.   1755
He, rolleth under foot as doth a bal.
He, foyneth on his feet with his tronchoun,
And he him hurtleth with his hors adoun.
He, thurgh the body is hurt, and sithen y-take,

1735. E., om. *they*; rest ins.   1752. E., *stierne*.
1750. E., *gooth*; rest *goon, goṅ(e)*.   1755. E., Cm., *semblen*.

1760 Maugree his heed, and broght unto the stake,
As forward was, right ther he moste abyde;
Another lad is on that other side.
And som tyme doth hem Theseus to reste,
Hem to refresshe, and drinken if hem leste.
1765 Ful ofte a-day han thise Thebanes two
Togidre y-met, and wroght his felawe wo;
Unhorsed hath ech other of hem tweye.
Ther nas no tygre in the vale of Galgopheye,
Whan that hir whelp is stole whan it is lyte,
1770 So cruel on the hunte, as is Arcite
For jelous herte upon this Palamoun;
Ne in Belmarie ther nis so fel leoun,
That hunted is, or for his hunger wood,
Ne of his praye desireth so the blood,
1775 As Palamon to sleen his foo Arcite.
The jelous strokes on hir helmes byte;
Out renneth blood on bothe hir sydes rede.

    Som tyme an ende ther is of every dede,
For er the sonne unto the reste wente,
1780 The stronge king Emetreus gan hente
This Palamon, as he faught with Arcite,
And made his swerd depe in his flesh to byte;
And by the force of twenty is he take
Unyolden, and y-drawe unto the stake.
1785 And in the rescous of this Palamoun
The stronge king Ligurge is born adoun;
And king Emetreus, for al his strengthe,

1764. E., *fresshen.*
1785. E., *rescus.*

Is born out of his sadel a swerdes lengthe,
So hitte him Palamon er he were take;
But al for noght; he was broght to the stake. 1790
His hardy herte mighte him helpe naught;
He moste abyde, whan that he was caught,
By force, and eek by composicioun.

Who sorweth now but woful Palamoun,
That moot namore goon agayn to fighte? 1795
And whan that Theseus hadde seyn this sighte,
Unto the folk that foghten thus echon
He cryde, 'Ho! namore, for it is don!
I wol be trewe juge, and no partye.
Arcite of Thebes shal have Emelye, 1800
That by his fortune hath hir faire y-wonne.'
Anon ther is a noyse of peple bigonne
For joye of this, so loude and heigh withalle,
It semed that the listes sholde falle.

What can now faire Venus doon above? 1805
What seith she now, what doth this quene of love,
But wepeth so, for wanting of hir wille,
Til that hir teeres in the listes fille?
She seyde, 'I am ashamed, doutelees.'
Saturnus seyde, 'Doghter, hold thy pees; 1810
Mars hath his wille, his knight hath al his bone,
And, by myn heed, thou shalt ben esed sone.'

The trompes with the loude minstralcye,
The heraudes, that ful loude yolle and crye,
Been in hir wele for joye of daun Arcite. 1815
But herkneth me, and stinteth now a lyte,
Which a miracle ther bifel anon.

This fierse Arcite hath of his helm y-don,

And on a courser, for to shewe his face,
1820 He priketh endelong the large place,
Loking upward upon this Emelye;
And she agayn him caste a frendlich yë,
—For wommen, as to speken in comune,
They folwen al the favour of fortune,—
1825 And she was al his chere, as in his herte.
Out of the ground a fyr infernal sterte,
From Pluto sent, at requeste of Saturne,
For which his hors for fere gan to turne,
And leep asyde, and foundred as he leep;
1830 And er that Arcite may taken keep,
He pighte him on the pomel of his heed,
That in the place he lay as he were deed,
His brest to-brosten with his sadel-bowe.
As blak he lay as any cole or crowe,
1835 So was the blood y-ronnen in his face.
Anon he was y-born out of the place
With herte soor, to Theseus paleys.
Tho was he corven out of his harneys,
And in a bed y-brought ful faire and blyve,
1840 For he was yet in memorie and alyve,
And alway crying after Emelye.

Duk Theseus, with al his compaignye,
Is comen hoom to Athenes his citee,
With alle blisse and greet solempnitee.
1845 Al be it that this aventure was falle,
He nolde noght disconforten hem alle.

1823. E., Hn., Cm., omit ll. 1823–1824.
1825. Hn., *she*; rest om.; E., *chiere*.
1826. E., *furie*; so Hn., Cm.; rest *fyr, fir*.

THE KNIGHTES TALE

Men seyden eek that Arcite shal nat dye,
He shal ben heled of his maladye.
And of another thing they were as fayn,
That of hem alle was ther noon y-slayn,   1850
Al were they sore y-hurt, and namely oon,
That with a spere was thirled his brest-boon.
To othere woundes and to broken armes,
Some hadden salves and some hadden charmes,
Fermacies of herbes, and eek save   1855
They dronken, for they wolde hir lymes have.
For which this noble duk, as he wel can,
Conforteth and honoureth every man,
And made revel al the longe night,
Unto the straunge lordes, as was right.   1860
Ne ther was holden no disconfitinge,
But as a justes or a tourneyinge;
For soothly ther was no disconfiture,
For falling nis nat but an aventure;
Ne to be lad with fors unto the stake   1865
Unyolden, and with twenty knightes take,
O persone allone, withouten mo,
And haried forth by arme, foot, and too,
And eek his steede driven forth with staves,
With foot-men, bothe yemen and eek knaves,—   1870
It nas aretted him no vileinye;
Ther may no man clepen it cowardye.
    For which anon duk Theseus leet crye,
To stinten alle rancour and envye,
The gree as wel of o syde as of other.   1875

1868. E., Hn., Cm., *arm*; rest *arme*.

And either syde y-lyk as otheres brother;
And yaf hem yiftes after hir degree,
And fully heeld a feste dayes three;
And conveyed the kinges worthily
1880 Out of his toun a journee largely.
And hoom wente every man the righte way;
Ther was namore, but 'Far wel, Have good day!'
Of this bataille I wol namore endyte,
But speke of Palamon and of Arcite.
1885 Swelleth the brest of Arcite, and the sore
Encreseth at his herte more and more.
The clothered blood, for any lechecraft,
Corrupteth, and is in his bouk y-laft,
That neither veyne-blood ne ventusinge,
1890 Ne drinke of herbes may ben his helpinge.
The vertu expulsif, or animal,
Fro thilke vertu cleped natural,
Ne may the venim voyden ne expelle.
The pipes of his longes gonne to swelle,
1895 And every lacerte in his brest adoun
Is shent with venim and corrupcioun.
Him gayneth neither, for to gete his lyf,
Vomyt upward, ne dounward laxatif;
Al is to-brosten thilke regioun;
1900 Nature hath now no dominacioun;
And certeynly, ther nature wol nat wirche,
Farewel, phisik! go ber the man to chirche.
This al and som, that Arcita moot dye,
For which he sendeth after Emelye,

1879. E., *conuoyed*; rest *conueyed*.
1882. E., *fare*.

THE KNIGHTES TALE 167

And Palamon, that was his cosyn dere; 1905
Than seyde he thus, as ye shul after here:
   'Naught may the woful spirit in myn herte
Declare o poynt of alle my sorwes smerte
To yow, my lady, that I love most:
But I biquethe the service of my gost 1910
To yow aboven every creature,
Sin that my lyf may no lenger dure.
Allas, the wo! allas, the peynes stronge,
That I for yow have suffred, and so longe!
Allas, the deeth! allas, myn Emelye! 1915
Allas, departing of our compaignye!
Allas, myn hertes quene! allas, my wyf!
Myn hertes lady, endere of my lyf!
What is this world? what asketh men to have?
Now with his love, now in his colde grave 1920
Allone, withouten any compaignye.
Farwel, my swete fo! myn Emelye!
And softe tak me in your armes tweye,
For love of God, and herkneth what I seye.
I have heer with my cosyn Palamon 1925
Had stryf and rancour, many a day a-gon,
For love of yow, and for my jelousye;
And Jupiter so wys my soule gye,
To speken of a servaunt proprely,
With alle circumstaunces trewely,— 1930
That is to seyn, trouthe, honour, knighthede,

1912. *ne* supplied by Tyrwhitt bef. *may*; not in MSS.
1916. E., *departynge*.
1927. E., Hn., Cp., *Ialousye*.
1931. Cp., Pt., Hl., ins. *and* bef. *knighthede*.

Wisdom, humblesse, estaat, and heigh kinrede,
Fredom, and al that longeth to that art,—
So Jupiter have of my soule part,
As in this world right now ne knowe I non
So worthy to ben loved as Palamon,
That serveth yow, and wol doon al his lyf.
And if that ever ye shul been a wyf,
Foryet nat Palamon, the gentil man.'
And with that word his speche faille gan,
For from his feet up to his brest was come
The cold of deeth, that hadde him overcome;
And yet moreover, for in his armes two
The vital strengthe is lost and al ago.
Only the intellect, withouten more,
That dwelled in his herte syk and sore,
Gan faillen when the herte felte deeth.
Dusked his eyen two and failled breeth,
But on his lady yet caste he his yë;
His laste word was, 'Mercy, Emelye!'
His spirit chaunged hous, and wente ther,
As I cam never, I can nat tellen wher.
Therfore I stinte, I nam no divinistre;
Of soules finde I nat in this registre,
Ne me ne list thilke opiniouns to telle
Of hem, though that they wryten wher they dwelle,
Arcite is cold, ther Mars his soule gye;
Now wol I speken forth of Emelye.

    Shrighte Emelye, and howleth Palamon,

1936. E., Hn., *ben*; rest *be*.
1941. E., *And fro*; E., Cm., Hl., *herte*.
1943. Only Hl., om. *for*.

THE KNIGHTES TALE 169

And Theseus his suster took anon 1960
Swowninge, and bar hir fro the corps away.
What helpeth it to tarien forth the day,
To tellen how she weep, both eve and morwe?
For in swich cas wommen have swich sorwe,
Whan that hir housbonds been from hem ago, 1965
That for the more part they sorwen so,
Or elles fallen in swich maladye,
That at the laste certeinly they dye.

    Infinite been the sorwes and the teres
Of olde folk, and folk of tendre yeres, 1970
In al the toun, for deeth of this Theban;
For him ther wepeth bothe child and man;
So greet a weping was ther noon, certayn,
Whan Ector was y-broght, al fresh y-slayn,
To Troye. Allas! the pitee that was ther, 1975
Cracching of chekes, rending eek of heer,—
'Why woldestow be deed,' thise wommen crye,
'And haddest gold ynough and Emelye?'
No man mighte gladen Theseus,
Savinge his olde fader Egeus, 1980
That knew this worldes transmutacioun,
As he had seyn it chaungen up and doun,
Joye after wo, and wo after gladnesse:
And shewed hem ensamples and liknesse.

    'Right as ther deyed never man,' quod he, 1985

1964. Hl., alone has *can have*.
1965. E., *housbond is*; rest pl.
1967. E., *ellis*.
1970. E., *and eek*; rest *and folk*.
1976. E., Hn., Cm., Pt., *rentynge*.
1982. E., *hadde*. All omit *chaungen* exc. Hn., *chaungen bothe*; Hl. has *torne*.

'That he ne livede in erthe in som degree,
Right so ther livede never man,' he seyde,
'In al this world, that som tyme he ne deyde.
This world nis but a thurghfare ful of wo,
1990 And we been pilgrimes, passinge to and fro;
Deeth is an ende of every worldly sore.'
And over al this yet seyde he muchel more
To this effect, ful wysly to enhorte
The peple that they sholde hem reconforte.
1995   Duk Theseus, with al his bisy cure,
Cáste now wher that the sepulture
Of good Arcite may best y-maked be,
And eek most honurable in his degree.
And at the laste he took conclusioun,
2000 That ther as first Arcite and Palamoun
Hadden for love the bataille hem bitwene,
That in that selve grove, swote and grene,
Ther as he hadde his amorous desires,
His compleynt, and for love his hote fires,
2005 He wolde make a fyr, in which thoffice
Fúneral he mighte all accomplice;
And leet comaunde anon to hakke and hewe
The okes olde, and leye hem on a rewe
In colpons wel arrayed for to brenne;
2010 His officers with swifte feet they renne,
And ryde anon at his comaundement.
And after this, Theseus hath y-sent

1991. E., *worldes*; rest *worldly*.
1996. E., Hl., *Cast*; Hn., *Caste*.
2003. E., *amorouse*.
2005. E., *the office*; Hl., *thoffice*.
2011. E., *ryden*; Pt., *right*; rest *ride*.

After a bere, and it al overspradde
With cloth of gold, the richest that he hadde;
And of the same suyte he cladde Arcite; 2015
Upon his hondes hadde he gloves whyte;
Eek on his heed a croune of laurer grene,
And in his hond a swerd ful bright and kene.
He leyde him bare the visage on the bere;
Therwith he weep that pitee was to here. 2020
And for the peple sholde seen him alle,
Whan it was day, he broghte him to the halle,
That roreth of the crying and the soun.
   Tho cam this woful Theban Palamoun,
With flotery berd, and ruggy ashy heres, 2025
In clothes blake, y-dropped al with teres;
And passing othere of weping, Emelye,
The rewfulleste of al the compaignye.
In as muche as the service sholde be
The more noble and riche in his degree, 2030
Duk Theseus leet forth three steedes bringe,
That trapped were in steel al gliteringe,
And covered with the armes of daun Arcite.
Upon thise steedes, that weren grete and white,
Ther seten folk, of which oon bar his sheeld, 2035
Another his spere up in his hondes heeld,
The thridde bar with him his bowe Turkeys,—
Of brend gold was the cas, and eek the harneys;
And riden forth a pas with sorweful chere
Toward the grove, as ye shul after here. 2040

2017. E,. *coroune*, so, Hn., Cm., Ln.
2025. E., *rugged*; rest *rogi, ruggy*.
2034. Only Hl., has *that weren*.
2035. E., Ln., *sitten*; Pt., *stoden*; rest *seten, setin*.

THE CANTERBURY TALES

The nobleste of the Grekes that ther were
Upon hir shuldres carieden the bere,
With slake pas, and eyen rede and wete,
Thurghout the citee, by the maister-strete,
2045 That sprad was al with blak, and wonder hye
Right of the same is al the strete y-wrye.
Upon the right hond wente old Egeus,
And on that other syde duk Theseus,
With vessels in hir hand of gold ful fyn,
2050 Al ful of hony, milk, and blood, and wyn;
Eek Palamon, with ful greet compaignye;
And after that cam woful Emelye,
With fyr in honde, as was that tyme the gyse,
To do thoffice of funeral servyse.

2055 Heigh labour, and ful greet apparaillinge
Was at the service and the fyr-makinge,
That with his grene top the heven raughte,
And twenty fadme of brede the armes straughte;
This is to seyn, the bowes were so brode.
2060 Of stree first ther was leyd ful many a lode.
But how the fyr was maked up on highte,
And eek the names how the treës highte,
As ook, firre, birch, asp, alder, holm, popler,
Wilow, elm, plane, ash, box, chasteyn, lind, laurer,
2065 Mapul, thorn, beech, hasel, ew, whippeltre,

2045. Only Hl., has *al*.
2049. E., *vessel*; rest pl.
2054. E., *the office*; Hl., Cp., as text.
2057. E., om. *raughte*, by mistake.
2059. E., *weren*; rest *were*.
2062. E., *that*; Hn., Cp., Ln., Pt., *how*; Cm., *what*.
2063. E., *firre . . . popeler*.
2064. E., *wilugh*.

THE KNIGHTES TALE

How they weren feld shal nat be told for me;
Ne how the goddes ronnen up and doun,
Disherited of hir habitacioun,
In which they woneden in reste and pees,
Nymphes, faunes, and amadrides; 2070
Ne how the bestes and the briddes alle
Fledden for fere, whan the wode was falle;
Ne how the ground agast was of the light,
That was nat wont to seen the sonne bright;
Ne how the fyr was couched first with stree, 2075
And than with drye stokkes cloven a three,
And than with grene wode and spicerye,
And than with cloth of gold and with perrye,
And gerlandes hanging with ful many a flour,
The mirre, thencens, with al so greet odour; 2080
Ne how Arcite lay among al this,
Ne what richesse aboute his body is;
Ne how that Emelye, as was the gyse,
Putte in the fyr of funeral servyse;
Ne how she swowned whan men made the fyr, 2085
Ne what she spak, ne what was hir desyr;
Ne what jewels men in the fyr tho caste,
Whan that the fyr was greet and brente faste;
Ne how som caste hir sheeld, and som hir spere,
And of hir vestiments, whiche that they were, 2090
And cuppes ful of wyn, and milk, and blood,

2066. E., *fild*; rest *felled(e)*.   2090. E., *hire . . . vestimentz*.
2070. E., Cm., *Nymphus*.   2091. E., *coppes*.
2076. E., *thanne*.
2085. E., *men made fyr*; Hn., Cm., *men made the fyr*; Cp., Pt., Ln. *maad was the fyr*.
2087. Hl. alone inserts *tho* before *caste*.

Into the fyr, that brente as it were wood;
Ne how the Grekes, with an huge route
Thryës riden al the fyr aboute
2095 Upon the left hand, with a loud shoutinge,
And thryës with hir speres clateringe;
And thryës how the ladies gonne crye;
Ne how that lad was homward Emelye;
Ne how Arcite is brent to asshen colde;
2100 Ne how that liche-wake was y-holde
Al thilke night, ne how the Grekes pleye
The wake-pleyes; ne kepe I nat to seye
Who wrastleth best naked, with oille enoynt,
Ne who that bar him best in no disjoynt.
2105 I wol nat tellen eek how that they goon
Hoom til Athenes whan the pley is doon.
But shortly to the poynt than wol I wende,
And maken of my longe tale an ende.

By processe and by lengthe of certeyn yeres
2110 Al stinted is the moorning and the teres
Of Grekes, by oon general assent.
Than semed me ther was a parlement
At Athenes, upon certeyn poynts and cas;
Among the whiche poynts y-spoken was
2115 To have with certeyn contrees alliaunce,
And have fully of Thebans obeisaunce.
For which this noble Theseus anon
Leet senden after gentil Palamon,
Unwist of him what was the cause and why;

2094. E., *Tries*; rest *Thryes*; E., *place* for *fyr*; Hl., *thre tymes*.
2110. E., *styntyd*. 2113, 14. E., *poyntz*.
2112. E., *thanne*.

THE KNIGHTES TALE

But in his blake clothes sorwefully 2120
He cam at his comaundement in hye.
Tho sente Theseus for Emelye.
Whan they were set, and hust was al the place,
And Theseus abiden hadde a space
Er any word cam from his wyse brest, 2125
His eyen sette he ther as was his lest,
And with a sad visage he syked stille,
And after that right thus he seyde his wille:
  'The Firste Moevere of the cause above,
Whan he first made the faire cheyne of love, 2130
Greet was theffect, and heigh was his entente;
Wel wiste he why, and what therof he mente;
For with that faire cheyne of love he bond
The fyr, the eyr, the water, and the lond
In certeyn boundes, that they may nat flee. 2135
That same Prince and that Moevere,' quod he,
'Hath stablissed in this wrecched world adoun
Certeyne dayes and duracioun
To al that is engendred in this place,
Over the whiche day they may nat pace, 2140
Al mowe they yet tho dayes wel abregge;
Ther needeth non auctoritee tallegge,
For it is preved by experience,
But that me list declaren my sentence.
Than may men by this ordre wel discerne, 2145
That thilke Moevere stable is and eterne.

2120. E., *hise*.
2136 E. repeats *that*; Hn., Ln., omit.
2139. E., *engendrid*.
2142. E., Cp., *noght non*; rest om. *nought*; E., *allegge*; rest ins. *to*.
2145. E., *Thanne*.

'Wel may men knowe, but it be a fool,
That every part deryveth from his hool.
For nature hath nat take his biginning
Of no partye ne cantel of a thing,
But of a thing that parfit is and stable,
Descending so, til it be corrumpable.
And therfore of his wise purveiaunce,
He hath so wel biset his ordinaunce,
That speces of thinges and progressiouns
Shullen enduren by successiouns,
And nat eterne, with-outen any lye:
This maistow understonde and seen at eye.

'Lo the ook, that hath so long a norisshinge
From tyme that it first biginneth springe,
And hath so long a lyf as we may see,
Yet at the laste wasted is the tree.

'Considereth eek, how that the harde stoon
Under our feet, on which we trede and goon,
Yit wasteth it, as it lyth by the weye.
The brode river somtyme wexeth dreye,
The grete tounes see we wane and wende;
Than may ye see that al this thing hath ende.

'Of man and womman seen we wel also,
That nedeth in oon of thise termes two,
This is to seyn, in youthe or elles age,
He moot ben deed, the king as shal a page;
Som in his bed, som in the depe see,
Som in the large feeld, as men may se.

2148. E., *dirryueth*.
2149. E., Cm., om. *nat*; rest ins.
2157. Hl., *eterne be withoute lye*.
2167. E., *toures*; rest *tounes*.
2168. E., *thanne*.

THE KNIGHTES TALE

Ther helpeth noght, al goth that ilke weye. 2175
Than may I seyn that al this thing moot deye.
What maketh this but Jupiter the king?
The which is prince and cause of alle thing,
Converting al unto his propre welle,
From which it is deryved, sooth to telle. 2180
And here-agayns no creature on lyve,
Of no degree, availleth for to stryve.

'Thanne is it wisdom, as it thinketh me,
To maken vertu of necessitee,
And take it wel that we may nat eschue, 2185
And namely that to us alle is due.
And whoso gruccheth ought, he doth folye,
And rebel is to him that al may gye
And certeynly a man hath most honour
To dyen in his excellence and flour, 2190
Whan he is siker of his gode name;
Than hath he doon his freend, ne him, no shame.
And gladder oghte his freend ben of his deeth,
Whan with honour up-yolden is his breeth,
Than whan his name apalled is for age; 2195
For al forgeten is his vasselage.
Than is it best, as for a worthy fame,
To dyen whan that he is best of name.
The contrarie of al this is wilfulnesse.
Why grucchen we, why have we hevinesse, 2200
That good Arcite, of chivalrye flour

2176. E., *Thanne*; Cm., om. *that*; Cm., *mote nedis*; rest as text.
2178. All have *That is prince*; exc. Hl., *The which is*.
2197. E., *Thanne*.
2201. Hl., Cp., Ln., Pt., ins. *the* bef. *flour*.

Departed is, with duetee and honour
Out of this foule prison of this lyf?
Why grucchen heer his cosyn and his wyf
2205 Of his welfare that loved hem so wel?
Can he hem thank? Nay, God woot, never a del
That bothe his soule and eek hemself offende,
And yet they mowe hir lustes nat amende.

'What may I conclude of this longe serie,
2210 But after wo I rede us to be merie,
And thanken Jupiter of al his grace?
And er that we departen from this place,
I rede that we make of sorwes two
O parfit joye, lasting evermo:
2215 And looketh now, wher most sorwe is her-inne,
Ther wol we first amenden and biginne.

'Suster,' quod he, 'this is my fulle assent,
With al thavys heer of my parlement,
That gentil Palamon, your owne knight,
2220 That serveth yow with wille, herte, and might,
And ever hath doon, sin that ye first him knewe,
That ye shul, of your grace, upon him rewe,
And taken him for housbonde and for lord:
Leen me your hond, for this is our acord.
2225 Lat see now of your wommanly pitee.
He is a kinges brother sone, pardee,
And, though he were a povre bacheler,
Sin he hath served yow so many a yeer,
And had for yow so greet adversitee,

2209. E., *concluden.*
2213. Hl., *that*; rest om.
2219. E., *thyn*; rest *your(e)*; E., *owene.*
2224. E., *Lene.*

THE KNIGHTES TALE

It moste been considered, leveth me; 2230
For gentil mercy oghte to passen right.
   Than seyde he thus to Palamon ful right:
'I trowe ther nedeth litel sermoning
To make yow assente to this thing.
Com neer, and tak your lady by the hond.' 2235
Betwixen hem was maad anon the bond,
That highte matrimoigne or mariage,
By al the counseil and the baronage.
And thus with alle blisse and melodye
Hath Palamon y-wedded Emelye. 2240
And God, that al this wyde world hath wroght,
Sende him his love, that hath it dere a-boght.
For now is Palamon in alle wele,
Living in blisse, in richesse, and in hele;
And Emelye him loveth so tendrely, 2245
And he hir serveth also gentilly,
That nevere was ther no word hem bitwene
Of jelousie, or any other tene.
Thus endeth Palamon and Emelye;
And God save al this faire compaignye! Amen. 2250

Here is ended the knightes tale.

2238. E., *conseil*; Cm., *cuntre*.
2242. E., om. *hath*.
2248. E., *ialousye*.
The colophon is from E.

THE MONK'S PROLOGUE

THE MERY WORDES OF THE HOST TO THE MONK

Whan ended was my tale of Melibee,
And of Prudence and hir benignitee,
Our hoste seyde, 'As I am faithful man,
And by the precious *corpus Madrian*,
5 I hadde lever than a barel ale
That goode lief my wyf hadde herd this tale!
For she nis no-thing of swich pacience
As was this Melibeus wyf Prudence.
By Goddes bones! whan I bete my knaves,
10 She bringth me forth the grete clobbed staves,
And cryeth, "Slee the dogges everichoon,
And brek hem, bothe bak and every boon."
And if that any neighebor of myne
Wol nat in chirche to my wyf enclyne,
15 Or be so hardy to hir to trespace,
Whan she comth hoom she rampeth in my face,
And cryeth, "False coward, wreek thy wyf!
By *corpus* bones! I wol have thy knyf,
And thou shalt have my distaf and go spinne!"
20 Fro day to night right thus she wol biginne;—
"Allas!" she seith, "that ever I was shape
To wedde a milksop or a coward ape,
That wol be overlad with every wight!
Thou darst nat stonden by thy wyves right!"
25 'This is my lyf, but-if that I wol fighte;

---

21. E., Hn., *euere that I.*

180

THE MONK'S PROLOGUE

And out at dore anon I moot me dighte,
Or elles I am but lost, but-if that I
Be lyk a wilde leoun fool-hardy.
I woot wel she wol do me slee som day
Som neighebore, and thanne go my way.　　　　　30
For I am perilous with knyf in honde,
Al be it that I dar nat hir withstonde,
For she is big in armes, by my feith,
That shal he finde, that hir misdooth or seith.
But lat us passe awey fro this matere.　　　　　35

'My lord the Monk,' quod he, 'be mery of chere;
For ye shul telle a tale trewely.
Lo! Rouchestre stant heer faste by!
Ryd forth, myn owene lord, brek nat our game,
But, by my trouthe, I knowe nat your name,　　　　　40
Wher shal I calle yow my lord dan John,
Or dan Thomas, or elles dan Albon?
Of what hous be ye, by your fader kin?
I vow to God, thou hast a ful fair skin,
It is a gentil pasture ther thou goost;　　　　　45
Thou art nat lyk a penaunt or a goost.
Upon my feith, thou art som officer,
Some worthy sexteyn, or som celerer,
For by my fader soule, as to my doom,
Thou art a maister whan thou art at hoom;　　　　　50
No povre cloisterer, ne no novys,
But a governour, wyly and wys.
And therwithal of brawnes and of bones

---
32. E., Cp., Ln., *hire nat*; rest as text.
36. E., *myrie*.
41, 42. E., *daun*.
51. E., Hn., Pt., Ln., *cloistre*.

A wel-faring persone for the nones.

75 But be nat wrooth, my lord, for that I pleye,
Ful ofte in game a sooth I have herd seye.'
  This worthy monk took al in pacience,
And seyde, 'I wol doon al my diligence,
As fer as souneth into honestee,
80 To telle yow a tale, or two, or three.
And if yow list to herkne hiderward,
I wol yow seyn the lyf of seint Edward;
Or elles first Tragedies wol I telle
Of whiche I have an hundred in my celle.
85 Tragedie is to seyn a certeyn storie,
As olde bokes maken us memorie,
Of him that stood in greet prosperitee
And is y-fallen out of heigh degree
Into miserie, and endeth wrecchedly.
90 And they ben versifyed comunly
Of six feet, which men clepe *exametron*.
In prose eek been endyted many oon,
And eek in metre, in many a sondry wyse.
Lo! this declaring oughte y-nough suffise.
95   Now herkneth, if yow lyketh for to here;
But first I yow biseke in this matere,
Though I by ordre telle nat thise thinges,
Be it of popes, emperours or kinges,
After hir ages, as men writen finde,
100 But telle hem som bifore and som bihinde,
As it now comth un-to my remembraunce;
Have me excused of myn ignoraunce.'

Explicit.

THE MONKES TALE

HERE BIGINNETH THE MONKES TALE, DE CASIBUS VIRORUM ILLUSTRIUM

I wol biwayle in maner of Tragedie
The harm of hem that stode in heigh degree,
And fillen so that ther nas no remedie
To bringe hem out of hir adversitee;
For certein, whan that Fortune list to flee,   5
Ther may no man the cours of hir withholde;
Lat no man truste on blind prosperitee;
Be war by thise ensamples trewe and olde.

DE HUGELINO, COMITE DE PIZE.

Of the erl Hugelyn of Pyse the langour
Ther may no tonge telle for pitee;
But litel out of Pyse stant a tour,
In whiche tour in prisoun put was he,   420
And with him been his litel children three.
The eldeste scarsly fyf yeer was of age.
Allas, Fortune! it was greet crueltee
Swiche briddes for to putte in swiche a cage!

Dampned was he to deye in that prisoun,   425
For Roger, which that bisshop was of Pyse,
Hadde on him maad a fals suggestioun,
Thurgh which the peple gan upon him ryse,
And putten him to prisoun in swich wyse
As ye han herd, and mete and drink he hadde   430

---

417. E., *Pyze*; Hn., *Pize*; rest *Pyse, Pise*, so also ll. 419, 426, 466.

So smal that wel unnethe it may suffyse,
And therwith-al it was ful povre and badde.

And on a day bifil that, in that hour,
Whan that his mete wont was to be broght,
435 The gayler shette the dores of the tour.
He herde it wel,—but he spak right noght,
And in his herte anon ther fil a thoght,
That they for hunger wolde doon him dyen.
'Allas!' quod he, 'allas! that I was wroght!'
440 Therwith the teres fillen from his yën.

His yonge sone, that three yeer was of age,
Unto him seyde, 'Fader, why do ye wepe?
Whan wol the gayler bringen our potage,
Is ther no morsel breed that ye do kepe?
445 I am so hungry that I may nat slepe.
Now wolde God that I mighte slepen ever!
Than sholde nat hunger in my wombe crepe;
Ther is no thing, save breed, that me were lever.'

Thus day by day this child bigan to crye,
450 Til in his fadres barme adoun it lay,
And seyde, 'Far-wel, fader, I moot dye,'
And kiste his fader, and deyde the same day.
And whan the woful fader deed it say,
For wo his armes two he gan to byte,
455 And seyde, 'Allas, Fortune! and weylaway!
Thy false wheel my wo al may I wyte!'

---

431. E., Pt., om. *wel*.
436. E., *spak*; rest *saugh, seegh, sawe*.

THE MONKES TALE

His children wende that it for hunger was
That he his armes gnow, and nat for wo,
And seyde, 'Fader, do nat so, allas!
But rather eet the flesh upon us two; 460
Our flesh thou yaf us, tak our flesh us fro
And eet y-nough:' right thus they to him seyde,
And after that, with-in a day or two,
They leyde hem in his lappe adoun, and deyde.

Himself, despeired, eek for hunger starf; 465
Thus ended is this mighty Erl of Pyse;
From heigh estaat Fortune awey him carf.
Of this Tragedie it oghte y-nough suffyse.
Whoso wol here it in a lenger wyse,
Redeth the grete poete of Itaille, 470
That highte Dant, for he can al devyse
Fro point to point, nat o word wol he faille.

---

461. E., Hn., om. *us* after *yaf.*

THE PROLOGUE OF THE NONNE PREESTES TALE

'Ho!' quod the Knight, 'good sir, na-more of this,
That ye han seyd is right y-nough, y-wis,
And muchel more; for litel hevinesse
Is right y-nough to muchel folk, I gesse.
5 I seye for me, it is a greet disese
Wher-as men han ben in greet welthe and ese,
To heren of hir sodeyn fal, allas!
And the contrarie is joie and greet solas,
As whan a man hath been in povre estaat,
10 And clymbeth up, and wexeth fortunat,
And ther abydeth in prosperitee,
Swich thing is gladsom, as it thinketh me,
And of swich thing were goodly for to telle.'
'Ye,' quod our Hoste, 'by Seinte Poules belle,
15 Ye seye right sooth; this monk, he clappeth loude,
He spak how "Fortune covered with a cloude"
I noot never what, and als of a "Tragedie"
Right now ye herde, and pardee! no remedie
It is for to biwaille, ne compleyne
20 That that is doon, and als it is a peyne,
As ye han seyd, to here of hevinesse.
Sir Monk, na-more of this, so God yow blesse!
Your tale anoyeth al this compaignye;
Swich talking is nat worth a boterflye;
25 For ther-in is ther no desport ne game.
Wherfore, sir Monk, or dan Piers by your name,

---

17. E., *also*; rest *als*.   26. Pt., *or*; Hn., *o*; rest om.

186

I preye yow hertely, telle us somwhat elles,
For sikerly, nere clinking of your belles,
That on your brydel hange on every syde,
By hevene king, that for us alle dyde, 30
I sholde er this han fallen doun for slepe,
Althogh the slough had never been so depe;
Than had your tale al be told in vayn,
For certeinly, as that thise clerkes seyn,
"Wher-as a man may have noon audience, 35
Noght helpeth it to tellen his sentence;"
And wel I woot the substance is in me,
If any thing shal wel reported be.
Sir, sey somwhat of hunting, I yow preye.'
'Nay,' quod this Monk, 'I have no lust to pleye; 40
Now let another telle, as I have told.'

   Than spak our Host, with rude speche and bold,
And seyde unto the Nonnes Preest anon,
'Com neer, thou preest, com hider, thou sir John,
Tel us swich thing as may our hertes glade, 45
Be blythe, though thou ryde upon a jade.
What thogh thyn hors be bothe foule and lene,
If he wol serve thee, rekke nat a bene;
Look that thyn herte be mery evermo.'
'Yis, sir,' quod he, 'yis, Host, so mote I go, 50
But I be mery, y-wis, I wol be blamed.'
And right anon his tale he hath attamed,
And thus he seyde unto us everichon,
This swete preest, this goodly man, sir John.

Explicit.

---

49. E., *murie*.   **51.** E., *myrie*.

THE NONNE PREESTES TALE

*HERE BIGINNETH THE NONNE PREESTES TALE OF THE
COK AND HEN, CHAUNTECLEER AND PERTELOTE*

A POVRE widwe somdel stope in age,
Was whilom dwelling in a narwe cotage,
Biside a grove, stonding in a dale.
This widwe, of which I telle yow my tale,
5   Sin thilke day that she was last a wyf,
In pacience ladde a ful simple lyf,
For litel was hir catel and hir rente.
By housbondrie of swich as God hir sente,
She fond hirself, and eek hir doghtren two.
10   Three large sowes hadde she, and namo.
Three kyn and eek a sheep that highte Malle.
Ful sooty was hir bour, and eek hir halle,
In which she eet ful many a sclendre meel;
Of poynaunt sauce hir neded never a deel.
15   No deyntee morsel passed thurgh hir throte,
Hir diete was accordant to hir cote.
Repleccioun ne made hir never sik;
Attempre dyete was al hir phisik,
And exercise, and hertes suffisaunce.
20   The goute lette hir no-thing for to daunce,
Napoplexie shente nat hir heed;
No wyn ne drank she, neither whyt ne reed;.
Hir bord was served most with whyt and blak,

---

1. E., Hn., *stape*; Ln., *stoupe*; rest *stope*.
3. E., *greue*.
11. E., *keen*; rest *kyn*.
21. E., Hn., *Napoplexie*; rest *Ne poplexie*.

THE NONNE PREESTES TALE

Milk and broun breed, in which she fond no lak,
Seynd bacoun, and somtyme an ey or tweye,   25
For she was as it were a maner deye.
   A yerd she hadde, enclosed al aboute
With stikkes, and a drye dych withoute,
In which she hadde a cok, hight Chauntecleer,
In al the land of crowing nas his peer.   30
His vois was merier than the merye orgon
On messe-dayes that in the chirche gon;
Wel sikerer was his crowing in his logge,
Than is a clokke, or an abbey orlogge.
By nature knew he ech ascencioun   35
Of equinoxial in thilke toun;
For whan degrees fiftene were ascended,
Than crew he, that it mighte nat ben amended.
His comb was redder than the fyn coral,
And batailled as it were a castel wal.   40
His byle was blak, and as the jeet it shoon;
Lyk asur were his legges and his toon;
His nayles whiter than the lilie flour,
And lyk the burned gold was his colour.
   This gentil cok hadde in his governaunce   45
Sevene hennes, for to doon al his plesaunce,
Whiche were his sustres and his paramours,
And wonder lyk to him, as of colours;
Of whiche the faireste hewed on hir throte
Was cleped faire damoysele Pertelote.   50
Curteys she was, discreet, and debonaire,

---
29. E., Hn., *heet*; rest *that hight(e)*.
31. E., Hn., Cm., *murier*; E., Cm., *murie*.
35. E., Pt., *he crew*; Hl., *knew he*; rest *he knew*.
36. E., Ln., ins. *the* after *of*.

And compaignable, and bar hirself so faire,
Sin thilke day that she was seven night old
That trewely she hath the herte in hold
55 Of Chauntecleer loken in every lith;
He loved hir so, that wel him was therwith.
But swich a joye was it to here hem singe,
Whan that the brighte sonne gan to springe,
In swete accord, 'My lief is faren in londe.'
60 For thilke tyme, as I have understonde,
Bestes and briddes coude speke and singe.

And so bifel, that in a daweninge,
As Chauntecleer among his wyves alle
Sat on his perche, that was in the halle,
65 And next him sat this faire Pertelote,
This Chauntecleer gan gronen in his throte,
As man that in his dreem is drecched sore.
And whan that Pertelote thus herde him rore,
She was agast, and seyde, 'O herte deere,
70 What eyleth yow, to grone in this manere?
Ye been a verray sleper, fy for shame!'
And he answerde and seyde thus, 'Madame,
I pray yow, that ye take it nat agrief:
By God, me mette I was in swich meschief
75 Right now, that yet myn herte is sore afright.
Now God,' quod he, 'my swevene rede aright,
And keep my body out of foul prisoun!
Me mette how that I romed up and doun
Withinne our yerde, wher as I saugh a beest,

---
58. E., Cm., Ln., *bigan*.
62. E., Pt., *the*; rest *a*.
74. E., *thoughte*; rest *mette*.
76. E., Hn., *recche*; Cm., *reche*; rest *rede*.

Was lyk an hound, and wolde han maad areest 80
Upon my body, and wolde han had me deed.
His colour was bitwixe yelwe and reed;
And tipped was his tail, and bothe his eres
With blak, unlyk the remenant of his heres;
His snowte smal, with glowing eyen tweye. 85
Yet of his look for fere almost I deye;
This caused me my groning, doutelees.'

'Avoy!' quod she, 'fy on yow, hertelees!
Allas!' quod she, 'for, by that God above,
Now han ye lost myn herte and al my love; 90
I can nat love a coward, by my feith.
For certes, what so any womman seith
We alle desiren, if it mighte be
To han housbondes hardy, wyse, and free,
And secree, and no nigard, ne no fool, 95
Ne him that is agast of every tool,
Ne noon avauntour, by that God above!
How dorste ye seyn for shame unto your love,
That any thing mighte make yow aferd?
Have ye no mannes herte, and han a berd? 100
Allas! and conne ye been agast of swevenis?
No-thing, God wot, but vanitee, in sweven is.
Swevenes engendren of replecciouns,
And ofte of fume, and of complecciouns,
Whan humours been to habundant in a wight. 105
Certes this dreem, which ye han met tonight,
Cometh of the grete superfluitee

---

81. E., Cm., Hn., om. *wolde*. 107. E., om. *the*.
82. E., Hn., *yelow*; Cp., *whit*.
83, 84. E., *eris, heris*.

Of youre rede *colera*, pardee,
Which causeth folk to dreden in here dremes
110 Of arwes, and of fyr with rede lemes,
Of rede bestes, that they wol hem byte,
Of contek and of whelpes grete and lyte;
Right as the humour of malencolye
Causeth ful many a man in sleep to crye,
115 For fere of blake beres, or boles blake,
Or elles, blake develes wole him take.
Of othere humours coude I telle also,
That werken many a man in sleep ful wo;
But I wol passe as lightly as I can.

120 'Lo Catoun, which that was so wys a man,
Seyde he nat thus, ne do no fors of dremes?
Now, sire,' quod she, 'whan we flee fro the bemes,
For Goddes love, as tak som laxatyf;
Up peril of my soule, and of my lyf,
125 I counseille yow the beste, I wol nat lye,
That bothe of colere, and of malencolye
Ye purge yow; and for ye shul nat tarie,
Though in this toun is noon apothecarie,
I shal myself to herbes techen yow,
130 That shul ben for your hele, and for your prow;
And in our yerd tho herbes shal I finde,
The whiche han of hir propretee, by kinde,
To purgen yow binethe, and eek above.
Forget not this, for Goddes owne love!
135 Ye been ful colerik of compleccioun.

---

109. H., Hn., Cm., *dreden*; rest *dremen*; E., *hir*.
111. E., *grete*; rest *rede*.
115. Cp., *of beres and of boles*; Ln., Pt., *of beres and boles*; rest as text.
122. E., *ye*; rest *we*.   127. E., Hn., Cm., *shal*.

THE NONNE PREESTES TALE

Ware the sonne in his ascencioun
Ne finde yow nat repleet of humours hote;
And if it do, I dar wel leye a grote,
That ye shul have a fevere terciane,
Or an agu, that may be youre bane.   140
A day or two ye shul have digestyves
Of wormes, er ye take your laxatyves,
Of lauriol, centaure, and fumetere,
Or elles of ellebor, that groweth there,
Of catapuce, or of gaytres beryis,   145
Of erbe yve, growing in our yerd, ther mery is;
Pekke hem up right as they growe, and ete hem in.
Be mery, housbond, for your fader kin!
Dredeth no dreem; I can say yow namore.'
   'Madame,' quod he, '*graunt mercy* of your lore.   150
But natheles, as touching daun Catoun,
That hath of wisdom such a greet renoun,
Though that he bad no dremes for to drede,
By God, men may in olde bookes rede
Of many a man, more of auctoritee   155
Than ever Catoun was, so moot I thee,
That al the revers seyn of his sentence,
And han wel founden by experience,
That dremes ben significaciouns,
As wel of joye as tribulaciouns   160
That folk enduren in this lyf present.
Ther nedeth make of this noon argument;

---

145. E., *gaitrys*.
146. Ln., *that*; E., Cm., Cp., Pt., *ther*; Hn., *they*.
148. E., *myrie*.
156. E., *Caton*.
160. E., Cm., Cp., Ln., Hl., ins. *of* after *as*.

The verray preve sheweth it in dede.
 'Oon of the gretteste auctours that men rede
165 Seith thus, that whylom two felawes wente
On pilgrimage, in a ful good entente,
And happed so, they comen in a toun,
Wheras ther was swich congregacioun
Of peple, and eek so streit of herbergage,
170 That they ne founde as muche as o cotage,
In which they bothe mighte y-logged be.
Wherfore they mosten, of necessitee,
As for that night, departen compaignye;
And ech of hem goth to his hostelrye,
175 And took his logging as it wolde falle.
That oon of hem was logged in a stalle,
Fer in a yerd, with oxen of the plough;
That other man was logged wel y-nough,
As was his aventure, or his fortune,
180 That us governeth alle as in commune.
And so bifel, that, long er it were day,
This man mette in his bed, ther as he lay,
How that his felawe gan upon him calle,
And seyde, "Allas! for in an oxes stalle
185 This night I shal be mordred ther I lye.
Now help me, dere brother, or I dye;
In alle haste com to me," he sayde.
 'This man out of his sleep for fere abrayde;
But whan that he was wakned of his sleep,

---

164. E., *auctour*; Hl., *auctorite*; Cm., *autourys*; rest pl.
167. E., Hn., *coomen in*; Cm., *comyn in*.
171. E., *logged*.
186. E., Hn., Hl., *or*; Ln., *ar*; rest *er*.
189. E., *wakened*.

He turned him, and took of this no keep; 190
Him thoughte his dreem nas but a vanitee.
Thus twyës in his sleping dremed he.
And atte thridde tyme yet his felawe
Cam, as him thoughte, and seyde, "I am now slawe;
Bihold my bloody woundes, depe and wyde! 195
Aryse up erly in the morwe-tyde,
And at the west gate of the toun," quod he,
"A carte ful of donge ther shaltow see,
In which my body is hid ful prively;
Do thilke carte arresten boldely. 200
My gold caused my mordre, sooth to sayn."
And tolde him every poynt how he was slayn,
With a ful pitous face, pale of hewe;
And truste wel, his dreem he fond ful trewe;
For on the morwe, as sone as it was day, 205
To his felawes in he took the way;
And whan that he cam to this oxes stalle,
After his felawe he bigan to calle.
The hostiler answerde him anon,
And seyde, "Sire, your felawe is agon, 210
As sone as day he wente out of the toun."
This man gan falle in gret suspecioun,
Remembring on his dremes that he mette,
And forth he goth, no lenger wolde he lette,
Unto the west gate of the toun, and fond 215
A dong-carte, as it were to donge lond,
That was arrayed in that same wyse

---

190. E., *it*; rest *this*.
212. Hl., om. *gret*, ins. *a*; E., om. *both*; rest as text.
216. Hn., Cm., Hl., *wente as it were*; Cp., Pt., Ln., *as he wente*.

As ye han herd the dede man devyse;
And with an hardy herte he gan to crye
220 Vengeaunce and justice of this felonye.
"My felawe mordred is this same night,
And in this carte he lyth gaping upright.
I crye out on the ministres," quod he,
"That sholden kepe and reulen this citee;
225 Harrow! allas! her lyth my felawe slayn!"
What sholde I more unto this tale sayn?
The peple out-sterte, and cast the cart to grounde,
And in the middel of the dong they founde
The dede man that mordred was al newe.

230 'O blisful God, that art so just and trewe!
Lo, how that thou biwreyest mordre alway!
Mordre wol out, that se we day by day.
Mordre is so wlatsom and abhominable
To God, that is so just and resonable,
235 That he ne wol nat suffre it heled be;
Though it abyde a yeer, or two, or three,
Mordre wol out, this my conclusioun.
And right anoon, ministres of that toun
Han hent the carter, and so sore him pyned,
240 And eek the hostiler so sore engyned,
That they biknewe hir wikkednesse anoon,
And were anhanged by the nekke-boon.

'Here may men seen that dremes been to drede.
And certes, in the same book I rede,
245 Right in the nexte chapitre after this,
—I gabbe nat, so have I joye or blis,—

222. E., Hn., Cm., *heere he.*
237. Cp., Pt., Ln., *this is*; rest *this.*

THE NONNE PREESTES TALE

Two men that wolde han passed over see,
For certeyn cause, into a fer contree,
If that the wind ne hadde been contrarie,
That made hem in a citee for to tarie,
That stood ful mery upon an haven-syde. 250
But on a day, agayn the eventyde,
The wind gan chaunge, and blew right as hem leste.
Jolif and glad they wente unto hir reste,
And casten hem ful erly for to saille; 255
But herkneth! to that oo man fil a greet mervaille.
That oon of hem, in sleping as he lay,
Him mette a wonder dreem, agayn the day;
Him thoughte a man stood by his beddes syde,
And him comaunded that he sholde abyde, 260
And seyde him thus, "If thou tomorwe wende,
Thou shalt be dreynt; my tale is at an ende."
He wook, and tolde his felawe what he mette,
And preyde him his viage for to lette;
As for that day, he preyde him to abyde. 265
His felawe, that lay by his beddes syde,
Gan for to laughe, and scorned him ful faste.
"No dreem," quod he, "may so myn herte agaste,
That I wol lette for to do my thinges.
I sette not a straw by thy dreminges, 270
For swevenes been but vanitees and japes.
Men dreme alday of owles or of apes,
And of many a mase therwithal;

---

250. E., *myrie*.
256. All MSS. as text; Skeat om. *herkneth*; Cp., Pt., Ln., *pereyle, perile*; rest *mervaille*.
264. E., Hn., om. *for*.
265. E., *byde*.

Men dreme of thing that nevere was ne shal.
275 But sith I see that thou wolt heer abyde,
And thus forslewthen wilfully thy tyde,
God wot it reweth me; and have good day!"
And thus he took his leve, and wente his way.
But er that he hadde halfe his cours y-seyled,
280 Noot I nat why, ne what mischaunce it eyled,
But casuelly the shippes botme rente,
And ship and man under the water wente
In sighte of othere shippes it bisyde,
That with hem seyled at the same tyde.
285 And therfore, faire Pertelote so dere,
By swiche ensamples olde maistow lere,
That no man sholde been to recchelees
Of dremes, for I sey thee, doutelees,
That many a dreem ful sore is for to drede.
290   'Lo, in the lyf of seint Kenelm, I rede,
That was Kenulphus sone, the noble king
Of Mercenrike, how Kenelm mette a thing;
A lytel er he was mordred, on a day,
His mordre in his avisioun he say.
295 His norice him expouned every del
His sweven, and bad him for to kepe him wel
For traisoun; but he nas but seven yeer old,
And therfore litel tale hath he told
Of any dreem, so holy was his herte.
300 By God, I hadde lever than my sherte
That ye had rad his legende, as have I.

---

283. Cp., Pt., *him*; rest *it*.
286. E., ins. *yet* after *olde*; rest om.
292. E., Hn., Cp., Pt., *Mertenrike*.
296. E., *swevene*.
299. E., *is*; rest *was*.

THE NONNE PREESTES TALE

Dame Pertelote, I sey yow trewely,
Macrobeus, that writ the avisioun
In Affrike of the worthy Cipioun,
Affermeth dremes, and seith that they been   305
Warning of thinges that men after seen.
And forthermore, I pray yow looketh wel
In the Olde Testament, of Daniel,
If he held dremes any vanitee.
Reed eek of Joseph, and ther shul ye see   310
Wher dremes ben somtyme, I sey nat alle,
Warning of thinges that shul after falle.
Loke of Egipt the king, daun Pharao,
His bakere and his boteler also,
Wher they ne felte noon effect in dremes.   315
Who so wol seken actes of sondry remes,
May rede of dremes many a wonder thing.
  'Lo Cresus, which that was of Lyde king.
Mette he nat that he sat upon a tree,
Which signified he sholde anhanged be?   320
Lo heer Andromacha, Ectores wyf,
That day that Ector sholde lese his lyf,
She dremed on the same night biforn,
How that the lyf of Ector sholde be lorn,
If thilke day he wente into bataille;   325
She warned him, but it mighte nat availle;
He wente for to fighte natheles,
But he was slayn anoon of Achilles.
But thilke tale is al to long to telle,
And eek it is ny day, I may nat dwelle.   330

---

314. E., Hn., *butiller*.
321. E., *Adro-*.

Shortly I seye, as for conclusioun,
That I shal han of this avisioun
Adversitee; and I seye forthermore,
That I ne telle of laxatyves no store,
335 For they ben venimous, I woot it wel;
I hem defye, I love hem never a del.
    'Now let us speke of mirthe, and stinte al this;
Madame Pertelote, so have I blis,
Of o thing God hath sent me large grace;
340 For whan I see the beautee of your face,
Ye been so scarlet-reed about youre yën,
It maketh al my drede for to dyen;
For, also siker as *In principio*,
Mulier est hominis confusio;
345 Madame, the sentence of this Latin is—
Womman is mannes joye and al his blis.

350 I am so ful of joye and of solas
That I defye bothe sweven and dreem.'
And with that word he fley doun fro the beem,
For it was day, and eek his hennes alle;
And with a chuk he gan hem for to calle,
355 For he had founde a corn, lay in the yerd.
Roial he was, he was namore aferd;

He looketh as it were a grim leoun;
360 And on his toos he rometh up and doun,
Him deyned nat to sette his foot to grounde.

---

335. E., Hn., Cm., *venymes*; Cp., Pt., Ln., *right*; rest *it*.
352. E., *fly*; rest *fley, fleigh*.
355. E., Hn., Cm., *hadde*.
356. All *Real* exc. Cm., Ln., *Royal*.

THE NONNE PREESTES TALE

He chukketh, whan he hath a corn y-founde,
And to him rennen thanne his wyves alle.
Thus roial, as a prince is in his halle,
Leve I this Chauntecleer in his pasture; 365
And after wol I telle his aventure.

Whan that the month in which the world bigan,
That highte March, whan God first maked man,
Was compleet, and passed were also
—Sin March bigan—thritty dayes and two, 370
Bifel that Chauntecleer in al his pryde,
His seven wyves walking by his syde,
Caste up his eyen to the brighte sonne,
That in the signe of Taurus hadde y-ronne
Twenty degrees and oon, and somwhat more. 375
He knew by kynde, and by noon other lore,
That it was pryme, and crew with blisful stevene.
'The sonne,' he sayde, 'is clomben up on hevene
Fourty degrees and oon, and more, y-wis.
Madame Pertelote, my worldes blis, 380
Herkneth thise blisful briddes how they singe,
And se the fresshe floures how they springe;
Ful is myn hert of revel and solas.'
But sodeynly him fil a sorweful cas;
For ever the latter ende of joye is wo. 385
God woot that worldly joye is sone ago;
And if a rethor coude faire endite,
He in a cronicle saufly mighte it write,
As for a sovereyn notabilitee.

---

364. E., Cm., *an*; rest *his*.
369. All MSS. have *passed*; Skeat emends, *y-passed*.
370. Hl., reads, *tway monthes and dayes two*.
388. Hl., Cp., *cronique*; rest *cronicle*.

390 Now every wys man, lat him herkne me;
This storie is also trewe, I undertake,
As is the book of Launcelot de Lake,
That wommen holde in ful gret reverence.
Now wol I torne agayn to my sentence.

395   A colfox, ful of sly iniquitee,
That in the grove hadde woned yeres three,
By heigh imaginacioun forn-cast,
The same night thurghout the hegges brast
Into the yerd, ther Chauntecleer the faire
400 Was wont, and eek his wyves, to repaire;
And in a bed of wortes stille he lay,
Til it was passed undern of the day,
Waiting his tyme on Chauntecleer to falle,
As gladly doon thise homicydes alle
405 That in await liggen to mordre men.
O false mordrer, lurking in thy den!
O newe Scariot, newe Genilon!
False dissimilour, O Greek Sinon,
That broghtest Troye al outrely to sorwe!
410 O Chauntecleer, acursed be that morwe,
That thou into that yerd fleigh fro the bemes!
Thou were ful wel y-warned by thy dremes
That thilke day was perilous to thee.
But what that God forwot mot nedes be
415 After the opinioun of certeyn clerkis.
Witnesse on him that any parfit clerk is,
That in scole is greet altercacioun

---

394. E., *come*; rest *torne*.
402. E., *undren*.
411. E., Hn., *flaugh*; Cm., *flaw*; Hl., *flough*.

THE NONNE PREESTES TALE

In this matere, and greet disputisoun,
And hath ben of an hundred thousand men.
But I ne can not bulte it to the bren, 420
As can the holy doctour Augustyn,
Or Boece, or the bishop Bradwardyn,
Whether that Goddes worthy forwiting
Streyneth me nedely for to doon a thing,—
Nedely clepe I simple necessitee,— 425
Or elles if free choys be graunted me
To do that same thing, or do it noght,
Though God forwot it, er that it was wroght;
Or if his witing streyneth never a del,
But by necessitee condicionel. 430
I wol not han to do of swich matere;
My tale is of a cok, as ye may here,
That took his counseil of his wyf, with sorwe,
To walken in the yerd upon that morwe
That he hadde met the dreem that I you tolde. 435
Wommennes counseils been ful ofte colde;
Wommannes counseil broghte us first to wo,
And made Adam fro paradys to go,
Ther as he was ful mery, and wel at ese.
But for I noot, to whom it might displese, 440
If I counseil of wommen wolde blame,
Passe over, for I seyde it in my game.
Rede auctours, wher they trete of swich matere,
And what they seyn of wommen ye may here.
Thise been the cokkes wordes, and nat myne; 445

---
423. E·, *Wheither*. 438. E., *out of p.*; rest *fro*.
424. E., *nedefully to*. 442. E., *seye*; rest *seyde*.
432. Hl., Cp., Pt., *schal, schuln*; rest *may*.
435. E., *of tolde*.

I can noon harme of no womman divyne.
    Faire in the sond, to bathe hire merily,
Lyth Pertelote, and alle hir sustres by,
Agayn the sonne; and Chauntecleer so free
450 Song merier than the mermayde in the see,
—For Phisiologus seith sikerly,
How that they singen wel and merily,—
And so bifel that as he caste his yë
Among the wortes, on a boterflye,
455 He was war of this fox that lay ful lowe.
Nothing ne liste him thanne for to crowe,
But cryde anon, 'cok, cok,' and up he sterte,
As man that was affrayed in his herte;
For naturelly a beest desyreth flee
460 Fro his contrarie, if he may it see,
Though he never erst hadde seyn it with his yë.
    This Chauntecleer, whan he gan him espye,
He wolde han fled, but that the fox anon
Seyde, 'Gentil sire, allas! wher wol ye gon?
465 Be ye affrayed of me that am your freend?
Now certes, I were worse than a feend,
If I to yow wolde harm or vileinye.
I am nat come your counseil for tespye;
But trewely, the cause of my cominge
470 Was only for to herkne how that ye singe.
For trewely ye have as mery a stevene,
As any aungel hath that is in hevene;
Therwith ye han in musik more felinge
Than hadde Boece, or any that can singe.

---

450. E., *murrier*.   472. E., om. *hath*.
452. E., *myrily*.

THE NONNE PREESTES TALE

My lord your fader—God his soule blesse!— 475
And eek your moder, of hir gentilesse,
Han in myn hous y-been, to my gret ese;
And certes, sire, ful fayn wolde I yow plese.
But for men speke of singing, I wol saye,
So mote I brouke wel myn eyen tweye, 480
Save yow, I herde never man so singe,
As dide your fader in the morweninge.
Certes, it was of herte, al that he song;
And for to make his voys the more strong,
He wolde so peyne him, that with both his yën 485
He moste winke, so loude he wolde cryen,
And stonden on his tiptoon therwithal,
And strecche forth his nekke long and smal.
And eek he was of swich discrecioun
That ther nas no man in no regioun 490
That him in song or wisdom mighte passe.
I have weel rad in daun Burnel the Asse,
Among his vers, how that ther was a kok,
For that a preestes sone yaf him a knok
Upon his leg, whyl he was yong and nyce, 495
He made him for to lese his benefice.
But certeyn, ther nis no comparisoun
Bitwix the wisdom and discrecioun
Of youre fader, and of his subtiltee.
Now singeth, sire, for seynte charitee, 500
Lat se, conne ye your fader countrefete?'

This Chauntecleer his winges gan to bete,
As man that coude his tresoun nat espye,

---

479. E., ins. *yow* after *wol*.   498. E., *Bitwixe*.
481. E., *herde I*; *yet* for *so*.

So was he ravisshed with his flaterye.
505 Allas! ye lordes, many a fals flatour
Is in your courtes, and many a losengeour,
That plesen yow wel more, by my feith,
Than he that soothfastnesse unto yow seith.
Redeth Ecclesiaste of flaterye;
510 Beth war, ye lordes, of hir trecherye.

    This Chauntecleer stood hye upon his toos,
Strecching his nekke, and held his eyen cloos,
And gan to crowe loude for the nones;
And daun Russel the fox sterte up at ones,
515 And by the gargat hente Chauntecleer,
And on his bak toward the wode him beer,
For yet ne was ther no man that him sewed.

    O destinee, that mayst nat been eschewed!
Allas, that Chauntecleer fleigh fro the bemes!
520 Allas, his wyf ne roghte nat of dremes!
And on a Friday fil al this meschaunce.
O Venus, that art goddesse of plesaunce,
Sin that thy servant was this Chauntecleer,
And in thy service dide al his poweer,
525 More for delyt than world to multiplye,
Why woltestow suffre him on thy day to dye?
O Gaufred, dere mayster soverayn,
That, whan thy worthy king Richard was slayn
With shot, compleynedest his deth so sore,
530 Why ne hadde I now thy sentence and thy lore,
The Friday for to chide, as diden ye?

---

    514. E., *stirte.*
    515. Ln., *gorge*; rest, *gargat, garget.*
    521. E., Hn., Cm., *fil*; rest *fel.*

—For on a Friday soothly slayn was he;—
Than wolde I shewe yow how that I coude pleyne
For Chauntecleres drede, and for his peyne.

    Certes, swich cry ne lamentacioun 535
Was nevere of ladies maad, whan Ilioun
Was wonne, and Pirrus with his streite swerd—
Whan he hadde hent king Priam by the berd,
And slayn him—as saith us *Eneydos*—
As maden alle the hennes in the clos, 540
Whan they had seyn of Chauntecleer the sighte.
But sovereynly dame Pertelote shrighte,
Ful louder than dide Hasdrubales wyf,
Whan that hir housbond hadde lost his lyf,
And that the Romayns hadde brend Cartage, 545
She was so ful of torment and of rage,
That wilfully into the fyr she sterte,
And brende hirselven with a stedfast herte.
O woful hennes, right so cryden ye,
As, whan that Nero brende the citee 550
Of Rome, cryden senatoures wyves,
For that hir housbondes losten alle hir lyves,
Withouten gilt,—this Nero hath hem slayn.—
Now wol I torne to my tale agayn.

    This sely widwe, and eek hir doghtres two, 555
Herden thise hennes crye and maken wo,
And out at dores sterten they anoon,
And syen the fox toward the grove goon,
And bar upon his bak the cok away;
And criden, 'Out! harrow! and weylaway! 560

---

542. E., *sodeynly*.   557. E., *stirten*.
554. E., *Now turne I wole*.

THE CANTERBURY TALES

Ha, ha, the fox!' and after him they ran,
And eek with staves many another man;
Ranne Colle our dogge, and Talbot, and Gerland,
And Malkin, with a distaf in hir hand;
565 Ran cow and calf, and eek the verray hogges,
So were they fered for berking of the dogges
And shouting of the men and wommen eke,
They ronne so, hem thoughte hir herte breke.
They yelleden as feendes doon in helle;
570 The dokes cryden as men wolde hem quelle;
The gees for fere flowen over the trees;
Out of the hyve cam the swarm of bees;
So hidous was the noyse, a! *benedicite!*
Certes, he Jakke Straw, and his meynee,
575 Ne made never shoutes half so shrille,
Whan that they wolden any Fleming kille,
As thilke day was maad upon the fox.
Of bras they broghten bemes, and of box,
Of horn, of boon, in whiche they blewe and pouped,
580 And therwithal they shryked and they houped;
It semed as that hevene sholde falle.
Now, goode men, I pray yow herkneth alle!

 Lo, how fortune turneth sodeynly
The hope and pryde eek of hir enemy!
585 This cok, that lay upon the foxes bak,
In al his drede unto the fox he spak,
And seyde, 'Sire, if that I were as ye,
Yet wolde I seyn—as wys God helpe me,—

---

565. E., om. *eek*.
566. Hl., *were they*; rest om.
569. E., *yolleden*.
575. E., Ln., *shille*.
580. E., Hn., *skriked*.
584. E., om. *eek*.

THE NONNE PREESTES TALE

Turneth agayn, ye proude cherles alle!
A verray pestilence upon yow falle! 590
Now am I come unto this wodes syde,
Maugree your heed, the cok shal heer abyde;
I wol him ete in feith, and that anon."
The fox answerde, 'In feith, it shal be don,'—
And as he spak that word, al sodeynly 595
This cok brak from his mouth delivery,
And heighe upon a tree he fleigh anon.
And whan the fox saugh that he was y-gon,
'Allas!' quod he, 'O Chauntecleer, allas!
I have to yow,' quod he, 'y-doon trespas, 600
In-as-muche as I maked yow aferd,
Whan I yow hente, and broghte out of the yerd;
But, sire, I dide it in no wikke entente;
Com doun, and I shal telle yow what I mente.
I shal seye sooth to yow, God help me so!' 605
'Nay, than,' quod he, 'I shrewe us bothe two,
And first I shrewe myself, bothe blood and bones,
If thou bigyle me ofter than ones.
Thou shalt namore, thurgh thy flaterye
Do me to singe and winken with myn yë. 610
For he that winketh, whan he sholde see,
Al wilfully, God lat him never thee!'
'Nay,' quod the fox, 'but God yeve him meschaunce,
That is so undiscreet of governaunce,

---

591. E., *the wodes.*
598. All *gon, goon,* exc. Hl., *i-goon.*
602. E., Hn., *into this yerd.*
603. E., *of no.*
608. E., Hn., Hl., ins. *any* after *me.*

615 That jangleth whan he sholde holde his pees.'
  Lo, swich it is for to be recchelees,
And necligent, and truste on flaterye.
But ye that holden this tale a folye,
As of a fox, or of a cok and hen,
620 Taketh the moralitee, good men.
For Seynt Paul seith, that al that writen is,
To our doctryne it is y-write, y-wis.
Taketh the fruyt, and lat the chaf be stille.
  Now, goode God, if that it be thy wille,
625 As seith my lord, so make us alle good men,
And bringe us to his heighe blisse. Amen.

Here is ended the Nonne preestes tale.

'By this gaude have I wonne, yeer by yeer,
An hundred mark sith I was Pardoner
I stonde lyk a clerk in my pulpet,
And whan the lewed peple is doun y-set,
I preche so as ye han herd bifore,   65
And telle an hundred false japes more,
Than peyne I me to strecche forth the nekke,
And est and west upon the peple I bekke
As doth a dowve sitting on a berne.
Myn hondes and my tonge goon so yerne,   70
That it is joye to see my bisinesse.
Of avaryce and of swich cursednesse
Is al my preching, for to make hem free
To yeven her pens, and namely unto me.
For my entente is nat but for to winne,   75
And nothing for correccioun of sinne,
I rekke nevere, whan that they ben beried,
Though that her soules goon a-blakeberied!
For certes, many a predicacioun
Comth ofte tyme of yvel entencioun,   80
Som for plesaunce of folk and flaterye,
To been avaunced by ypocrisye,
And som for veyne glorie and som for hate.
For, whan I dar non other weyes debate,
Than wol I stinge him with my tonge smerte   85
In preching, so that he shal nat asterte
To been defamed falsly, if that he
Hath trespased to my brethren or to me.
For, though I telle noght his propre name,
Men shal wel knowe that it is the same   90

77. E., Hl., om. *that*.

By signes and by other circumstances,
Thus quyte I folk that doon us displesances;
Thus spitte I out my venim under hewe
Of holinesse, to seme holy and trewe,
95 'But shortly myn entente I wol devyse;
I preche of nothing but for coveityse,
Therfore my theme is yet, and ever was—
Radix malorum est cupiditas.
Thus can I preche agayn that same vyce
100 Which that I use, and that is avaryce,
But though myself be gilty in that sinne,
Yet can I maken other folk to twinne
From avaryce, and sore to repente,
But that is nat my principal entente.
105 I preche no-thing but for coveityse;
Of this matere it oughte y-nogh suffyse.
   'Than telle I hem ensamples many oon
Of olde stories longe tyme agoon,—
For lewed pepel loven tales olde,—
110 Swich thinges can they wel reporte and holde.
What! trowe ye, the whyles I may preche,
And winne gold and silver for I teche,
That I wol live in poverte wilfully?
Nay, nay, I thoghte it nevere trewely!
115 For I wol preche and begge in sondry londes;
I wol nat do no labour with myn hondes;
Ne make baskettes, and lyve therby,
Because I wol nat beggen ydelly.
I wol noon of the apostles counterfete;
120 I wol have money, wolle, chese, and whete,
Al were it yeven of the povreste page,

THE PARDONER'S TALE

Or of the povreste widwe in a village,
Al sholde hir children sterve for famyne.
Nay! I wol drinke licour of the vyne,
And have a joly wenche in every toun. 125
But herkneth, lordinges, in conclusioun;
Your lyking is that I shal telle a tale.
Now have I dronke a draughte of corny ale,
By God, I hope I shal yow telle a thing
That shal, by resoun, been at your lyking. 130
For, though myself be a ful vicious man,
A moral tale yet I yow telle can,
Which I am wont to preche, for to winne,
Now holde your pees, my tale I wol beginne.'

HERE BIGINNETH THE PARDONERS TALE.

In Flaundres whylom was a compaignye
Of yonge folk, that haunteden folye,
As ryot, hasard, stewes, and tavernes,
Wher-as, with harpes, lutes, and giternes,
They daunce and pleye at dees bothe day and night, 5
And ete also and drinken over hir might,
Thurgh which they doon the devel sacrifyse
Within that develes temple, in cursed wyse,
By superfluitee abhominable.
Hir othes been so grete and so dampnable, 10
That it is grisly for to here hem swere;
Our blissed lordes body they to-tere;
Hem thoughte Jewes rente him noght y-nough;
And ech of hem at otheres sinne lough.
And right anon than comen tombesteres 15

---
6. E., *eten.*

Fetys and smale, and yonge fruytesteres,
Singers with harpes, baudes, wafereres,
Whiche been the verray develes officeres
To kindle and blowe the fyr of lecherye,
20 That is annexed unto glotonye;
The holy writ take I to my witnesse,
That luxurie is in wyn and dronkenesse.

Lo, how that dronken Loth, unkindely,
Lay by his doghtres two unwitingly;
25 So dronke he was, he niste what he wroghte.
Herodes, (who-so wel the stories soghte),
Whan he of wyn was replet at his feste,
Right at his owene table he yaf his heste
To sleen the Baptist John, ful giltelees.

30 Senek seith eek a good word douteless;
He seith, he can no difference finde
Bitwix a man that is out of his minde
And a man which that is dronkelewe,
But that woodnesse, y-fallen in a shrewe,
35 Persevereth lenger than doth dronkenesse.
O glotonye, ful of cursednesse;
O cause first of our confusioun;
O original of our dampnacioun;
Til Crist had boght us with his blood agayn!
40 Lo, how dere, shortly for to sayn,
Aboght was thilke cursed vileinye;
Corrupt was al this world for glotonye!

Adam our fader, and his wyf also,
Fro Paradys to labour and to wo
45 Were driven for that vyce, it is no drede;

---

34. E., *fallen.*

THE PARDONER'S TALE

For whyl that Adam fasted, as I rede,
He was in Paradys; and whan that he
Eet of the fruyt defended on the tree,
Anon he was out-cast to wo and peyne.
O glotonye, on thee wel oghte us pleyne!   50
O, wiste a man how many maladyes
Folwen of excesse and of glotonyes,
He wolde been the more mesurable
Of his diete, sittinge at his table.
Allas! the shorte throte, the tendre mouth,   55
Maketh that, Est and West, and North and South,
In erthe, in eir, in water men to-swinke
To gete a glotoun deyntee mete and drinke!
Of this matere, O Paul, wel canstow trete!
'Mete unto wombe, and wombe eek unto mete,   60
Shal God destroyen bothe,' as Paulus seith.

But sirs, now wol I telle forth my tale.

  Thise ryotoures three, of whiche I telle,
Longe erst er pryme rong of any belle,   200
Were set hem in a taverne for to drinke;
And as they satte, they herde a belle clinke
Biforn a cors, was caried to his grave.
That oon of hem gan callen to his knave,
'Go bet,' quod he, 'and axe redily,   205
What cors is this that passeth heer forby;
And look that thou reporte his name wel.'
  'Sir,' quod this boy, 'it nedeth never-a-del.
It was me told, er ye cam heer, two houres;

---
59. E., *matiere*.

210 He was, pardee, an old felawe of youres;
And sodeynly he was y-slayn to-nyght,
For-dronke, as he sat on his bench up-right;
Ther cam a privee theef, men clepeth Deeth,
That in this contree al the peple sleeth,
215 And with his spere he smoot his herte a-two,
And wente his wey withouten wordes mo.
He hath a thousand slayn this pestilence:
And, maister, er ye come in his presence,
Me thinketh that it were necessarie
220 For to be war of swich an adversarie
Beth redy for to mete him evermore.
Thus taughte me my dame, I sey na-more.'
'By seinte Marie,' seyde this taverner,
'The child seith sooth, for he hath slayn this yeer,
225 Henne over a myle, within a greet village,
Both man and womman, child, and hyne, and page.
I trowe his habitacioun be there;
To been avysed greet wisdom it were,
Er that he dide a man a dishonour.'
230   'Ye, Goddes armes,' quod this ryotour,
'Is it swich peril with him for to mete?
I shal him seke by wey and eek by strete,
I make avow to Goddes digne bones!
Herkneth, felawes, we three been al ones;
235 Lat ech of us holde up his hond til other,
And ech of us bicomen otheres brother,
And we wol sleen this false traytour Deeth;
He shal be slayn, which that so many sleeth,
By Goddes dignitee, er it be night.'
240   Togidres han thise three her trouthes plight,

THE PARDONER'S TALE

To live and dyen ech of hem for other,
As though he were his owene y-boren brother.
And up they sterte al dronken, in this rage,
And forth they goon towardes that village
Of which the taverner had spoke biforn,   245
And many a grisly ooth than han they sworn,
And Cristes blessed body they to-rente—
'Deeth shal be deed, if that they may him hente.'

    Whan they han goon nat fully half a myle,
Right as they wolde han troden over a style,   250
An old man and a povre with hem mette.
This olde man ful mekely hem grette,
And seyde thus, 'Now, lordes, God yow see!'

    The proudest of thise ryotoures three
Answerde agayn, 'What, carl, with sory grace,   255
Why artow al forwrapped save thy face?
Why livestow so longe in so greet age?'

    This olde man gan loke in his visage,
And seyde thus, 'For I ne can nat finde
A man, though that I walked into Inde,   260
Neither in citee nor in no village,
That wolde chaunge his youthe for myn age;
And therfore moot I han myn age stille,
As longe tyme as it is Goddes wille.
Ne deeth, allas! ne wol nat han my lyf;   265
Thus walke I, lyk a restelees caityf,
And on the ground, which is my modres gate,
I knokke with my staf, bothe erly and late,
And seye, "Leve moder, leet me in!

---

242. E., *yborn*.   245. E., *hadde*.
243. E., *stirte*.   254. E., *ryotours*.

270 Lo, how I vanish, flesh, and blood, and skin!
Allas! whan shul my bones been at reste?
Moder, with yow wolde I chaunge my cheste,
That in my chambre longe tyme hath be,
Ye! for an heyre clout to wrappe me!"
275 But yet to me she wol nat do that grace,
For which ful pale and welked is my face.

But, sirs, to yow it is no curteisye
To speken to an old man vileinye,
But he trespasse in worde, or elles in dede.
280 In holy writ ye may yourself wel rede,
"Agayns an old man, hoor upon his head,
Ye sholde aryse;" wherfore I yeve yow reed,
Ne dooth unto an old man noon harm now,
Namore than ye wolde men dide to yow
285 In age, if that ye so longe abyde;
And God be with yow, wher ye go or ryde.
I moot go thider as I have to go.'

'Nay, olde cherl, by God, thou shalt nat so,'
Seyde this other hasardour anon;
290 'Thou partest nat so lightly, by seint John!
Thou spak right now of thilke traitour Deeth,
That in this contree alle our frendes sleeth.
Have heer my trouthe, as thou art his espye,
Tel wher he is, or thou shalt it abye,
295 By God, and by the holy sacrament!
For soothly thou art oon of his assent,
To sleen us yonge folk, thou false theef!'

'Now, sires,' quod he, 'if that yow be so leef
To finde Deeth, turne up this croked wey,

---

284. E., *that ye*.   295. E., *sacrement*.

THE PARDONER'S TALE.

For in that grove I lafte him, by my fey,   300
Under a tree, and ther he wol abyde;
Nat for your boost he wol him no-thing hyde.
See ye that ook? right ther ye shul him finde.
God save yow, that boghte agayn mankinde,
And yow amende!' —thus seyde this olde man.   305
And everich of thise ryotoures ran,
Til he cam to that tree, and ther they founde
Of florins fyne of golde y-coyned rounde
Wel ny an eighte busshels, as hem thoughte.
Ne lenger thanne after Deeth they soughte,   310
But ech of hem so glad was of that sighte,
For that the florins been so faire and brighte,
That doun they sette hem by this precious hord.
The worste of hem he spake the firste word:
'Brethren,' quod he, 'tak kepe what I seye;   315
My wit is greet, though that I bourde and pleye,
This tresor hath fortune unto us yiven,
In mirthe and jolitee our lyf to liven,
And lightly as it comth, so wol we spende,
Ey! Goddes precious dignitee! who wende   320
To-day that we sholde han so fair a grace?
But mighte this gold be caried fro this place
Hoom to myn hous, or elles unto youres—
For wel ye woot that al this gold is oures—
Than were we in heigh felicitee.   325
But trewely, by daye it may nat be;
Men wolde seyn that we were theves stronge,
And for our owene tresor doon us honge,

---

302. E., *Noght*; Hn., Cm., *Nat*; rest *Ne*.
318. E., *ioliftee*.

This tresor moste y-caried be by nighte
As wysly and as slyly as it mighte,
Wherfore I rede that cut among us alle
Be drawe, and lat see wher the cut wol falle;
And he that hath the cut with herte blythe
Shal renne to the toune, and that ful swythe,
And bringe us breed and wyn ful prively,
And two of us shul kepen subtilly
This tresor wel; and if he wol nat tarie,
Whan it is night, we wol this tresor carie
By oon assent, wher as us thinketh best.'
That oon of hem the cut broughte in his fest,
And bad hem drawe, and loke wher it wol falle;
And it fil on the yongeste of hem alle;
And forth toward the toun he wente anon,
And al-so sone as that he was gon,
That oon of hem spak thus unto that other,
'Thou knowest wel thou art my sworne brother,
Thy profit wol I telle thee anon.
Thou woost wel that our felawe is agon;
And heere is gold, and that ful greet plentee,
That shal departed been among us three,
But natheles, if I can shape it so
That it departed were among us two,
Hadde I nat doon a freendes torn to thee?'

That othere answerde, 'I noot how that may be;
He woot how that the gold is with us tweye,
What shal we doon, what shal we to him seye?'

'Shal it be conseil?' seyde the firste shrewe,
'And I shal tellen, in a wordes fewe,

---
341. E., *hym*: rest *hem*.   345. E., om. *of hem*.

THE PARDONER'S TALE

What we shal doon, and bringen it wel aboute.'
   'I graunte,' quod that other, 'out of doute,   360
That by my trouthe, I wol thee nat biwreye.'
   'Now,' quod the firste, 'thou woost wel we be tweye,
And two of us shul strenger be than oon,
Look whan that he is set, and right anoon
Arys, as though thou woldest with him pleye;   365
And I shal ryve him thurgh the sydes tweye
Whyl that thou strogelest with him as in game,
And with thy dagger look thou do the same;
And thanne shal al this gold departed be,
My dere freend, bitwixen me and thee;   370
Thanne may we bothe our lustes al fulfille,
And pleye at dees right at our owene wille.'
And thus acorded been thise shrewes tweye
To sleen the thridde, as ye han herd me seye.

   This yongest, which that wente unto the toun,   375
Ful ofte in herte he rolleth up and doun
The beautee of thise florins newe and brighte.
'O lord!' quod he, 'if so were that I mighte
Have al this tresor to myself allone,
Ther is no man that liveth under the trone   380
Of God, that sholde live so mery as I!'
And atte laste the feend, our enemy,
Putte in his thought that he shold poyson beye,
With which he mighte sleen his felawes tweye;
For-why the feend fond him in swich lyvinge,   385
That he had leve him to sorwe bringe,

---

361. E., *shal*; rest *wol*.
364. E., ins. *right* bef. *he*.
386. E., Cm., *hem*; rest *hym, him*.

For this was outrely his fulle entente
To sleen hem bothe, and never to repente.
And forth he gooth, no lenger wolde he tarie,
390 Into the toun, unto a pothecarie,
And preyde him, that he him wolde selle
Som poyson, that he mighte his rattes quelle;
And eek ther was a polcat in his hawe,
That, as he seyde, his capouns hadde y-slawe,
395 And fayn he wolde wreke him, if he mighte,
On vermin, that destroyed him by nighte.

The pothecarie answerde, 'And thou shalt have
A thing that, also God my soule save,
In al this world ther nis no creature,
400 That ete or dronke hath of this confiture
Noght but the mountance of a corn of whete,
That he ne shal his lyf anon forlete;
Ye, sterve he shal, and that in lasse whyle
Than thou wolt goon a paas nat but a myle;
405 This poyson is so strong and violent.'

This cursed man hath in his hond y-hent
This poyson in a box, and sith he ran
Into the nexte strete, unto a man,
And borwed [of] him large botels three;
410 And in the two his poyson poured he;
The thridde he kepte clene for his drinke.
For al the night he shoop him for to swinke
In caryinge of the gold out of that place.
And whan this ryotour, with sory grace,

---
387. Cm., Cp., Pt., Ln., *utterly*; E., *outrely*.
399. E., *is*.
400. E., *eten, dronken*.
409. All om. *of.*; Skeat emends.

THE PARDONER'S TALE

Had filled with wyn his grete botels three, 415
To his felawes agayn repaireth he.
   What nedeth it to sermone of it more?
For right as they had cast his deeth bifore,
Right so they han him slayn, and that anon.
And whan that this was doon, thus spak that oon, 420
'Now lat us sitte and drinke, and make us merie,
And afterward we wol his body berie.'
And with that word it happed him, par cas,
To take the botel ther the poyson was,
And drank, and yaf his felawe drinke also, 425
For which anon they storven bothe two.
   But, certes, I suppose that Avicen
Wroot never in no canon, ne in no fen,
Mo wonder signes of empoisoning
Than hadde thise wrecches two, er hir ending. 430
Thus ended been thise homicydes two,
And eek the false empoysoner also.

   O cursed sinne, ful of cursednesse!
O traytours homicyde, o wikkednesse!
O glotonye, luxurie, and hasardrye! 435
Thou blasphemour of Crist with vileinye
And othes grete, of usage and of pryde!
Allas! mankinde, how may it bityde,
That to thy creatour which that thee wroghte,
And with his precious herte-blood thee boghte, 440
Thou art so fals and so unkinde, allas!

---

418. E., *so as*; rest om. *so*.
429. E., Hn., Cm., *signes*; rest *sorwes, sorowes*.
433. All but Hl., Cp., Pt., Ln., om. *ful*.

Now, goode men, God foryeve yow your trespas,
And ware yow fro the sinne of avaryce.
Myn holy pardoun may yow alle waryce,
445 So that ye offre nobles or sterlinges,
Or elles silver broches, spoones, ringes.
Boweth your heed under this holy bulle!
Cometh up, ye wyves, offreth of your wolle!
Your name I entre heer in my rolle anon;
450 Into the blisse of hevene shul ye gon;
I yow assoile, by myn heigh power,
Yow that wol offre, as clene and eek as cleer
As ye were born; and, lo, sires, thus I preche,
And Jesu Crist, that is our soules leche,
455 So graunte yow his pardon to receyve;
For that is best; I wol yow nat deceyve.

But sires, o word forgat I in my tale,
I have relikes and pardon in my male,
As faire as any man in Engelond,
460 Whiche were me yeven by the popes hond,
If any of yow wol, of devocioun,
Offren, and han myn absolucioun,
Cometh forth anon, and kneleth heer adoun,
And mekely receyveth my pardoun:
465 Or elles, taketh pardon as ye wende,
Al newe and fresh, at every myles ende,
So that ye offren alwey newe and newe
Nobles and pens, which that be gode and trewe.
It is an honour to everich that is heer

---

448. E., *Com.*
449. E., *names.*
466. E., Hn., Cm., *myles*; rest *tounes.*
468. E., Hn., *or*; rest *and.*

THE PARDONER'S TALE

That ye mowe have a suffisant pardoneer 470
Tassoille yow in contree as ye ryde,
For aventures which that may bityde.
Peraventure ther may fallen oon or two
Doun of his hors, and breke his nekke atwo.
Looke which a seuretee is it to yow alle 475
That I am in your felaweship y-falle,
That may assoille yow, bothe more and lasse,
Whan that the soule shal fro the body passe,
I rede that oure Hoste heer shal biginne,
For he is most enveluped in sinne, 480
Com forth, sir Hoste, and offre first anon,
And thou shalt kisse my reliks everichon
Ye, for a grote; unbokel anon thy purs.'

SELECTIONS FROM CHAUCER'S LYRICS

I. ROUNDEL FROM "THE PARLEMENT OF FOULES"

Qui bien aime, a tard oublie

Now welcom, somer, with thy sonne softe,
That hast this wintres wedres overshake,
And driven away the longe nightes blake.

Seynt Valentine, that art ful hye on lofte,
Thus singen smale foules for thy sake:
   Now welcom, somer, with thy sonne softe,
   That hast this wintres wedres overshake.

Wel han they cause for to gladen ofte,
Sith ech of hem recovered hath his make;
Ful blisful may they singen, when they wake:
   Now welcom, somer, with thy sonne softe,
   That hast this wintres wedres overshake,
   And driven away the longe nightes blake.

II. MERCILES BEAUTÈ

I. CAPTIVITY

Your yën two wol slee me sodenly,
I may the beautè of hem not sustene,
So woundeth hit through-out my herte kene.

3, 13. MS., *large* (for *longe*).
10. MS., *Ful blissful mowe they ben when they wake.*

And but your word wol helen hastily
My hertes wounde, whyl that hit is grene, 5
   Your yën two wol slee me sodenly,
   I may the beautè of hem not sustene.

Upon my trouthe I sey yow feithfully,
That ye ben of my lyf and deeth the quene;
For with my deeth the trouthe shal be sene. 10
   Your yën two wol slee me sodenly,
   I may the beautè of hem not sustene,
   So woundeth hit through-out my herte kene.

II. REJECTION

So hath your beautè fro your herte chaced
Pitee, that me ne availeth not to pleyne; 15
For Daunger halt your mercy in his cheyne.

Giltles my deeth thus han ye me purchaced;
I sey yow sooth, me nedeth not to feyne;
   So hath your beautè fro your herte chaced
   Pitee, that me ne availeth not to pleyne. 20

Allas! that nature hath in yow compassed
So greet beautè, that no man may atteyne
To mercy, though he sterve for the peyne.
   So hath your beautè fro your herte chaced
   Pitee, that me ne availeth not to pleyne; 25
   For Daunger halt your mercy in his cheyne.

III. ESCAPE

Sin I fro Love escaped am so fat,
I nevere thenk to ben in his prison lene;
Sin I am free, I counte him not a bene.

30 He may answere, and seye this or that;
I do no fors, I speke right as I mene.
   Sin I fro Love escaped am so fat,
   I nevere thenk to ben in his prison lene.

Love hath my name y-strike out of his sclat,
35 And he is strike out of my bokes clene
For ever-mo; [ther] is non other mene.
   Sin I fro Love escaped am so fat,
   I nevere thenk to ben in his prison lene;
   Sin I am free, I count him not a bene.

III. TRUTH

BALADE DE BON CONSEYL

FLEE fro the prees, and dwelle with sothfastnesse,
Suffyce thin owen thing, though hit be smal;
For hord hath hate, and climbing tikelnesse,
Prees hath envye, and wele blent overal;
5 Savour no more than thee bihove shal;
Werk wel thy-self, that other folk canst rede;
And trouthe shal delivere, hit is no drede.

Tempest thee noght al croked to redresse,
In trust of hir that turneth as a bal;
10 Gret reste stant in litel besinesse;

---

6. MS., *Reule*; E., *Werk*.   10. MS., *myche wele*.

Beth war therfore to sporne ageyn an al;
Stryve noght, as doth the crokke with the wal.
Daunte thy-self, that dauntest otheres dede;
And trouthe shal delivere, hit is no drede.

That thee is sent, receyve in buxumnesse, 15
The wrastling for this worlde axeth a fal.
Her nis non hoom, her nis but wildernesse:
Forth, pilgrim, forth! Forth, beste, out of thy stal!
Know thy contree; look up, thank God of al;
Hold the hye wey, and lat thy gost thee lede: 20
And trouthe shal delivere, hit is no drede.

ENVOY

Therfore, thou vache, leve thyn old wrecchednesse;
Unto the worlde leve now to be thral;
Crye him mercy that of his hy goodnesse
Made thee of noght, and in especial 25
Draw unto him, and pray in general
For thee, and eek for other, hevenlich mede;
And trouthe shal delivere, hit is no drede.

Explicit Le bon counseill de G. Chaucer.

IV. GENTILESSE

MORAL BALADE OF CHAUCER

THE firste stok, fader of gentilesse—
What man that claymeth gentil for to be,
Must folowe his trace, and alle his wittes dresse
Vertu to sewe, and vyces for to flee.

---

13. MS., *Conquer*, E., *daunte*.
2. MS., *Desireth* for *that claymeth*.

5 For unto vertu longeth dignitee,
   And noght the revers, saufly dar I deme,
   Al were he mytre, croune, or diademe.

   This firste stok was ful of rightwisnesse,
   Trewe of his word, sobre, pitous, and free,
10 Clene of his goste, and loved besinesse,
   Ageinst the vyce of slouthe, in honestee;
   And, but his heir love vertu, as dide he,
   He is noght gentil, thogh he riche seme,
   Al were he mytre, croune, or diademe.

15 Vyce may wel be heir to old richesse;
   But ther may no man, as men may wel see,
   Bequethe his heir his vertuous noblesse;
   That is appropred unto no degree,
   But to the firste fader in magestee,
20 That maketh him his heir, that can him queme,
   Al were he mytre, croune, or diademe.

Explicit.

V. LAK OF STEDFASTNESSE

BALADE

Som tyme the world was so stedfast and stable,
That mannes word was obligacioun,
And now hit is so fals and deceivable
That word and deed, as in conclusioun,

---

20. MS., *That maketh his heires hem that hym queme.*

Ben no-thing lyk, for turned up so doun
Is al this world for mede and wilfulnesse,
That al is lost for lak of stedfastnesse.

What maketh this world to be so variable,
But lust that folk have in dissensioun?
Among us now a man is holde unable,
But-if he can, by som collusioun,
Don his neighbour wrong or oppressioun.
What causeth this, but wilful wrecchednesse,
That al is lost, for lak of stedfastnesse?

Trouthe is put doun, resoun is holden fable;
Vertu hath now no dominacioun,
Pitee exyled, no man is merciable.
Through covetyse is blent discrecioun;
The world hath mad a permutacioun
Fro right to wrong, fro trouthe to fikelnesse,
That al is lost, for lak of stedfastnesse.

LENVOY TO KING RICHARD

O prince, desyre to be honourable,
Cherish thy folk and hate extorcioun!
Suffre no thing, that may be reprevable
To thyn estat, don in thy regioun.
Shew forth thy swerd of castigacioun,
Dred God, do law, love trouthe and worthinesse,
And wed thy folk agein to stedfastnesse.

Explicit.

VI. CHAUCERS WORDES UNTO ADAM HIS OWEN SCRYVEYNE

Adam scriveyn, if ever it thee bifalle
Boece or Troylus for to wryten newe,
Under thy long lokkes thowe most have the scalle,
But after my making thowe wryte more trewe,
5 So ofte a daye I mot thy werk renewe,
Hit to corecte and eke to rubbe and scrape;
And al is through thy necgligence and rape.

VII. THE COMPLEINT OF CHAUCER TO HIS EMPTY PURSE

To you, my purse, and to non other wight
Compleyne I, for ye be my lady dere!
I am so sory, now that ye be light;
For certes, but ye make me hevy chere,
5 Me were as leef be leyd upon my bere;
For whiche unto your mercy thus I crye:
Beth hevy ageyn, or elles mot I dye!

Now voucheth sauf this day, or hit be night,
That I of you the blisful soun may here,
10 Or see your colour lyk the sonne bright,
That of yelownesse hadde never pere.
Ye be my lyf, ye be myn hertes stere,
Quene of comfort and of good companye:
Beth hevy ageyn, or elles mot I dye!

15 Now purs, that be to me my lyves light,
And saveour, as doun in this worlde here,

Out of this toune help me through your might,
Sin that ye wole nat been my tresorere;
For I am shave as nye as any frere.
But yit I pray unto your curtesye: 20
Beth hevy ageyn, or elles mot I dye

LENVOY DE CHAUCER

O conquerour of Brutes Albioun!
Which that by lyne and free eleccioun
Ben verray king, this song to you I sende;
And ye, that mowen al myn harm amende, 25
Have minde upon my supplicacioun!

NOTES

[The texts in this edition are based upon the following MSS.: For the selections from the Canterbury Tales, the Ellesmere MS. has been made the basis, but this has been collated with the other five principal MSS., and in some cases other readings than the Ellesmere have been adopted. Important variations are noted at the foot of every page. The abbreviations are as follows: E. (Ellesmere), Hn. (Hengwrt), Cm. (Cambridge), Cp. (Corpus College, Oxford), Pt. (Petworth), Ln. (Lansdowne), and Hl. (Harleian). All of these MSS. were reprinted by the Chaucer Society, the first six in a single edition arranged in parallel columns, and the last (Hl.) separately. Of these, E., Hn., Cm., are the oldest, Hl. is intermediate, and Cp., Ln., and Pt. late texts. E., the most complete MS., is also the most accurate grammatically and the best in spelling. There are numerous other MSS. of the Canterbury Tales, all more or less fragmentary, and of little value except for purposes of text-criticism. For a complete catalogue see the Oxford Chaucer, Vol. IV, pp. vii ff.

As to the selections from the lyrics, the Roundel from the *Parlement of Foules* is from MS. GG. 427 Cambr. Univ. Lib., the only one preserving the complete text.

Merciles Beautè is from Pepys 2006, unique.

Truth is from Addit. MS. 10,340, Brit. Mus., the only one with the Envoy.

Gentilesse is mainly from Cotton Cleopatra D VII (c. 1430 A.D.).

Lak of Stedfastnesse is from Cot. Cleopatra D VII.

The selection from the Prologue to the *Legend of Good Women* is from Fairfax 16, the later version.

To Adam Scriveyne is from Trinity MS.

Compleint of Chaucer to his Empty Purs is from the Fairfax MS.]

NOTES TO THE PROLOGUE

Line 1 ff. It was a literary convention during the mediæval period to begin a poem with a description of the coming of Spring. In some cases the description fits the theme of the poem, as here; in others there is no connection whatever. For example, in the metrical romance of *Alexander*, each *fit*, or canto, begins in this fashion, with a result often ludicrous. Hundreds of poems, especially love allegories, in French, Italian, Spanish, and English, show this stereotyped method of beginning. (Cf. Neilson, *Origins and Sources of the*

Court of Love, s.v. "May.") Chaucer was thus employing a form very well known to him, and his power here, as elsewhere, consists in his ability to breathe the spirit of life into what in other poets was simply the accepted form of beginning a poem. Of the passage Lowell says, "I repeat it to myself a thousand times, and still at the thousandth time a breath of uncontaminate springtide seems to lift the hair upon my forehead."

1. *soote.* Compare the form *swete* (l. 5). '*Soote* is a less correct form of *swote* and . . . corresponds to A. S. *swot,* adv., sweetly, and *swete* to A. S. *swēte,* adj., sweet." (Skeat.)

4. *flour,* flower, is the subject; *vertu,* vital power.

6. Consult the dictionary for *holt,* and, in general, for unfamiliar words not given in the notes or the glossary. *Holt and heeth.* Chaucer, like other writers of his time, uses many of these alliterative phrases; cf. *meeke as is a mayde* (Prol. 69); *long and lene* (Prol. 591); *dyke and delve* (Prol. 536); *looth ne leef* (Knight's T. 979), etc.

7. The sun is called "young" because in Chaucer's time the beginning of the year was reckoned from the Vernal Equinox.

8. The time is about April 15. The sun passes through the Ram (Aries) from March 12 to April 11; it had therefore passed the *April half course,* i.e. had entered the next zodiacal sign, the Bull (Taurus).

11. "So nature excites them in their feelings (instincts)." (Skeat.) Note the form *hir,* their. The *th* of the modern word is due to Northern influence. Chaucer's dialect was Midland, and it is from this dialect that Modern English is descended. For a short, authoritative, and interesting account of early English dialects consult Greenough and Kittredge, *Words and Their Ways,* pp. 80–92.

12. Chaucer rightly holds that one cause for the pilgrimages of his day was a desire for change after a winter of confinement. The pilgrimages of modern life are not to shrines but to seashore and mountains.

13. Supply *longen* as a verb. *To seken* is a gerund, expressive of purpose. Cf. "What went ye out *for to see.*" (Matt. 11:9.)

14. *halwes,* really saints; here shrines. Cf. Halloween, the eve of All Saints Day. *couthe,* ppl., known, from *cunnan.* Cf. Milton's use of *uncouth* (L'Allegro, l. 5), unknown.

15. *shires.* Connection of this word with modern sheriff?

16. *wende* is pres., the pret. being *wente.* Cf. modern forms *go, went, gone,* where another verb has supplied the pres. and ppl. forms. *Wends* is used now only in poetry.

17. Thomas à Becket (1118–1170; canonized 1173), the famous chancellor, later Archbishop of Canterbury. The shrine at Canterbury was destroyed by Henry VIII.

20. *Tabard.* It was common to name inns from their signs. Houses were not numbered, as in modern cities, and the signs were necessary in a time when few could read. The tabard was a herald's coat-of-arms. Skeat says it was not sleeveless, though the sleeves were very short.

24. *wel.* Fully, at least.

27. *wolden* has here, as often, the force of wished.

29. *esed atte beste,* made comfortable.

30. *to reste,* at rest. Account for the-*e*.
Shortly, i.e. to make a long story short.

33. *for to ryse.* Cf. l. 13, note.

34. *ther as,* lit. where that. The *as* is redundant, and need not be translated. Observe other uses of *as* in your reading.

37. *me thinketh,* it seems to me; an impersonal use of the verb.

40. *whiche,* Lat. *qualis.*

45. *to riden out,* i.e. in search of adventures; the chivalric ideal.

46. *freedom.* See glossary, and cf. N. P. T. (ll. 93, 94) where Pertelote says:
 "We alle desyren, if it mighte be,
  To han housbondes hardy, wise, and free."
To be "free" was one of the cardinal virtues in the mediæval times.

51. Alexandria (Egypt) was taken by Pierre de Lusignan, king of Cyprus, in 1365. The other campaigns mentioned took place a few years earlier. Chaucer is telling what was the ordinary practice of knights, who besides fighting in their lord's wars (l. 47) in addition (*therto*) campaigned under many flags. In the XIV century, the chief glory of a knight was fighting against the heathen nations (*hethenesse*). Skeat's note on this passage gives numerous examples.

52. That is, he had sat at the head of the table, as the warrior most honored among the knights of various nationalities who were engaged in warring on the infidels.

53. It was a common occurrence for English knights to go to Prussia (*Pruce*) and there fight with the Teutonic knights against the heathen of Lithuania (*Lettow*) and Russia (*Ruce*).

56-8. *Gernade,* Granada. Algezir (the modern Algeciras) was taken from the Moorish king of Granada in 1344. The other places named in the passage are as follows: *Belmarye* and *Tramissene,* Moorish kingdoms in Northern Africa; *Satalye,* now Adalia, in Asia Minor, this campaign taking place in 1361; *Lyeys,* now Ayas, in Armenia, taken in 1367; *Palatye,* a Christian lordship in Asia Minor.

59. *Grete See,* the Mediterranean, to distinguish it from the Dead Sea and the Sea of Galilee. Skeat cites Numb. 34:6; Josh. 1:4.

60. *at . . . armee,* i.e. he had been in many noble armies. The word was formerly applied also to naval expeditions (Oxford Dictionary, army, 1). The better MSS. read *armee;* some late MSS. have *aryve,* which is very awkward to translate. Skeat adopts *aryve,* and translates it *debarkation.* But in the next line *at* =*in*; why not here?

74. *hors* is plural, the same form serving for both numbers.

75. *wered*, a weak verb in Chaucer as in A. S. (*werede*); now we have a strong pret. *wore*. The *gipoun* was rusted (*bismotered*) by contact with the iron coat of mail.

79. The description which follows is typical of the ideal lover. Cf. Neilson, *Court of Love* s.v. "Statutes of Love." A "squire" attended on a knight and bore his arms and shield.

80. *bacheler*. See Glossary. Cf. the college degree, bachelor of arts.

82. *yeer*. "In the older stages of the language, *year, goat, swine*, etc., being neuter nouns underwent no change in the nom. case of the pl. number." Skeat. Cf. *hors*, l. 74.

83. *evene*, medium.

87. *As of so litel space*, i.e. considering his youth.

88. *lady*. The A.S. form of this word has no *-s* in the gen. sing.; the Mid. Eng. form also omits the *-s*. Cf. the modern phrase Lady Day, which preserves the old form.

95. *endyte*, compose, not "write," as the next line shows. Cf. Knight's Tale, l. 522, and especially the *Legende of Good Women*, ll. 2356–8:

"And couthe eke rede and wel ynogh endyte,
But with a penne couthe she nat wryte,
But letteres can she weave to and fro."

The reference in the last line of the quotation is to embroidery.

101. *he*, the knight.

102. *him liste*. Construction? Cf. l. 37.

107. That is, they did not droop in such a way as to be of no use in the wind in flight. *lowe*, worn out, clipped short.

110. *coude*, knew, as often.

115. *Christofre*, an image of the saint, which was supposed to be especially efficacious in shielding the owner from hidden dangers.

120. *Loy*, <*Eloy*, <*Eligius*. He was a goldsmith, master of the mint to Dagobert and other kings of France. There is a story that when Dagobert asked Eligius to swear upon the sacred relics Eligius refused. Hence to swear by St. Loy was not to swear at all, or, at most, to swear very mildly.

125. *scole*, school, in the sense of style, or custom. Her dialect was the Anglo-French of the Benedictine nunnery at Stratford-at-Bow, near London. Professor Skeat (V, 15) thinks that Chaucer is not jesting at the lady's pronunciation; there are some indications, however, that Anglo-French was often ridiculed during the period. Examples are given by G. H. McKnight in *Modern Language Notes*, XIX, 62.

127 ff. Mediæval books on Courtesy and Nurture contain similar rules of conduct. In the *Roman de la Rose* (ll. 13, 612 ff.) is a description of good manners at mealtime much like the one in the text; probably Chaucer had this in mind.

NOTES

149. *men*, any one.

152. *greye as glas*, a favorite simile in the romances. Gray, not blue, was then the color thought beautiful for a woman's eyes.

162. Of course the lady prioress meant by *amor* the love spoken of in 1 Cor. 13, but the motto might well serve for the conventional love poetry of the time. Cf. Virgil, *Ecl. X*, 69. The line is a specimen of Chaucer's sly irony.

165. "a fair (one) for the championship," or "for the highest place."

166. *out-ridere*, i.e. he had charge of the farms of the abbey.

168. *deyntee*. The word comes from the Latin *dignitas*, through the French. Account for the modern meaning.

170. In Chaucer's day, small bells were hung upon bridles and harness.

172. That is, he had charge of a small monastery or cell, dependent upon the abbey.

173. Saint Maur was a disciple of Saint Benedict and established the Benedictine order in France.

177. There is no reference to any particular words of scripture, but to the view of the church that hunters were always sinners. Nimrod and Esau were frequently referred to in this connection. Professor O. F. Emerson (*Modern Philology* I, 105 ff.) thinks the particular "text" Chaucer refers to is in the *Decretum* of Gratian, reading "Hieronymus in Psalm xc. ad vers: Sperabo in Domino. Esau venator erat, quoniam peccator erat. Et penitus non invenimus, in Scripturis sanctis, sanctum aliquem venatorem; piscatores invenimus sanctos." That the idea was widespread is proved by the numerous similar "texts" in the decretals and elsewhere.

A "pulled hen" is a plucked hen; it was said that hens which had lost part or all of their feathers would not lay.

179. *recchelees*, negligent of the rules and duties of monastic life, especially applicable to the wandering monks (*out of his cloistre*), who were held to be particularly wicked. The Harleian MS. reads *cloysterlees*, which fits the simile very well, but involves a tautology in l. 181. As all the MSS., with this one exception, read *recchelees* or *rekeles* this seems the proper reading. Professor Emerson, in the article referred to just above, cites numerous instances where the word was applied to negligent and worthless monks.

180. Cf. the Decretal of Gratian, "Sicut pisces sine aqua caret vita, ita sine monasterio monachus."

183 ff. Observe that the poet contrives to give the impression that he conversed with the Monk, and that he courteously expressed some assent to that gentleman's rather radical views; *seyde* (pret. tense) helps convey this impression. There is not a little irony in the passage.

184 ff. *What sholde he studie*, why should he study, etc. Cf. Milton, Lycidas (ll. 64 ff.):

> "Alas, what boots it with uncessant care
> To ply the homely, slighted shepherd's trade,
> And strictly meditate the thankless Muse."

187. *bit*, is a shortened form of *biddeth*.

187. *Austin*, St. Augustine of Hippo, d. 430 A.D., who advised monks to practice manual labor.

202. "Shone like the fire under a cauldron."

205. *for-pyned*. The *for* is intensive, as in "forswear." Cf. Lanier's lines,

> "Into the woods my Master went,
> Clean forspent, forspent."

205 ff. For much interesting information about the friars, see Jusserand's *English Wayfaring Life in the XIV Century*, pp. 279 ff.

208. *wantown*. From *wan*-(un) and *towen* (A. S. *togen*, drawn; related to L. *duco*). Thus it originally meant "untrained"; it came to be applied to a spoiled child, hence the M. E. meaning "sportive," "playful."

210. The four orders were as follows: The Franciscans, or Grey Friars, founded 1209 by St. Francis of Assisi; the Augustines, founded in the XII century; the Dominicans or Black Friars, XIII century; and the Carmelites, or White Friars, XIII century.

227. *he . . . he*, the man . . . the friar.

232. *men moot*, one ought to. Cf. l. 149.

241. *tappestere*. Note the feminine ending. Does this ending remain in any modern English words?

242. *lazar*. Etymology?

252. One MS. (Hn.) inserts after this line two lines, as follows:

> "And yaf a certeyn ferme for the graunt,
> Noon of his bretheren cam ther in his haunt."

254. *In principio*. The friars often quoted John 1:1. "In the beginning was the word," etc.

256. The line is based on one in the *Romaunt of the Rose* (Eng. version, l. 6838),

> "My purchase is bettir than my rente."

Skeat explains that the proceeds of his begging were greater than his rent or regular income. Flügel (*Anglia*, 23:233 ff.) believes *rente*= *ferme*, as used in the line quoted in the note at l. 252 above, which he defines as the sum to be paid the order for his "limits." Thus his income from all sources exceeded the sum he paid his order. Cf. the Roman custom of "farming" the revenues. But one of the characters in the Townley Mystery play of *Coliphizacio* says:

> 'Whoso kepis the lawe, I gess,
> He gettis more by purches
> Then by his fre rent."

The sense is here that the government official, if unscrupulous, can make far more money (*purches*) than his legal salary (*rent*) would amount to. Moreover in almost every other case in which Chaucer uses the word *rent*, the sense is clearly "income," always without suggestion of fraud. Similarly, *purchas* always implies illegality, this being the sense even in Shakspere's time. Hence it seems safe to follow Skeat's interpretation.

257. "He could play about, just as if he were a puppy."

258. *love-dayes*, days on which differences could be settled by umpires, out of court. These umpires usually belonged to the clergy, and though the practice, as calculated to prevent litigation, was at first commendable, it later degenerated into a source of great abuses. *Piers Ploughman*, a contemporary poem, speaks of the evil done by the bribetaking friars who acted as umpires. (See Skeat's note in his edition of P. P., III, 137.)

263. The sense probably is "his semi-cope, that, rounded like a bell, was just out of the press."

268. Cf. John Heywood (*Give place, you ladies*, etc.), for a parallel simile:

> "Her beauty twinkleth like a star
> Within the frosty night."

271. *on horse*. Note the petrified dative *-e*.

272. Flemish (*Flaundrish*) hats were favorites in England.

276. *for anything*, at any cost.

277. *Middleburgh*, a port on an island off the Netherlands; *Orewelle*, now Harwich, on the English coast directly opposite Middleburgh. In 1386 Chaucer was directed to survey Orewell because of a rumor that the French king was intending to invade England at that port. Middleburgh was a wool-port, 1384–88. These facts help to fix the date of the Prologue.

285. Look up the etymology and history of "clerk."

285 ff. This is one of the most admirable of the portraits. Note the kindly humor with which the poor student is described.

292. i.e. a secular position.

297. In the Middle Ages a "philosopher" was also an alchemist. This makes the next line clear; it is one of Chaucer's many good-humored flings at the superstitions of his time.

301 ff. Poor scholars preparing for the priesthood often supported themselves by begging, praying for the souls of their benefactors as a reward for the kindness they received.

308. The sympathy with which the clerk is portrayed is partly due to Chaucer's own love for books and scholarship. See the

NOTES

highly characteristic passage in the *Legende of Good Women*, Prol. ll. 29 ff.

309 ff. There are one or two malicious touches in this portrait.

310. *parvys* is from the Old Fr. *parvis*, from Lat. *paradisus*. The reference is to the portico of St. Paul's, a common meeting place for lawyers.

319. If a landed estate were entailed or held by will, the learned lawyer knew how to evade the difficulty by making the estate held in fee-simple, and (l. 320) his conveyancing (*purchasing*) was never invalid (*infect*). Cf. Spenser, *Mother Hubberds Tale*, ll. 866 ff.:

> "Now like a lawyer, when he land would lett,
> Or sell fee-simples in his master's name,
> Which he had never, nor ought like the same."

323. He had definite knowledge of all legal precedents since the time of William.

327. Cf. the common expression "to learn by rote."

331. The franklin was a man of considerable importance in English society and was a householder.

332. *dayesye.* Etymology? What does the *-es-* represent? Note that *ye* is dissyllabic.

333. An interesting account of the "complexions" will be found in *Words and Their Ways*, pp. 30 ff. Cf. also Nun's Priest's Tale, ll. 104 ff., and the note.

339. There is no real reason for the modern spelling of *delyt*; it is an example of the irrational character of much English spelling.

340. St. Julian was the patron saint of hospitality, and thus the pattern for landlords. Note the description of an English householder's hospitality. In a metrical romance of the XIV century, *The Avowing of Arthur*, one of Arthur's knights is especially lauded because, during a test lasting for a considerable time, the king found that no stranger was refused hospitality, no matter how slight his claims or even if the knight had strong provocation for turning the applicant away.

341. *after oon*, i.e. always of the same high standard.

346. Cf. the use of *coude* here with that of l. 327.

353. A "table dormant" was a fixed, irremovable table, thus a proof of abundant hospitality. At this time most tables were merely boards thrown across saw-horses and easily removed; hence our terms "to board," "festal board," "boarding house," etc.

362. *Webbe* is a masculine form, the feminine being "webster." These words are the sources of the proper names Webb and Webster. Shakspere uses this old feminine suffix in the word "spinsters," meaning "female spinners," in *Twelfth Night*, II, iv. 68; *Othello*, I, i, 24; and *Henry VIII*, I, ii. 33.

364. *fraternitee*, guild. Look up the subject of guilds in the en-

NOTES

cyclopedia or in L. Toulmin Smith's *English Gilds*. Look up also the etymology of the word *liveree*, and trace the modern meaning.

371. cf. *can* with *coude* (l. 383). Is *can* pres. or pret.?

372. *alderman*, head of the guild. Etymology?

373. *catel*, property, chattel. Cf. Lat. *pecunia* < *pecus*, which yields such words as pecuniary, impecunious, etc.

379. *for the nones* was originally *for then ones*, i.e. *for then once*. Similar transference of an initial or final letter, due to frequent use in a phrase, is shown in *apron*, originally *napperon* or *napron; adder*, originally *nadder*, etc.

385. *it thoughte me*, it seemed to me. An impersonal construction common in Chaucer but not often met in modern Eng. Cf. *methinks* or *meseems*.

390. i.e. as well as he knew how, which of course was not well at all.

398. *nyce*, foolish, the usual sense in Chaucer. The word comes (through the French) from Lat. *nescius*. Later, the word came to mean "foolish about small matters," which in turn developed into "particular about details." This sense still remains, as when we speak of a "nice distinction"; but a colloquial use of the word has also developed, as when one speaks of anything attractive or pleasing as "nice."

400. He made them walk the plank.

414. The mediæval physician was grounded in *astronomye* because medicines, to be effective, were to be administered with due regard to the rules of astrology.

415 ff. He watched (*kepte*) his patient carefully through the astrological hours in order to discover a favorable star in the ascendant. For the contribution of mediæval astrology to our modern vocabulary see *Words and Their Ways*, pp. 31, 33 ff.

418. Astrologers were in the habit of making wax images which they believed could be so treated as to bring good or evil fortune to the person they represented. Physicians used such images in their treatment. See an interesting reference to the practice in Chaucer's *Hous of Fame*, ll. 1259–70.

420. The four elements of which all matter was composed were hot, cold, moist, and dry. See *Paradise Lost*, Bk. II, ll. 898 ff. It was supposed that these elements exercised an influence upon the humours (blood, phlegm, bile, and black bile), thus affecting a person's *temperament* (L. *tempero;* hence the "balance" or mixture of the humours which determined what we call a person's "temperament"), and also causing disease. Cf. *Prol.* ll. 104 ff., and the note.

429 ff. Æsculapius was the son of Apollo, and reputed the father of medicine; Hippocrates, Galen, Rufus, Dioscorides, Greek writers on the subject; Haly, Rhasis, Damascenus, Serapion, Avicen, all Arabian authorities; Averroës, born at Cordova 1126; Gilbertyn, an English writer on medicine, XIII century; Bernard, a French professor of medicine, and John Gatesden, physician to Edward II., both contemporary with Chaucer.

438. Dante (*Inferno*, iv, 143) names Hippocrates, Dioscorides, Galen, Avicen, and Averroës among those in the first circle of hell, where were confined all who had lived "without faith in Christ." In the first paragraph of the *Religio Medici*, Sir Thomas Browne speaks of "the general scandal" of his profession in matters of religion.

442. The great plague of 1348-9 is probably referred to. Other plagues occurred in 1362, 1369, 1376.

448. Ypres (West Flanders) and Ghent were great clothing markets.

453. *coverchiefs* is a variant of kerchief. Look up the etymology and history of this interesting word in *Words and Their Ways*, pp. 270 ff., or in a large dictionary. *Fyne of ground* is fine of texture.

454. Skeat remarks that while this is a playful exaggeration, the headdress was undeniably very heavy. Cuts illustrating XIV century millinery may be found in Fairholt's *Costume*, figs. 125, 129, 130, 151, and in Jusserand's *English Wayfaring Life*.

460. The marriage service was said at the church door; the couple afterwards went to the altar to hear mass.

461. *withouten*, to say nothing of.

465-466. An image of the Virgin was at Boulogne; the shrine of St. James was in Galicia, in Spain; and at Cologne the bones of the Three Wise Men were supposed to be preserved.

476. She knew the old game or custom about love philters; a slang phrase.

478 ff. With this portrait of the "povre persoun" compare Goldsmith's description of the village preacher in *The Deserted Village*. Note, especially, such parallels as those existing between l. 490 and

"And passing rich with forty pounds a year."
(*Des. Vil.*, l. 142.)

Again, cf. ll. 491 ff. with

"In his duty prompt at every call,
He watched and wept, he prayed and felt for all."
(*Ibid*, ll. 165, 166.)

And ll. 496, 497, 518, 519 correspond to

"As a bird each fond endearment tries
To tempt its new-fledged offspring to the skies,
He tried each art, reproved each dull delay,
Allured to brighter worlds, and led the way."
(*Ibid*, ll. 167 ff.)

NOTES

With ll. 507 ff. cf.

> "Remote from towns he ran his godly race,
> Nor e'er had changed, nor wished to change, his place;
> Unpractised he to fawn, or seek for power."
>
> (*Ibid*, ll. 143 ff.)

Finally, cf. ll. 515 ff. with ll. 149 ff. of Goldsmith's poem. Other parallels may be noted.

486. He would not treat harshly delinquent tithe payers.

494. *muche and lite*, rich and poor.

496 ff. Professor Kittredge has pointed out a striking parallel between this passage and a portion of the *Roman de Carité* by the Renclus de Moiliens (end of the XII century). See *Mod. Lang. Notes*, XII, pp. 113 ff. In a long exhortation to parish priests are the lines:

> "Prestre, tu dois faire et puis dire,
>   Se ors enrunge, queus ert fers?
> . . . Quel mervaille est, se mervaille ai
>   De fol pastour, de sage oeille?"

502. Etymology and history of *lewd*?

503. If a priest will only take heed to it.

507 ff. "He did not hire out his benefice, leaving his sheep encumbered in the mire, while he went to St. Paul's seeking a chantry for souls." These chantries were endowed by men who desired to employ priests to pray for their souls or those of their relatives. The position was a sinecure, and was eagerly sought by ease-loving monks.

511. Or with a fraternity to be kept away (from his sheep).

517. *daungerous* < *dominus*. "Daunger" was often used in the sense of a guardian, etc. A girl was called "daungerous" who was shy or reserved. Here, the word means "sparing," "difficult," "reserved."

534. Though it gamed (was pleasant to) him or smarted him. Impersonal construction.

548. The ram was the prize.

550 ff. Favorite sports at the time among the country louts.

557. *nose-thirles*. Modern form?

560. *goliardeys*, buffoons of the XII century and after, ribald jesters gaining a parasitical living by flattering rich men.

563. A reference to the common proverb, "An honest miller has a golden thumb." Chaucer implies that he was as honest as most millers, even if he did collect toll three times instead of once. As to "golden thumb," it was said that the miller's thumb acquired a peculiar shape from his constant testing of grain, and, since his profits depended upon his skill in testing, his thumb was "golden" to him. Perhaps, however, the sense is purely satirical; no millers have golden thumbs; hence, there are no honest millers.

564. *wered*. Note the weak pret.

567. *temple.* One of the Inns of Court, so called because the building originally belonged to the Knights Templar.

581. *his propre good,* his own income or property.

582. *but he were wood,* unless he were mad.

586. *sette hir aller cappe,* got the best of them; literally, "set the caps of them all." Cf. the modern phrase, "to set one's cap for a man."

604. *he,* the Reeve.

605. *the deeth,* the Plague.

622. *hindreste.* Note the double comparison, hind-r-este.

624. *fyr-reed.* In the Middle Ages cherubim were usually represented as having red faces.

638. Though during the XIV century English began to be used in civil courts, the ecclesiastical courts continued to use Latin.

643. i.e. a jay can say Walter or any other name as well as if it were a man.

646. *Questio quid iuris,* the question is "What is the law?"

647. *harlot,* usually referred to a young person of either sex, and with no evil implication. Cf. "lewd" and "wanton," other instances of words which have degenerated in meaning. Words, like people, are known by the company they keep.

652. To pull a finch meant to cheat a gull, to pluck a greenhorn, to shear a lamb.

654 ff. The sense is he need not fear excommunication, or any other punishment than being relieved of some of his money. *But-if* = unless.

659 ff. Is Chaucer serious, or is this another example of his irony?

662. The *significavit* was the writ issued by the secular authorities for the taking of an excommunicated person. *War* is pres. subj.

664. *yonge girles,* "young people, of either sex" (Skeat).

667. The sign of an ale-house was a pole on which was fastened a "bush," made of ivy leaves, and also a "garland," made of three ribbon covered hoops, set at right-angles.

669. Consult Jusserand's *English Wayfaring Life,* pp. 309 ff. for material proving that Chaucer did not overdraw his picture of the Pardoner.

670. The Pardoner was from the hospital of Rouncival, London.

685. *vernicle,* a copy of the picture of Christ, supposed to have been miraculously printed upon the handkerchief with which St. Veronica wiped the face of Jesus on the way to Calvary. The name "Veronica" (i.e. *vera iconica,* " true likeness") was given to both the handkerchief and the maiden.

687. *al hoot.* One of the London street cries. The Pardoner sold his wares as a peddler would sell popcorn and peanuts.

695. *lady veyl.* Cf. note to l. 88.

NOTES

702. *upon lond*, in the country. Cf. "upland" and also "outlandish."

716. *thestat*, the estate.

723. *viage*, journey, either by land or sea.

725 ff. This is one of the passages in which Chaucer tells us something of his theory of art.

742. Chaucer got the saying, not from Plato, but from Boëthius, one of Chaucer's favorite authorities.

751. Harry Bailly, the host, is one of the best of Chaucer's creations. The lines which follow, together with the links connecting the various tales, show that Chaucer had a rich sense of the dramatic in life.

760. It is business before pleasure with the host. Note, too, that Harry's proposition involves more suppers at his inn.

777. *if yow lyketh*, if it pleases you.

785. "It seemed to us not worth while to make it a subject for deliberation."

799. *our aller cost*, the cost of us all. *Aller* is a genitive plural. A. S. *ealra*. Cf. l. 586.

823. *our aller cok*, i.e. waked us all. Cf. note to l. 799.

825. i.e. a little faster than a foot-pace.

826. The Watering of St. Thomas was a place for watering horses, at a brook two miles on the road to the shrine of St. Thomas, i.e. to Canterbury.

830. "If evening song and morning song agree," i.e. if you still hold to the resolution you made last night.

840. The title "sir" was given to university graduates and to priests.

shamfastnesse. The proper form of the word. The modern "shamefaced" is an irregular form, an example of popular etymology. "Shamfast" means held by shame; since the "shamfast" person showed his shame in his face, the word came to be pronounced and spelled "shamefaced."

850. Account for the *e-* in *goode*.

THE KNIGHTES TALE

The Knight's Tale differs from most of the *Canterbury Tales* in that it is a metrical romance. Most literature of the XIII and XIV conturies was drawn from one of two sources; chivalric or popular. The first class dealt with the heroes of chivalry—Arthur and his knights, Charlemagne, Roland, and the contests between the Christians and the pagans. The second was made up of *fabliaux*, folk-tales, ballads, and rude stories, told without the art and elaborateness of the chivalric romances, and distinguished rather by coarseness, humor, and cynicism than by dignity and the pomp and circumstance of war. The most famous of the chivalric romances flourished in France in the XII and XIII centuries. The best of these were very good indeed; but as time went on they degenerated into interminable recitals of the deeds of heroes, with little or no characterization and with the most wooden descriptions. It is small wonder that Chaucer satirized these weak imitations in his *Sir Thopas*.

Some of the most popular romances, particularly in Italy, dealt with classical or pseudo-classical subjects in the manner of the chivalric tales about Charlemagne and Arthur. The Knight's Tale is based upon one of these Italian romances, the story having been told by Boccaccio in his *Teseide*. In Chaucer's version, as in his Italian original, there is nothing classical except the names. The characters are heroes of the age of chivalry, not of the Greek heroic age; such questions as the debate proposed at the end of Part I, whether Palamon or Arcite had the first claim to Emily, illustrate very well the mediæval causuistry of love; the account of the tournament as a means for settling the dispute between the lovers, together with the description of the temples, is purely chivalric.

Many years before he thought of writing the *Canterbury Tales*, Chaucer had become interested in the love of the two Theban knights for Emily, sister of Queen Hippolyta. In the Prologue to the *Legend of Good Women* he gives us a list of the works he had written up to that time.

> "He made the book that hight the Hous of Fame,
> And eek the Deeth of Blaunche the Duchesse,
> And the Parlement of Foules, as I gesse,
> And al the love of Palamon and Arcyte
> Of Thebes, thogh the story is knowen lyte.
> And many an ympne[1] for your holydayes,
> That highten Balades, Roundels, Verelayes:
> And, for to speke of other holynesse,
> He hath in prose translated Boëce."

There can be no doubt that this story of the love of Palamon and Arcite was the same as that told by the Knight. Since it was early work it was pretty certainly written in seven line stanzas, and it was also probably incomplete.

Another of Chaucer's early works, *Anelida and Arcite*, has also some relation to the knight's story. This poem shows familiarity with Boccaccio's *Teseide* and with the *Thebes* of Statius. It opens with an account of the home-coming of Theseus with Hippolyta and Emily, then turns suddenly to tell of the woe of Anelida, a fair young Armenian queen. Arcite, who may or may not be the same as the joint-hero of the Knight's Tale, is a false Theban who has won the love of Anelida only to desert her for another. The foolish Anelida

---

[1] *Ympne* = hymn.

was too submissive to her lover; she told him all that other men said to her; she showed him all her letters, and she complied in every way with his will. Being so easily won, she soon tired Arcite, for,

> "The kinde of mannes herte is to delyte
> In thing that straunge is, also God me save!
> For what he may not gete, that wolde he have."

It is interesting to observe that Arcite's new mistress knew better how to deal with him, for he became her slave and had a hard life of it. The poem is unfinished, and is not very good.

A comparison of the Knight's Tale with its original throws much light upon Chaucer's methods of recasting old stories and proves him to have been a not unworthy predecessor of Shakespere in this respect. The *Teseide* is extremely long, being written in twelve books. Of the 2,250 lines in Chaucer's poem, only 270 are drawn directly from Boccaccio, and only about 500 more bear even a general resemblance to lines in the Italian poem. For the rest, Chaucer merely took his plot from the *Teseide*, exhibiting extraordinary skill in condensation. An abstract of the plot of Boccaccio's work will show the principal variations made by the English poet.

The war of Theseus with the Amazons is told in detail, together with the account of their submission and the marriage of Theseus with Hippolyta. Theseus spends two years in Scythia, but finally has a vision which leads him to turn homewards. Then the story, as Chaucer tells it, begins, the chief difference being that at first Palamon and Arcite are on friendly terms. Arcite is freed and passes some time away from Emily and Palamon. On his return, he takes the disguise of a servant, but is known to Emily, though to no one else. Palamon becomes jealous when he learns from his servant that Arcite has returned; the servant, not Palamon, overhears Arcite's complainings in a grove. Mad with jealousy, Palamon contrives to escape from prison, seeks out Arcite, and they fight. Emily finds them and summons Theseus, who promptly forgives them and proposes a tournament as a means of settling the claim for Emily's hand. The preliminary arrangements are recounted in great detail, the principal variation from Chaucer's version being that the prayers of the heroes are personified and are represented as seeking out the divinities to whom they are addressed. Many other details are given, such as the harangues of Palamon and Arcite to their respective bands before the contest. The battle is described at length; there are numerous fatalities; Palamon is taken prisoner, but the horse of Arcite is frightened by a Fury sent from Hell at the request of Venus. On his deathbed, Arcite is married to Emily; he makes his will, giving both Emily and his possessions to his rival, and dies. The funeral of the warriors slain in the combat is described. Book XI recounts the passage of Arcite's soul to heaven. The ceremonies attending the burial of the dead hero are described at great length, six stanzas being devoted to the account of the wood felled for the pyre. Palamon builds a temple in honor of Arcite, on the walls of which is painted the complete history of the hero's exploits; this history is given in detail and is an abridgment of all the preceding part of the *Teseide*. In the last book, Theseus proposes to carry out the will of Arcite; Emily and Palamon demur for a time, but at length are married.

The Knight's Tale was probably written in 1381, as is shown by an interesting bit of internal evidence. Near the beginning of his poem, Chaucer tells us that he has no time to give us in detail,

> "How wonnen was the regne of Femenye
> By Theseus, and by his chivalrye.

Nor can he describe the marriage of Theseus and Hippolyta.

> "And of the feste that was at hir weddinge
> And of the tempest at hir hoom-cominge."

All these details had been given by Boccaccio, with the exception of any reference to a tempest. It is hghly probable that we have here a complimentary reference to the marriage of Richard II. to Anne of Bohemia. Contemporary accounts tell of a "watershake" which destroyed the ship in which Anne journeyed on her way from Brussels to London, a few minutes after the queen had landed. This was December 18, 1381 (O.S.). What caused the "watershake" is not known, perhaps an earthquake or a tidal wave.[1]

The chief excellences of the Knight's Tale are the skilful condensation of the borrowed plot; the admirable way in which the tale is suited to the character and the personality of the Knight (see the description of him in the Prologue), and the interest which is aroused by the rapidity and vividness of the narrative. In characterization the tale is weak, owing partly to the fact that there is little characterization in the original, and partly to the remoteness of the persons and incidents from those which Chaucer knew best and of which he was such a keen-eyed observer. Palamon, Arcite, Emily, are all lay figures; we have no real acquaintance with them, no impression of individuality. One has only to contrast them with the living men and women who are so vivdly portrayed in the Prologue, or with Chanticleer and Pertelote in the Nun's Priest's Tale, to realize how far inferior the Knight's Tale is, in these respects, to some of Chaucer's other work. The tale gets tedious at times, especially when Chaucer describes the preliminaries to the contest; but if the reader becomes a little weary, he has only to reflect on the immense amount of material which Chaucer rejected from his source, and a proper spirit of appreciation will no doubt carry him on his way with resignation, if not with rejoicing. Chaucer's merit in this respect deserves the more praise, because as has already been pointed out in the introduction, and as Chaucer himself tells us in the Prologue, the chief duty of a man, according to the canons of art in force in the XIV century, was to tell the story, the whole story, and nothing but the story, as he found it in his source.

---

[1] These facts were recently pointed out by Professor J. L. Lowes, in an article in *Mod. Lang. Notes*. Vol. XIX, p. 240. Dr. Lowes also proves that the word "tempest" might at that time be used to describe such a phenomenon.

THE KNIGHTES TALE

The Latin printed under the title is from the *Thebaid* of Statius, XII, 519, 520. Chaucer refers to the passage in ll. 9, 11, 12, below, and in *Anelida and Arcite* (ll. 22 ff.) he translates as follows:

> "Whan Theseus with werres long and grete
> The aspre folk of Cithe hadde overcome,
> With laurer crouned, in his char, gold bete,
> Home to his contre houses is y-come."

8. *regne of Femenye*, the country of the Amazons.
10. The same Hippolyta appears in *A Midsummer Night's Dream*.
26. This "tempest" has greatly perturbed some students of Chaucer because Boccaccio makes no mention of any irregularity in the weather. See the introduction to the Knight's Tale, p. 254 above.
55. In the chivalric romances one of the chief characteristics of the ladies is their ability to swoon upon the slightest provocation.
60. *biseken*. Cf. *seche*, Prol. l. 784, etc. The *k* shows Northern influence; *ch* is Southern. Cf. "kirk," "church;" "dike," "ditch," etc.
66. A middle sense of "caitiff" (Lat. *captivus*) is well shown. The word meant, originally (1) "captive," hence (2) miserable or wretched one; more recently (3) contemptible or cowardly one.
68. *estat* is accusative.
74. Capaneus was one of the seven heroes who besieged Thebes.
116. Tense of *rit?* Cf. Prol. l. 187, note.
117. *statue* refers to the image of Mars on the banner.
119. *feeldes* is usually explained as the field or ground on which the device is emblazoned. But if so, this is the only case in Chaucer in which the word is used in an heraldic sense. Perhaps the line means that the splendor of the banner made the ground glisten.
135. *obsequies*. Accent on the second syllable.
142. Find other phrases showing that Chaucer is trying to cut out all unnecessary elements in his story.
153. *by and by*, side by side. This is the original meaning of the phrase. Later it was transferred from place to time, signifying "immediately," "at once." This sense is shown in the biblical phrase "the end is not by and by" (Luke xvi: 9). The modern use of the phrase is an interesting example of degeneration in meaning.
179. In the romances the heroines were always "fresher than the May." In contrast with this trite comparison note the vividness of the next line.
193. *sonne*. Gen. case. The A. S. form had no *-s* in the gen.
196. *sotil*, finely woven. How does the modern meaning of 'subtle' come from this?
229. *Aspect* and *disposicioun* are both astrological terms. *Aspect*

(Lat. *aspectus*, "looking at") refers to the manner in which the planets " look at" each other or at the earth. The word is thus a contribution of mediæval astrology to our language. *Disposicioun* means "position." Saturn was supposed to exert a baleful influence. Cf. "saturnine," "jovial," etc.

231. i.e. even if we had sworn to the contrary. Cf. ll. 808, 809.

248. *wrecche*. Cf. *wikke*, l. 229. In both words; the -*d* was a later addition.

260. *The fresshe beautee sleeth me sodeynly*. Cf. Chaucer's little poem, "Mercilles Beautè":

> "Your yën two wol slee me sodenly,
> I may the beaute of hem not sustene."

262. "And except I have."

273. *brother* means brother-in-arms. It was common for knights to make compacts of brotherhood, on the terms named in the next few lines, their oaths being sealed with their blood.

275. The sense is, "on pain of death by torture."

289. *counseil* gives some difficulty, as the word was not used in the sense of "counsel," "adviser," in the XIV century. If the word *cosin* be substituted, as has been proposed, the line becomes the same as line 303.

295. *shalt*, in the sense of "art sure to be." The original sense of "shall" implies obligation.

297. *par amour*, i.e. he loved her as a woman, not as a goddess.

300. Like Wordsworth after him, Arcite longed for a woman

> "not too bright or good
> For human nature's daily food."

Such debates as this were very common in the mediæval casuistry of love.

305. Chaucer is again thinking of Boëthius. See his translation, bk. iii, met. xii, and cf. *Troilus*, iv, l. 618.

309. *positif lawe*, law made by man.

311. *nedes*, adverbial genitive. Cf. "must needs."

319 ff. Fables similar to this, but with different animals, are found in several of the Æsopic collections.

340. *olde bokes*. Chaucer refers to the *Romaunt of the Rose*. The story is in Plutarch, but there is no evidence that Chaucer read it there. In the *Teseide* is merely a reference to the visit of Pirithous to Athens.

343. Observe the slip in *write*.

367. *me shape*, it is shaped or decreed to me.

388. Earth, water, fire, and air were the four elements, according to mediæval physics, from which all things were made.

391. *wanhope*. The prefix *wan-* indicates lack. Cf. *wanton* which originally meant lacking education or breeding.

NOTES

402. Cf. Rom. 8:26.

403 ff. This passage comes from Boëthius.

421. *pure*, here, "very." For a similar emphatic use of pure cf. "pure and simple."

428. *kinrede*. The suffix *-rede* corresponds to -ship, as in "kinship"; the *d* in the modern word is intrusive. Cf. hatred.

444. *asshen*. Note the old plural ending *-en*, which survives in a few such words as oxen, children, brethren, etc.

459. *letten* does not mean "allow."

475. *him Arcite*, this Arcite. Cf. l. 352.

489. A specimen of the debates in the mediæval Courts of Love already referred to (l. 300, note). Poems and tales often ended with similar propositions for debate; Heywood's comedy of *Love* is an excellent example.

503 ff. These lines give the conventional signs of love as found everywhere in mediæval love literature. Cf. Neilson's *Court of Love* s.v. "Statutes of Love."

516. *Hereos*, Eros.

518. The "fantastic" cell, which caused insanity, was supposed to be in the front of the head (*biforen*).

519. *up-so-doun*. The older form; "upsidedown" is an example of popular etymology.

527 ff. Consult some work on mythology for the story of Mercury and Argus.

529. *slepy yerde*, the caduceus.

547. *bar him lowe*, conducted himself humbly.

555. *nexte*, nearest. Cf. Mark 1:38.

570. *Philostrate*, "one conquered by love." Chaucer got the name from Boccaccio's version of the story of Troilus.

586. *slyly*. See Glossary; cf. "cunning," "craft," etc. for similar degeneration of meaning. *Honestly* here means honorably.

601. Observe how carefully Chaucer avoids situations calling for the expression of violent emotion and tears.

621. *dredful*, full of dread. Cf. Milton's use of "careful."

633 ff. Another instance of the literary convention, already noted, making divisions or sections of a poem begin with a reference to the season or the hour of day. Here, however, as in the beginning of the Prologue, Chaucer is exceedingly happy.

636. Note the beauty of the figure, which, as Skeat points out was suggested by Dante, *Purg.*, I, 20.

642. *observaunce to May*. For interesting accounts of May Day customs consult Chambers, *Mediæval Stage*, Vol. I, index, and Brand's *Popular Antiquities*. Cf. also Herrick's poem, "Corinna's Going a-Maying."

664. A proverb found in Lat., Ger., and other languages.

665-6. "It is wise for a man to bear himself calmly, for men are always meeting at unexpected times."

671. For comment on *roundel*, see the introduction to the Roundel from the Parlement of Foules.

681. This is a widely known proverb in rural England.

701. *felle.* Note the vocative *-e*.

708. "My death was decreed before my baby shirt was made," i.e. before my birth. Cf. *Troilus* III, 733, 734.

> "O fatal sustren, which, er any clooth
> Me shapen was, my destinè me sponne."

722 ff. Note the energy of this speech, as well as that of Arcite's (ll. 741 ff.).

767-8. The proverb is found in both the *Romaunt of the Rose* and in Ovid. Spenser copies it from Chaucer in *Mother Hubberd's Tale*, l. 1026. *Hir thankes*, willingly.

780 ff. Note that this is an Homeric simile, something very rare in Chaucer. The figure, however, is very old, being found in Statius, Dante, and Boccaccio.

788. *me mishappe. Me* is dative.

791. Note the grimness of the situation; Chaucer is at his best here.

807. *seyn biforn*, foreseen.

814. *sighte above*, cf. the idea of "sight" in "providence"; also in "*purveiaunce*" (l. 807), which comes through the French.

818. *daweth.* The *n* in the modern word is intrusive, the sign of the infinitive having been mistaken as part of the root.

841. *breme*, furiously. The word meant originally the line between sea and land (cf. "filled to the brim"); since the coast line was the region of much froth and foam, the word developed the sense in which Chaucer uses it. "Broom" is a related word, meaning that which whirls together.

903. This has been called Chaucer's favorite line, for it occurs three times in the *Canterbury Tales* and once in the *Legend of Good Women*.

913. Whether the reference is to women in general, or to these particular supplicants, is not very clear; Chaucer's statement is pretty generally true of the heroines of the romances. *Evere in oon*, incessantly.

922. *can*, knows.

923. *after oon.* Cf. note to Prol. l. 341.

927 ff. Theseus is the most clearly drawn character in the poem; the two youths differ but slightly from each other, while Ipolita and Emily are as colorless as the average ladies of the romances. Theseus, however, as this passage shows, is a genuine creation.

NOTES

941. "Who can be a fool, unless he love;" i.e. a fool *par excellence.*

949. *Iolitee.* The meaning here is "gay dress," referring to their clothing, stained with blood and torn into ribbons; a superb bit of irony.

956. *servant.* The regular term designating a knight who had sworn himself to the service of some particular lady.

980. *pypen in an ivy-leef,* whistle for his trouble.

992. The line means, "This day a year hence, no later or sooner."

1008. "Except that one of you shall be slain or taken prisoner."

1060 ff. This passage constitutes a typical description of the Court of Love. Three groups will be noted among the courtiers: (1) the symptoms (ll. 1062–1065); (2) qualities or characteristics, personified (ll. 1067–1072); (3) famous lovers. This exceedingly conventional passage was full of meaning to Chaucer's readers. Cf. Neilson, *Court of Love.* Chaucer describes temples of Venus in the *Parl. of Foules,* 183–294 (a passage, like this, imitated from the *Teseide*) and in the *Hous of Fame* 119–139.

1070–1073. *Dispense* refers to gifts made to love or to the minstrels. There are frequent references to the *cuckoo* as being an unlucky bird in love matters. The *caroles* were accompaniments to the dance.

1078. Chaucer confuses the island of Cytherea, the home of Venus, with a Mount Cithæron, in Attica, which had nothing to do with the goddess.

1082. *Ydelnesse* is the porter of the garden in which the Rose is kept in the *Roman.* The references to famous lovers, except that to Solomon may be looked up in a work on mythology or a classical dictionary.

1149. See the story of Jael and Sisera, Judges, ch. iv.

1159. *hoppesteres,* literally, female dancers. The awkward figure is due to Chaucer's failure to translate correctly the Italian *nave bellatrici,* warships. He read it *ballatrici,* dancing.

1163. Chaucer has confused Mars, the god of war, and Mars, the planet which causes ill-luck; the following passage refers to the planet.

1167. *barbour,* barber-surgeon.

1171. To whom is the reference?

1187. Puella and Rubeus are names of figures in geomancy, or earth-divination, so-called because the figures were originally made on the ground. To form such figures, jot down hurriedly a series of dots, without counting, in a straight line. Do the same thing four times in all. Count the dots in each line, and, if the result be odd, put one dot in the middle of a piece of paper; if even, put two dots, one on each side, arranging the whole in four rows, one beneath the other. Of the sixteen possible figures, three may be noted:

The first, Puella, was sacred to Venus; the second, Rubeus, and the third, Puer, to Mars. Chaucer should have named Puer and Rubeus, since he is speaking of Mars. See Skeat's very interesting note in Oxf. Chaucer, V, 82–83.

1198 ff. Callisto was changed into the Great Bear, while the l ode star is in the lesser bear; Chaucer's astronomy is mixed.

1203. Callisto's son, Arcas, was changed into the constellation Boötes.

1204. *Dane*, Daphne. Look up the story of Daphne and Apollo, and read Lowell's delightful lines at the beginning of the *Fable for Critics*.

1207. *Attheon*, Actæon.

1212. *Atthalante*, Atalanta.

1217. Look up the characteristics of Diana in any book on mythology. Cf. l. 1455.

1230. There is a good deal of unconscious humor in this estimate of the value of the paintings.

1254. *paramours*, passionately.

1257. *benedicite*, pronounced *ben'cite*, as commonly in Chaucer.

1267. Chaucer suddenly realizes that he is perpetrating anachronisms in every line, hence his rather lame apology that there is nothing new under the sun.

1270. Chaucer describes but one champion on each side. As there were two hundred in all, and as the literary convention of his time called for a description of a good number of these, his self-restraint is unusual. Boccaccio gives an entire book to the mere enumeration of the contestants.

1329. *alle and some*, one and all.

1339. Look up the various meanings of "minstrelsy" in a large dictionary. l. 1345 is very characteristic of the time.

1353. The astrology involved in this and the following lines has been fully explained by Professor Skeat (Oxf. Chaucer, V, 86). To condense somewhat: In the astrology of the time the planets were arranged in the order named in the table below. Each day was particularly assigned to the planet whose hour was the first, i.e. sunrise. Thus, Sunday belonged to Sol; Monday to Luna; Tuesday, Mars; Wednesday, Mercury; Thursday, Jupiter; Friday, Venus; Saturday, Saturn. In the table, the numerals refer to the hour of day, beginning with sunrise on Sunday. Thus it is seen that each hour of the day was influenced by some one planet.

	Sunday hours.				Monday.
Saturn		5	12	19	2
Jupiter		6	13	20	3
Mars		7	14	21	4
Sol	1	8	15	22	5
Venus	2	9	16	23	6
Mercury	3	10	17	24	7
Luna	4	11	18	1	8 etc.

Emily goes forth at sunrise on Monday, the hour sacred to Luna (Diana); Palamon, two hours before sunrise (twenty-third hour of Sunday), the hour sacred to Venus; and Arcite the fourth hour of Monday, the hour sacred to Mars.

1363. The three prayers follow Boccaccio more closely than any other part of the poem; the chief difference is that in the *Teseide* the prayers are personified and go at once to seek the divinities addressed.

1366. *Adoun*, Adonis.

1394. *go*, i.e. go on foot, the usual meaning in Chaucer's time.

1413. The day and the night were divided into twelve hours each, the result being that in winter the hours of the night were longer than those of the day, while in the summer the reverse was true. Thus the hours were never equal except at the equinox.

1415. This line has been much admired as illustrative of Chaucerian humor.

1436. Chaucer's references cannot be depended upon. The real source is not Statius, but Boccaccio, whose books were anything but "olde."

1444. *As keep me*. "As" is frequently used with the imperative. Cf. 1459 and 1467.

1445. *Aboghte*, paid for. In former times to buy meant to pay for, which is not always the case to-day.

1455. *thre formes*. Diana was goddess of the moon; and was also Diana and Lucina on earth, and Proserpina in the nether world. Cf. ll. 1217–1230.

1480 ff. The simile comes from Dante, Inf. xiii, 40.

1525. Referring to the love of Mars for Venus.

1538. *doth* is causative. Cf. *do*, l. 1547.

1577. *fare . . . fare*. Almost an identical rhyme. Chaucer often permits himself to use rhyme words of the same spelling and sound, if the meaning varies, as in 1475-6; 1499-1509; Prol. 17-18, etc. Here, however, he has merely different forms of the same word.

1579. A common proverb, as is also l. 1591, where the meaning is "Men may outrun the old, but not outwit."

1592. Saturn was generally considered an instigator of strife, hence this kindness was "against his nature." The lines next following show a confusion between Saturn the divinity and Saturn the planet of baleful influence analogous to the treatment of Mars already noted. In l. 596, allusion is made to the planet's orbit, then supposed to be the largest of all.

1601. The constant terror of Chaucer's time was the "cherles rebelling." See the Introduction, p. 11.

1603. *signe of the leoun,* properly the "mansion" of the sun, in astrology, but the first ten degrees were assigned to Saturn.

1639. *uncouth.* Cf. Milton's similar use. Note the picturesque vigor of the following lines.

1723. *under Marte,* under the shrine, or oratory, of Mars. Cf. l. 1727.

1744. In go the spears full firmly into the rest."

1754 ff. *He . . . He . . .* One . . . Another.

1758. *he him hurtleth,* one overthrows another.

1763. *doth,* causative use.

1768. *Galgopheye.* Probably the Vale of Gargaphia, in Bœotia, where Actæon was turned into a stag. (Skeat.)

1772. *Belmarie,* Benmarin, a Moorish kingdom in Africa. See Prol. l. 57.

1808. *hir teres in the listes fille.* Cf. Chaucer's *Envoy to Scogan,* ll. 11, 12.

> But now so wepeth Venus in hir spere,
> That with hir teres she wol drenche us here.

1815. *Been in hir wele,* are overjoyed. This indicates the popularity of Arcite. *Daun* (<Lat. *dominus*) was a title usually given to monks, but might be given to others. Cf. the phrase "Dan Cupid." The title was often given to Chaucer himself by his admirers in later times.

1817. *which a,* what a.

1823-1824. Three of the MSS. (E., Hn., Cm.) omit these lines.

1825. "She was all his joy, so far as his heart was concerned."

1826. Three of the MSS. (E., Hn., Cm.) have *furie, furye.* The rest have *fyr, fir, fire, tyre.* In Boccaccio it is a fury who causes the accident; so also Statius.

1840. *In memorie,* conscious.

1875. *gree,* superiority, prize. Cf. Burns's "For a' That":

> "May bear the gree, and a' that."

1877. *after hir degree,* according to their rank.

1882. Another evidence that Chaucer is conscious of the length of this tale and is hurrying to the conclusion.

1891. According to the physiology of the time the *vertu expulsif* represents the powers of recuperation; the *animal* virtue is seated in the brain; *natural* refers to the liver.

1902. Note the grim humor.

1903. *al and som,* this is the long and short of it.

1907 ff. Note the pathos of the following lines, and observe how, at the most affecting moment, Chaucer suddenly becomes himself again, with characteristic humor refusing to discuss the theological bearings of the case. Boccaccio has no such scruples.

1929. *Servant*, i.e. in the cause of Love. Cf. 956.

1945. *Only* modifies *gan faillen* (1947).

1957. Again evidence that Chaucer is hurrying to the end. *Gye*, may he guide.

1962 ff. Chaucer usually hastens over such scenes as this. Cf. the exaggeration and lack of real pathos in this passage with the simplicity of the description of Arcite's death.

2062 ff. Such lists of trees were conventional. They are found in Ovid, Virgil, Lucan, Statius, Boccaccio, Chaucer (*Parl. of Foules*, and here), Tasso, Spenser, etc.

2070. *Amadrides*, hamadryads.

2076. *a three*, in three, we say *in two*. Chaucer's is the usual Middle English idiom. It occurs repeatedly in the Mystery plays.

2079. The *gerlandes hanging with ful many a flour* were characteristic of Elizabethan funerals of unmarried girls. Cf. the grave scene in Hamlet.

2100. The *liche-wake* was anything but classical. Wake-plays were common in England and Ireland. See Chambers, *Mediæval Stage*, I, index.

2109. In the *Teseide*, Palamon and Emily are married a few days after the death of Arcite; Chaucer represents several years as having elapsed. Boccaccio makes the lovers decline, in set speeches, and their scruples are overcome only with difficulty. Chaucer's account of the sermon of Theseus comes mainly from Boëthius.

2129. According to the Ptolemaic astronomy the planets were set in spheres; outside all was the *Primum Mobile*, Milton's "first moved" (P. L. III. 483) which kept the planets in their courses. Chaucer considers God the mover of the *Primum Mobile*, and makes Love the first cause of the universe, binding all things with its "faire cheyne."

2137. *adoun*, below.

2148, 9. Note *his* for *its* in each of these lines, and again in l. 2179. "Its" did not come into general use until the XVII century.

2158. *at eye*, at a glance.

2184. This was a proverb even in Chaucer's time.

2193, 4. The purpose of Theseus' long sermon is to show that they should not grieve, because Arcite died at the height of his fame. Chaucer has elsewhere shown such good judgment in cutting out unnecessary passages that it is a little disappointing to find this homily here. The explanation is that he admired Boëthius so highly that he was always dragging in references to him on the slightest occasion. Perhaps, too, he takes a little sly pleasure out of keeping the reader in suspense.

2226. *brother sone*. Nouns of relationship had no *-s* in the genitive singular in A.S., and sometimes the same rule was observed in Middle English.

Though it had been very long, the story told by the knight was well received by the travelers. Chaucer tells us

> Whan that the Knight had thus his tale y-told,
> In al the route was ther yong ne old
> That he ne seyde it was a noble storie,
> And worthy for to drawen to memorie;
> And namely the gentils everichoon.
> Our Hoste lough and swoor, 'So moot I goon,
> This gooth aright; unbokeled is the male;[1]
> Lat see now who shal telle another tale:
> For trewely, the game is wel bigonne.
> Now telleth ye, sir Monk, if that ye conne,
> Sumwhat, to quyte with the Knightes tale.'

Evidently the Host wanted some man of learning to continue the story-telling, but the Miller, who "fordronken was al pale," interrupted

> He wolde avalen neither hood ne hat,
> Ne abyde no man for his curteisye,
> But in Pilates vois[2] he gan to crye,
> And swoor by armes and by blood and bones,
> 'I can a noble tale for the nones.'

The Host tries to dissuade him, but in vain, and though a quarrel very nearly ensues between the Miller and the Reve, the Miller is victorious and tells a rather rough story. It is not for a long time that the Monk is allowed to give his "tragedies."

STUDY TOPICS

1. Theseus is more a feudal lord than a Greek hero. Find evidence of this (a) in the tale itself, (b) by reference to more characteristic stories of Greek heroes, such as Ulysses, for example.

2. Read Dryden's *Palamon and Arcite* and compare it in as many ways as you can with the Knight's Tale.

3. Note as many examples as you can find of the characteristics of Chaucer's style, such as his peculiar humor; his treatment of his

---

[1] *male*, bag.

[2] In the miracle plays, thoroughly familiar to Chaucer and the pilgrims, Pilate, Herod, and such potentates were always represented as ranting, blustering fellows, much given to oaths and swaggering about the stage. Evidently they were popular heroes with such fellows as the Miller.

sources (effort to condense, reference to authorities, etc.); narrative power; attitude toward medicine, theology, science, philosophy, etc.

4. Test what has been said concerning the weakness of the tale in characterization by setting down the characteristics of Emily, Arcite, Palamon, as made clear in the text, and comparing them with some of the portraits in the Prologue.

5. In spite of length, weakness of characterization, and failure to reproduce accurately the life of the time with which it deals, why is the Knight's Tale worthy of admiration?

THE MONK'S PROLOGUE

1. *Tale of Melibee.* This was the second of the tales Chaucer represents himself to have told. After the lady Prioress had told her story of the martyred Hugh of Lincoln, the Host sought to relieve the gloom which fell upon the company by poking fun at Chaucer.

> WHAN seyd was al this miracle, every man
> As sobre was that wonder was to see,
> Til that our hoste japen tho bigan,
> And than at erst he loked up-on me,
> And seyde thus, 'What man artow?' quod he;
> 'Thou lokest as thou woldest finde an hare,
> For ever up-on the ground I see thee stare.
>
> Approche neer, and loke up merily.
> Now war yow, sirs, and lat this man have place;
> He in the waast is shape as wel as I;
> This were a popet in an arm tenbrace
> For any womman, smal and fair of face.
> He semeth elvish by his contenaunce,
> For un-to no wight dooth he daliaunce.
>
> Sey now somwhat, sin other folk han sayd;
> Tel us a tale of mirthe, and that anoon.'
> 'Hoste,' quod I, 'ne beth nat yvel apayd,
> For other tale certes can I noon,
> But of a ryme I lerned longe agoon.'
> 'Ye, that is good,' quod he; 'now shul we here
> Som deyntee thing, me thinketh by his chere.'

In response, Chaucer tells, or tries to tell, about Sir Thopas. The tale is a delightful parody on some of the poorer metrical romances, being filled with conventional phrases and having the story carefully squeezed out through wearisome repetitions. The humor of the parody is quite lost upon the practical-minded host, who cares for naught but a good story. As a result, he bursts forth with

> 'No more of this, for Goddes dignitee,
> Quod oure hoste, 'for thou makest me
> So wery of thy verray lewednesse
> That, also wisly God my soule blesse,
> Myn eres aken of thy drasty speche;
> Now swiche a rym the devel I biteche!
> This may wel be rym dogerel,' quod he.

Chaucer remonstrates, but to no avail, so he tells a long prose story about Melibeus and his wife Prudence. The wife is remarkable for her long-suffering, for though she and her daughter have been severely wounded by enemies of Melibeus who broke into the house during his absence, she advises him to forgive them, and her husband yields to her wishes.

4. *corpus Madrian.* St. Mathurin, of whom it is said in the Golden Legend that his body would not stay in the earth until it had been carried back to France, in accordance with the wish expressed by the saint before his death.

5. "I had rather that my wife had heard this story than to have a barrel of ale."

29. *do* is causative.

35. The subject is too painful for him.

46. *penaunt or a goost,* a penitent or a spirit.

49. "According to my judgment."

82. Edward the Confessor is meant.

85. Note the definition of "tragedy," then the prevalent conception of the term. In Chaucer's time there was no drama, other than the Mysteries and the Miracle Plays. "Comedy," which was also non-dramatic, was used of a poem or tale which had a happy ending, such as Dante's Divine Comedy.

THE MONK'S TALE – HUGELINO

The Monk's Tale is based upon a Latin work by Boccaccio, *De Casibus Virorum Illustrium,* which is named in the sub-title. Much of the Tale had been written earlier, and Chaucer simply made some additions, humorously apologized for the lack of chronological sequence, and assigned it to the Monk. It must have been a surprise to the Host to hear the fat and jolly Monk begin to bewail, "in maner of Tragedie," the lives of men who had been less fortunate in this world than he. Yet the tale is not unsuited to the narrator, for, taken in connection with the lines about the Monk in the Prologue, it shows the mixture of seeming piety with worldliness found also in the Pardoner. It is, moreover, an example of the many collections of tales having a didactic purpose which were characteristic of mediævalism.

The Tale contains brief accounts of such characters as Lucifer,

NOTES

Adam, Samson, Hercules, Nebuchadnezzar, Nero, Holofernes, Alexander, Crœsus, and Julius Caesar. As the tales were written at various times and have no connection with each other, no violence is done by selecting the story of Hugelino, or Ugolino as representative of the whole. The story is based upon Dante's account of him in the *Inferno*, canto XXXIII. Ugolino was a noble Guelph of Pisa, who made himself master of the city after expelling his grandson, Nino de' Visconti, judge of Gallura. The archbishop, who hated the count, fomented a rebellion, and Ugolino's house was surrounded by a mob. The count was made prisoner, together with his two sons and his two grandsons. After seven months' confinement in the tower of the Gualandi the prisoners were starved to death, the archbishop having made the people believe that Ugolino was a traitor who had covenanted with the Florentines to deliver certain castles to them.

Chaucer tells the story with not a little of the simplicity and pathos of Dante, the English poet merely condensing and adapting. It is the best of the stories told by the Monk, whose tale soon grew wearisome to his auditors because of the monotony and gloom which its method entailed.

As already pointed out, the Monk's Tale is for the most part early work. The use of the stanza is one of the indications of this, since Chaucer in his later work generally used the heroic couplet. The stanza, which rhymes ababbcbc, is of interest, because it was derived from the French and afterwards was developed by Spenser, through the addition of an Alexandrine, into the famous stanza of the *Faërie Queene*. This is not the only influence exerted by the Monk's Tale upon English literature, for Chaucer's disciple Lydgate refers to it as his model in *The Falls of Princes*. The Elizabethan *Mirror for Magistrates*, by Sackville and others, is also a continuation of the same influence.

419. The tower of the Gualandi.

421 Dante represents Ugolino as having four sons with him in prison; in reality two were grandsons.

426. *Roger*, Archbishop Ruggieri degli Ubaldini, who had been associated with Ugolino in the expulsion of Nino from Pisa.

427. *suggestioun*, accusation that he had plotted to betray Pisa.

433 ff. Dante (Cary's translation) says,

> When I awoke,
> Before the dawn, amid their sleep I heard
> My sons, for they were with me, weep and ask
> For bread. Right cruel art thou, if no pang
> Thou feel at thinking what my heart foretold;
> And if not now, why use thy tears to flow?
> Now had they wakened; and the hour drew near
> When they were wont to bring us food; the mind
> Of each misgave him through his dream, and I

> Heard, at its outlet underneath locked up
> The horrible tower; whence, uttering not a word,
> I looked upon the visage of my sons.
> I wept not; so all stone I felt within,
> They wept: and one, my little Anselm, cried,
> 'Thou lookest so! Father, what ails thee?' Yet
> I shed no tear.

438. *doon* is causative.

443-448. These pathetic lines are Chaucer's own.

454 ff. Cf. Dante.

> When a faint beam
> Had to our doleful prison made its way,
> And in four countenances I descried
> The image of my own, on either hand
> Through agony I bit; and they, who thought
> I did it through desire of feeding, rose
> O' the sudden, and cried, 'Father, we should grieve
> Far less, if thou wouldst eat of us: thou gavest
> These weeds of miserable flesh we wear;
> And do thou strip them off from us again.'
> Then, not to make them sadder, I kept down
> My spirit in stillness. That day and the next
> We all were silent. Ah, obdurate earth!
> Why open'dst not upon us? When we came
> To the fourth day, then Gaddo at my feet
> Outstretched did fling him, crying, 'Hast no help
> For me, my father!' There he died; and e'en
> Plainly as thou seest me, saw I the three
> Fall one by one 'twixt the fifth day and the sixth;
> Whence I betook me, now grown blind, to grope
> Over them all, and for three days aloud
> Called on them who were dead. Then, fasting got
> The mastery of grief.

471. Chaucer does not often give, as he does here, a *correct* reference to his source.

THE NUN'S PRIEST'S PROLOGUE

1. The gloom of the Monk's Tale has become deeper and deeper, and there seems no end to the number of sad stories he has in store. It is too much for the Knight, who would far rather hear stories of

> "Whan a man hath been in poore estaat
> And clymbeth up, and wexeth fortunate."

Perhaps the Knight is a little fearful lest his own life may become a "tragedie," and he cannot bear to hear these stories. The Host agrees that the Monk must stop, because, he says, "it is a peyne to here of hevinesse."

28. Cf. Prologue, l. 170.

38. Cf. the description of the Monk in the Prologue, in order to realize how grievously the Host is disappointed in the character of the story told by him, and note that he cannot give up the hope that a racy story may yet be secured.

44. "Sir John" was a common designation of a priest in Chaucer's time, no matter what his real name.

THE NUN'S PRIEST'S TALE

In the Knight's Tale we have a specimen of the chivalric romance at its best; in the tale told by the Nun's Priest we are introduced to another great *genre* of mediæval literature, the animal epic. The sources of the romances of chivalry were courtly; the animal epic was originally of the people, though in its later forms in France it was modified by the great influence exerted by the heroic romances. Though probably not the direct source of Chaucer's poem, the great French *Roman de Renart* contains in its second branch, all the elements of the story. The hero of the *Roman* is the fox, who is continually at war with the other animals and is as constantly escaping from the results of his attacks upon them.[1] The romance was very popular in England; Caxton, the famous XV century printer, published a translation of part of it, and Spenser gives us a specimen in his *Mother Hubberd's Tale*.

The *Roman* was made up of innumerable fables which had been developing for centuries. A strong element of satire was introduced, and in the later portions of the cycle the constant tendency was to get farther away from animal life into the realm of human life. Thus the animal epic served during the latter part of the mediæval period much the same purpose as the pastoral did later in the Renaissance, i.e. as a means for satirizing, under a perfectly transparent device, court life, the corrupt clergy, and even men too powerful to be attacked directly. In Chaucer's story there is plenty of satire, though it is quite subordinate to the narrative interest; and Pertelote and Chauntecleer are far more real to us than Palamon and Emily.

Much of the material in Chaucer's poem, however, is not drawn directly from the *Roman de Renart*. The discussions as to the significance of dreams and of the power of destiny, favorite subjects with Chaucer are independent of such influence, and are also characteristic

---

[1] Miss K. O. Petersen (*The Sources of the Nonne Prestes Tale*, Boston 1898) thinks that Chaucer's immediate source was more directly related to the German version of the romance than to the French.

of the mediæval sermons.[1] These sermons included discussions of dreams, freewill, the evil influence of women, flattery, homicide, earthly fortune and joy, etc., all of which are found in the Tale. In addition, we have two or three excellent *exempla* (little stories illustrating some precept), with appeal to authorities and exhortations to give attention, all sermon-characteristics. Thus the Tale is admirably suited to the narrator, as it is quite as "professional" as the tale told by the Pardoner a little later.

In the presence of such wholly satisfying work as the story of Chauntecleer there seems little need for further introduction. Perhaps nothing that Chaucer ever wrote, excepting the Prologue, gives such clear proof of his surpassing genius. The Knight's Tale, excellent as it is in many ways, affords us no such intimacy with the author. In the history of Emily and her lovers we find a good story, told by an excellent craftsman, but in the Nun's Priest's Tale we are conscious that Chaucer is enjoying the telling as thoroughly as we enjoy listening. He pokes fun at himself, at us, at his beloved books on freewill and foreordination, at women, and at literary conventions. And how wonderfully real are the chief personages of this little drama. No barnyard fowl is Chauntecleer, but a lordly hero who scarcely deigns to put his foot to ground. He is learned, and completely overwhelms poor Pertelote with his array of authorities before telling her flatly that, as for medicine, he will none of it. True, with all his cleverness, he is no match for that Judas, that Genilon, that Greek Sinon, the fox, when the first attack comes. But how beautifully he escapes, and how touching the scene in which these masters of cleverness berate themselves, in chorus, for their momentary folly. Pertelote is not less a masterpiece.

31. *orgon* is plural, as *gon* (l. 32) proves. The word was considered plural until comparatively recent times and was often written "organs." References have been found to "a pair of organs."

35 ff. Instinct told him the hours for the latitude he lived in, and whenever the sun had ascended 15°, i.e. every hour, he crew, so accurately that no one could gainsay his marking of time.

59. Professor Skeat has found this song, a stanza of which reads,

> 'My lefe is faren in lond
> Allas why is she so?
> And I am so sore bound
> I may not com her to.
> She hath my hert in hold
> Wherever she ride or go.
> With trew love a thousand-fold.'

The fifth line of this stanza is referred to in l. 54, above.

---

[1] The material in this paragraph is based upon Miss Petersen's important study, referred to a moment ago.

NOTES

74. *me mette*, literally, "it dreamed to me."

94. Chaucer uses this combination of good qualities several times:

> "They wolde that hir housbondes sholde be,
> Hardy, and wyse and riche, and ther-to free."
>   Shipman's Tale, ll. 175, 176.

> "And ther-to he was hardy, wys, and riche."
>   Squire's Tale, l. 11.

> "That half so trewe a man ther nas of love
> Under the cope of heven that is above;
> And he was wys, hardy, secree, and riche."
>   L. G. W. ll. 1526–1528.

These qualities were especially emphasized as necessary to the ideal lover in the mediæval statutes of love, where a complete code was drawn up for all matters relating to women. That bravery and wisdom were not requirements peculiar to the Middle Ages, however, may be seen from a passage in Bidpai's Fables (Keith-Falconer edition, p. 149) in which we are told that a man, upon asking his daughter what kind of a husband she desired, received the reply: "I desire a mighty man whom defeat shall never overtake, intelligent, and unaffected by foolishness, a man who will not succumb to an enemy, a lamp the oil of whose brightness is never lacking."

104. According to mediæval physiology, repletion either of food or drink caused *fumes*, or vapors, to rise from the stomach into the brain. Cf. *Macbeth*, I, VII, 66, and *Tempest*, V, I, 67, for analogous uses. The original meaning of complexion is very well illustrated by the next line. The four liquids, called *humours* (from the Latin word for liquid) were blood, phlegm, bile, and black bile. The mixture of these humours in a man's body was called his *temperament* (L. *tempero*, to mix) or his *complexion* (*complecto*, to weave). When any one humour was "to habundant in a wight," disease resulted. (See *Words and Their Ways*, pp. 30 ff. and cf. *Prol.*, ll. 333 and 420, and the notes.)

120. *Catoun.* Dionysius Cato, in *De Moribus* (II, 32) says, *Somnia ne cures*, which Chaucer translates (l. 121) *ne do no fors of dremes*.

123. *As* is often used with the imperative.

126. *colere*, red bile, causes red dreams (ll. 108, 110, 111); *malencolye*, black bile, causes black dreams (ll. 113 ff). Chauntecleer was in a bad way, having an excess of two out of the four humours.

146-148. As to take so many bitter herbs can hardly have been pleasant, even for a cock, Pertelote seems a trifle heartless.

148. *fader*. Note the genitive and cf. K. T. 2226.

150. *graunt mercy*, great thanks; later corrupted into *gramercy*. Chauntecleer is ironical.

164. The *auctour* is perhaps Cicero; if so, Chauntecleer refers to *De Divinatione*. Valerius Maximus (*de Somniis*) also tells the story, and some think he is the one from whom Chaucer got it. Probably, however, Chaucer was using a XIV century book (*Super Libros Sapientiae*), by Richard Holkot, and, as often, names another source with the intention of misleading the reader. Such is the opinion of Miss K. O. Petersen, in her book cited above. (pp. 103 ff.)

165 ff. This is a typical *exemplum*, a story told with the idea of illustrating some precept, and either incorporated into a sermon or made part of a collection for the use of priests in constructing their sermons. Great collections of *exempla* were made during the Middle Ages, and these afford some of the most valuable material for the study of popular literature that we possess. In the present case the moral, or precept illustrated by the *exemplum*, is found in ll. 230 ff.

200. "Cause that cart to be stopped."

222. *gaping upright*. Cf. K. T. l. 1150.

247. *that* goes with *rede* (l. 244).

258. Dreams just before daybreak were held to be most likely to come true. Dante often refers to this belief, as in the *Inferno*, xxvi, 7, 8 and xxxiii, 36, 290. *Kenelm* was the seven year old king of Mercia who was murdered by his sister Quendrith in 821. The story occurs in a number of early chronicles, and is mentioned by Milton in his *History of Britain*. The premonitory dream was added to the account in the chronicles by some of the writers of legends shortly before Chaucer's time.

303. The *Somnium Scipionis* of Cicero, edited by Macrobius, exerted great influence upon the dream literature of the Middle Ages. Probably Chaucer refers to this book at second-hand, his direct source being Holkot, mentioned above (note to l. 164). An abstract of the *Somnium* is given by Chaucer in *The Parlement of Foules*, ll. 36–84.

318. The story of Crœsus had been told by Chaucer in the Monk's Tale. It was a favorite story in the Middle Ages, having been told by Boccaccio in his *De Casibus Virorum*, by Vincent of Beauvais, and by Boëthius, in his *De Consolatione*. It also occurs in the French *Roman de la Rose*.

321. The story of Andromache's dream is not found in Homer, but is a part of the Troy legend which grew up during the Middle Ages. Dares Phrygius, who pretended to have been at the Trojan war, and who wrote the most famous account of it from the Trojan point of view, has the story to which Chaucer refers. The *Historia* of Dares was probably written in the VI century, and was considered of great importance by the western nations of Europe, which, including England, believed themselves descended from the Trojans.

334. After his long defense, Chauntecleer comes to the real point, which is that he has an insuperable aversion to all bitter herbs.

338 ff. The contrast between the lordly, brilliant Chauntecleer and his domestic, practical, but wholly unlearned wife is delightfully brought out here. Madame Pertelote is an expert on simple household remedies, but she knows no Latin, and her learned husband mischievously pokes fun at her. The Latin really means, In the beginning, woman is man's destruction.

359. Note the mock-heroic touch: Chauntecleer is described as if he were some hero of romance.

361. *to grounde*, petrified dative.

368. Mediæval theologians held that the world was created in March, chiefly because we are told in Genesis that the earth brought forth grass, thus proving that it was spring; and, since light was divided equally from darkness, it was the time of the equinox.

370. Therefore it was the third of May. *Bigan* gives some trouble, as we should expect *ended* or *passed*. One MS. (Hl.) emends the line, but in a very awkward manner (see foot-note to l. 370 in the text). Professor Skeat suggests that *sin March bigan* is merely parenthetical. (March "began" the year in the old calendar.) The reference to Taurus (l. 374) leaves no doubt as to the date intended.

376. The astronomical expertness of Chauntecleer has already been dwelt upon (ll. 33 ff.).

385. This digression is quite in the manner of the mediæval sermon-writers, as Miss Petersen points out. Particularly delightful is the combined thrust in ll. 391–393, at a very popular and extremely exaggerated romance and at women. Then Chaucer gravely catches himself and turns again to his "sentence."

401. *wort*, root, yielded *wort-yard*, which degenerated into the more easily pronounced *orchard*.

406 ff. Another sermon-like digression, especially in the naming of examples. Genilon, next to Judas, was the type of treachery. In the *Chanson de Roland*, the most famous of the French *chansons de geste*, he betrayed and caused the death of Roland, thus bringing about the defeat of Charlemagne. Sinon was the spy who induced the Trojans to haul the wooden horse into Troy. The comparison of the fox to these famous traitors is an example of the mock-heroic vein which runs throughout this tale.

420 ff. Chaucer says he cannot sift the matter to the bran, referring to the disputes about fate, freewill, foreordination, etc., which form so large a part of the theological treatises of the time. *Augustyn*, Saint Augustine (IV century); *Boëce*, Boëthius, another of the frequent references which Chaucer makes to *De Consolatione*; *Bradwardyn*, a professor and also Archbishop of Canterbury in Chaucer's own time; the reference is to his *De Causa Dei*.

425. *simple necessitee* implies no choice, as contrasted with *necessitee condicionél* (l. 430), which admits of a certain freedom of the will. Boëthius discusses such questions at length, as does Chaucer in *Troilus* IV, 960 ff.

431 ff. Note the ironical touch, the thrust at women, and the skilful way in which Chaucer extricates himself from a position which might cause him trouble with his feminine readers. But does he retract any whit? Ll. 440 ff. contain a reference to the mass of mediæval literature about women, such as the *Roman de la Rose*. Much of this is satirical.

451. The reference is to a book by Theobaldus, named *Physiologus de Naturis XII Animalium*. It is a bestiary, or a book which tells about animals and then draws some religious lesson from each description. Some of these descriptions are very amusing. Extracts from bestiaries may be found in Morris's *Old English Miscellany* and in Emerson's *Middle English Reader*.

474. Boëthius wrote *De Musica*.

492. *daun Burnel the Asse.* Nigellus Wireker wrote a satirical poem in the reign of Richard I., entitled *Burnellus seu Speculum Stultorum*. Burnell was a stock name for an ass, as Russell was for a fox.

496. Made him lose it by failing to awake the priest by his crowing on the morning of ordination.

505 ff. Another conventional passage imitated from the sermons. *Ecclesiaste* is Ecclesiasticus.

521. Cf. the references to Friday, the day of Venus, as being changeable and unlucky, in K. T. ll. 676–681.

527 ff. Chaucer is ridiculing a poem by Geoffrey de Vinsauf in which Friday is blamed as being the cause of the death of Richard I. Geoffrey (XIII century) wrote a *Nova Poetria* in which he gave examples of his own composition. One of the worst of these is the lamentation to which Chaucer refers.

535 ff. The mock-heroic element here is in Chaucer's best style, and the rhetorical passage is well concluded by the sudden solemnity of "Now wol I torne to my tale again" (l. 554).

543. Hasdrubal was king of Carthage.

574. The reference is to Jack Straw's rebellion, 1381. Many Flemish merchants were killed, because the English objected to their competition.

585 ff. Miss Petersen cites a large number of instances in which a captured animal gets free by quickness of wit. At times the victim saves himself by suggesting what seems to be a particularly terrible punishment for himself. Thus the Turtle says, Fire and knives won't hurt me, but don't throw me into the water. The Crow tells the Fox, throw me down the cliff, and let me be dismembered. Often the prisoner tells the Fox or the Wolf that he ought to say grace before eating. Peculiarly interesting are the stories in which phonetics play a part. Thus the Hare, caught by a Crocodile who threatens him "Hic," "Hic," "Hic," says, "I don't mind your Hic, Hic, Hic, but if you should say, Ha, Ha, Ha, I should be scared."

621. 2 Timothy 3:16.

625. *my lord*, the Archbishop of Canterbury. Miss Petersen considers this "benediction" another instance of the imitation of the mediæval sermon, but one must remember that romances, as well as early dramatic pieces, commonly ended in some such way.

THE PARDONER'S TALE

The Pardoner's Tale, with its long prologue, is important for several reasons: (1) it is an authentic document bearing witness to the credulity and superstition of the time; (2) it shows how clear-headed Chaucer was, and also illustrates his method of dealing with such abuses; (3) it affords another illustration of the apt fitting of the tale to the narrator which we have already noted in the case of the Knight's Tale and the tale told by the Nun's Priest; (4) the *exemplum* which is the central part of the whole is told in Chaucer's best manner, and illustrates some characteristics not found in the stories with which we have just been concerned.

(1). As to the first point, there is plenty of evidence that Chaucer did not exaggerate his portrait in the least.[1] Originally, pardoners were sent out by the Pope and their powers were pretty carefully circumscribed. But in a time when the masses were too ignorant to read, and were superstitious to the last degree, nothing was easier than for unscrupulous men to forge papal decrees, covered with gaudy seals, and to collect a number of spurious relics, in order to rob the people and interfere with regular church services. The Popes tried in vain to stop the frauds and there are many documents proving that the methods used by these rascals were repudiated by the ecclesiastical authorities. But it was a time when even kings did not scruple to forge papal bulls and to collect spurious relics, a time when every form of superstition was eagerly embraced by the illiterate commoners; it is small wonder, then, that fellows like Chaucer's Pardoner flourished.

(2). In respect to these superstitions, as well as much of the false contemporary science, Chaucer proved himself in advance of his age. He shows the Pardoner to be the thorough-going knave that he was. At the same time, Chaucer, as has already been pointed out, was no zealous reformer. He had, apparently, no passion for correcting abuses; he was in no sense a Wycliffite. Life interested him, life in all its phases, and he studied the Pardoner as coolly and dispassionately as a surgeon studies a desperate disease. He even admires artistic rascality, in an intellectual way, and his Pardoner is certainly an artist in his

---

[1] The chapter on Pardoners in Jusserand's *English Wayfaring Life*, pp. 308–337 is extremely interesting and furnishes a large amount of supplementary material.

line. It is a question whether Chaucer's keen irony, slowly working its way into the thought of the people, was not a more effective weapon for reform than any amount of zealous preaching could have been. However this may be, it was nowhere Chaucer's purpose to preach indignantly against the abuses he saw. He merely looks on, with keen interest, and dissects and analyzes with unerring insight.

(3). Like the Nun's Priest's Tale, the story of the Pardoner is in many respects similar to a mediæval sermon. The pardoners were, of course, pseudo-priests, and they used the ordinary sermon forms. We have here the text, the appeal to authorities, the impassioned digressions, the mingling of sound ethical doctrine with the fraud, the use of *exempla*, the appeals for attention, etc.

(4). The principal part of the tale, the story of the three *ryotoures* who went forth to seek Death in order to slay him, is of the *exemplum* type and is told with marvelous skill. The story itself was very old. In one version,[1] Christ is represented as finding, when accompanied by his disciples, a sum of money. The disciples wish to take the money, but are restrained. Soon after, two men find the gold and meet death in a way similar to that narrated by Chaucer. In another version,[2] the story is told of a hermit, who runs away from a cave where he has discovered a heap of gold. Three robbers meet him, and ask why he runs. He replies that Death is pursuing him. "Show him us." The hermit takes them to the cave, and the robbers are overjoyed. Then the robbers plot against each other, with the result that all meet Death. There are also numerous Oriental versions. A very striking parallel has recently been pointed out in Coryat's *Crudities*, one of the curious books abounding in out-of-the-way material published in the XVII century.[3] Four porphyry figures stand at the corner of the treasury of St. Mark, Venice. Coryat in 1608 heard the legend regarding them, according to which the four figures represent four noble gentlemen of Albania who came to Venice with a richly laden ship. Two went ashore, and plotted to poison the two who remained; these other two made a similar plot, with the result that all four died at a banquet. The seignory of Venice seized the goods, and erected the statues.

But in none of the analogues so far published is the story told with anything approaching the dramatic tenseness and compression that Chaucer has contrived to work in. There is a suggestion of unutterable things, a weirdness, a familiarity with one of life's tremendous mysteries, that one finds nowhere else in Chaucer. Indeed, for the

---

[1] Printed by Dr. Furnivall in his *Originals and Analogues* etc., from *Le Ciento Novelle Antike*.

[2] Printed in the same work, from *Libro di Novelle*. Both these stories are quoted in the Oxford Chaucer, III, 439, 440.

[3] Noted by Professor Kittredge, in *Mod. Lang. Notes* XV, 193 ff.

best parallel to the atmosphere of the tale, one must go to a modern poet, and read Burns's *Death and Doctor Hornbook*, and a few other of the poems in which he deals with old Nickie Ben, such as the *Address to the Deil*. Chaucer has caught the same spirit here, with the result that we are introduced to a Chaucer who can be terse, tense, tragic, in a way not illustrated by the other tales we have read, if indeed by anything else he wrote.

THE WORDS OF THE HOST

2. *Harrow*, the ancient hue and cry against an outlaw; *by nayles, and by blood*, oaths referring to the crucifixion.

3. The tale just finished had been told by the Physician and dealt with the story of Virginia. The *cherl* was Claudius; and the *justyse* Appius. The story is in Livy, and is also in Macaulay's *Lays of Ancient Rome*.

4. "May as shameful death . . . come."

6. *sely mayde*, Virginia. *Sely* originally meant "blessed," then "innocent," "simple," "foolish," in the order named.

13. Gifts of fortune and of beauty (l. 8).

17. *is no fors*, it is no matter; it is too painful to dwell upon. The Host is tender-hearted and he likes pleasant stories best.

20. *Ypocras*. Hippocrates was the father of medicine; a Greek physician born about 460 B.C. The reference here is to a drink named after him, made of wine, spices and sugar. *Galianes* (from Galen, a famous physician) would seem also to mean a drink (Skeat).

24. *Lyk a prelat*, i.e. a learned man. *St. Ronyan*, or Ronan, a Scottish priest about whom little is known.

25. *in terme*, in learned fashion.

35. *ale-stake*. The sign of an inn, which projected horizontally from above the door, and at the end of which was a garland or *bush*. Cf. the saying "Good wine needs no bush," and also Prologue, l. 667.

36. *Cake* was bread.

37. The Pardoner's character was so well-known that they do not wish to hear him.

THE PARDONER'S PROLOGUE

6. See 1 Timothy, 6:10.

9. *lige lord*, the Pope, bulls from whom he pretends to show.

17. "To color my preaching with."

19. *cristal stones*, receptacles for the relics.

27. "That any snake hath bitten or stung." Observe how in this and the following lines the Pardoner appeals to the superstitions and the passions of his auditors.

64. *lewed*, unlearned. The word originally had no bad sense.

78. *goon a-blakeberied*, go wandering wherever they like, go blackberrying. This difficult phrase was first explained by Professor Skeat (Oxford Chaucer, V, 272-3). The *-ed* is not really a sign of the past ppl., but a corruption of the ending *-eth* sometimes found in verbal substantives. In *Piers Plowman*, C, ix, 138 we read of "folk that gon a-begged" (= a-begging).

100 ff. Avarice is a sin, and the knave boldly avows that he is guilty of it; yet does he not do valiant service to the cause of righteousness by freeing others from the clutches of such deadly iniquity?

109. There is a deal of human nature in this observation; the Pardoner knows how to interest his crowd.

112. *for I teche*, because I teach.

123. *sterve for famyn*, die of hunger. There is no tautology. *Sterven* originally meant "to die," no matter how.

133. Observe that he expressly says that his tale is to be a specimen sermon.

THE PARDONER'S TALE

15, 16. *tombesteres . . . fruytesteres*. Note the feminine suffix *-ster* and cf. note to *Prologue* l. 362.

30. The appeal to authorities, as already noted, is a characteristic of sermons.

39. *boght us . . . agayn*, redeemed us.

48. *defended*, forbidden.

60. See 1 Corinthians, 6:13.

205. *go bet*, go better, go quickly.

208. "There's no need of going."

210. *felawe*, companion.

217. An allusion to the Plague which devastated England in the reign of Edward III.

234. *been al ones*, are all at one.

242. Cf. *Knight's Tale* l. 273 and note.

260. *Inde*, India.

265 ff. Professor Kittredge has pointed out that this touching and beautiful passage is imitated from the first Elegy of Maximian, part of which is as follows:

> Almula cur cessas finem properare senectus?
>   Cur et in hoc fesso corpore tarda sedes?
> Solue, precor, miseram tali de carcere uitam;
>   Mors est iam requies, uiuere poena mihi . . .
> Hinc est quod baculo incumbens ruitura senectus
>   Assiduo pigram uerbere pulsat humum.
> Et numerosa mouens certo uestigia passu
>   Talia rugato creditur ore loqui;
> 'Suspice me, genetrix nati miserere laborum,
>   Membra uelis gremio fessa fouere tuo.'

272. He is ready to exchange the chest which contains all his earthly possessions for a hair-cloth to wrap his body in (Skeat).

231. *Agayns*, in the presence of. Levit. 19:32.

286. *go or ryde*, cf. K. T. l. 1394 and note.

296. *oon of his assent*, i.e. you have an understanding with him, you are of his party.

304. Cf. note to l. 39.

309. "Very near eight bushels."

328. *doon* is causative. "Cause us to be hanged."

330. *slyly.* This word had formerly a good reputation. The meaning is "secretly" "carefully."

331. "I advise that we draw cuts."

398. "As may God save my soul."

403. See note to l. 123 of the Pardoner's Prologue.

404. *a paas* at an ordinary walk.

423. *par cas*, by chance.

427. *Avicen*, Avicenna. Cf. *Prologue*, l. 432. He was an Arabian physician of the early XI century. *Canon* refers to the whole work; *fen* to a section or chapter (Skeat).

441. *unkinde*, unnatural.

442. *goode men.* Note the imitation of the sermon.

465 ff. His enthusiasm for his calling, together with the consciousness that he has told a good story, leads him to try to do business with his fellow-travelers.

483. "Even for so small a sum as a groat." He makes a special rate to the Host.

SELECTIONS FROM CHAUCER'S LYRICS

Most of Chaucer's purely lyrical poems belong to his earlier work, and are due to French influence. In the Prologue to the *Legend of Good Women*, Alceste defends Chaucer against the charge that he is the mortal foe of Love by giving a list of the poems which he had written

>   To serve you, in preysing of your name.

Among these she finds

>   Many an ympne for your halydayes
>   That highten Balades, Roundels, Virelayes.

In these poems, Chaucer imitates such French versifiers as Machault (1284–1377), and Deschamps (1328–1415). Villon, who lived in the XV century, was another distinguished French writer of balades and rondels. Recently there has been a revival of interest in these ancient verse-forms, particularly due to Andrew Lang, Austin Dobson, and Edmund Gosse.[1]

---

[1] For an interesting account of this type of verse together with specimens from French and English poets, see Alden's *English Verse*,

In the roundel or rondel (modern "rondeau") there are not less than nine or more than fourteen lines, with but two rhymes. Chaucer's rhyme-scheme was, as a rule, abb, abab, abbabb, and thirteen lines are usually found. It will be noted that the refrain links together the parts of the poem, so that the effect of the whole is very charming. The first two selections belong to this type.

In the balade, the theme is usually somewhat more dignified than that of the roundel. There are commonly three stanzas, with an envoy. This envoy, in the ancient poems, was generally addressed to royalty, and in all cases if well-written, was of a more elevated tone, a peroration in fact. The envoy was sometimes omitted. The rhyme-scheme of all stanzas must be the same, but the rhyming words must be different, in sense if not in spelling. The refrain is the keynote of the poem, and is repeated at the end of each stanza and of the envoy.

The artificial form, the limitations as to rhyme and the use of the refrain, make balads and roundels admirably suited to *vers de société*. One does not often find them used for the expression of the deepest poetical thought. Their charm lies in absence of strain and lightness of touch and the slightest suspicion of effort is disastrous.

I. ROUNDEL FROM "THE PARLEMENT OF FOULES."

This song concludes Chaucer's poem, and is introduced in the following words:

> But first were chosen foules for to singe,
> As yeer by yeer was alwey hir usaunce
> To singe a roundel at hir departinge,
> To do Nature honour and plesaunce,
> The note I trowe, maked was in Fraunce;
> The wordes were swich as ye may heer finde,
> The nexte vers as I now have in minde.

The poet tells us that the "note," or the tune, came from France. Probably the words printed beneath the title, *Qui bien aime, a tard oublie* (He who loves well is slow to forget), refer to this tune. Both Machault and Deschamps composed poems beginning with this line.

II. MERCILES BEAUTE

This is a triple roundel; the third poem is thoroughly Chaucerian in its roguish humor.

1. Cf. K. T. 260.

> The fresshe beautee sleeth me sodeynly.

---

pp. 358 ff. Gummere's *Handbook of Poetics*, pp. 241 ff. contains a brief note.

NOTES

3. So keenly your beauty wounds me through the heart.
15. It does not avail me to complain.
16. *Daunger* here means "haughtiness," "unwillingness to be wooed."
28. Lovers were always supposed to be lean.
29. Observe the characteristic *counte him not a bene*, and also *I do no fors* (l. 31).

III. TRUTH

This magnificent poem is original with Chaucer, so far as is known. Scattered through it are hints which show that the poet was thinking of his favorite writer Boëthius, but there is little if any direct translation. Shirley says that it is a 'balade that Chaucer made on his deeth-bedde," but there is no certainty of the truth of his statement. The sturdy, noble note struck by the poem is one not often found in Chaucer.

2. The sense is, Let your own possessions satisfy you.
4. *blent*, blindeth; a contracted form of the present tense.
5. Have an appetite for no more than may be fitting for you.
6. *that*, thou who. *rede*, advise.
7. "The Truth shall make you free."
8. Do not have a violent zeal for reforming the world.
9. *hir that turneth as a bal* refers to Fortune and her wheel.
10. "Much repose consists in abstinence from fussiness" (Skeat).
11. *to sporne agayn an al:* Cf. Acts 9: 5. "It is hard for thee to kick against the pricks."
19. *of al*, for all things.

IV. GENTILESSE

Most of the ideas in this poem Chaucer drew from Boëthius and from the *Roman de la Rose*. Similar ideas are not infrequently met with in the literature of the Middle Ages, and may be indicative of protests against feudalism. Thus one cannot claim for Chaucer the credit of anticipating the tenets of modern democracy, since he is expressing ideas which were in a sense commonplaces of the time; yet his expression of those ideas was doubtless sincere. The Canterbury Tales give sufficient indications that he was no respecter of persons. One particularly important passage, from the Wife of Bath's Tale, deserves to be quoted in full:

> But for ye speken of swich gentilesse
> As is descended out of old richesse,
> That therfore sholden ye be gentil men,
> Swich arrogance is nat worth an hen.
> Loke who that is most vertuous alway

Pryvee and apert,[1] and most entendeth ay
To do the gentil dedes that he can,
And take him for the grettest gentil man.
Crist wol, we clayme of him our gentilesse,
Nat of our eldres for hir old richesse,
For thogh they yeve us al hir heritage,
For which we clayme to been of heigh parage,[2]
Yet may they not biquethe, for no thing
To noon of us hir vertuous living
That made hem gentil men y-called be;
And bad us folwen hem in swich degree.
Wel can the wyse poete of Florence,
That highte Dant, speken in this sentence;
Lo in swich maner rym is Dantes tale:
'Ful selde up ryseth by his branches smale
Prowesse of man; for God, of his goodnesse,
Wol that of him we clayme our gentilesse;'[3]
For of our eldres may we no-thing clayme
But temporel thing, that man may hurte and mayme.

Eek every wight wot this as wel as I,
If gentillesse were planted naturelly
Un-to a certeyn lynage, doun the lyne,
Privee ne apert, than wolde they never fyne[4]
To doon of gentillesse the faire office;
They mighte do no vileinye or vice.

Tak fyr, and ber it in the derkeste hous
Bitwix this and the mount of Caucasus,
And lat men shette the dores and go thenne;
Yet wol the fyr as faire lye and brenne,[5]
As twenty thousand men mighte it biholde;
His office naturel ay wol it holde,
Up peril of my lyf, til that it dye.

Heere may ye see wel how that genterye
Is nat annexed to possessioun,
Sith folk ne doon hir operacioun
Alwey, as dooth the fyr, lo! in his kinde.
For God it woot, men may wel often finde
A lordes sone do shame and vileinye;
And he that wol han prys of his gentrye
For he was boren of a gentil hous,
And hadde hise eldres noble and vertuous,
And nil him-selven do no gentil dedis,
Ne folwe his gentil auncestre that deed is,

---

[1] *Secretly and openly.* [3] *Purgatorio, VII, 121.* [5] *burn.*
[2] *Parentage, descent.* [4] *end.*

NOTES

> He nis nat gentil, be he duk or erl;
> For vileyns sinful dedes make a cherl.
> For gentillesse nis but renomee
> Of thyne auncestres, for hir heigh bountee,
> Which is a strange¹ thing to thy persone.
> Thy gentillesse cometh fro God allone;
> Than comth our verray gentillesse of grace,
> It was no-thing biquethe us with our place.
>
> (D. 1109–1164.)

1. *firste stok*, Christ.

3. The first *his* refers to *fader;* the second to *man*.

7. "Although he wear," etc.

V. LAK OF STEDFASTNESSE

This ballade, which also owes much to Boëthius (II, 8) belongs to the last decade of Chaucer's life, a time when he was turning back to his favorite philosopher for help against the coming of adversity and of old age. The envoy, in its address to King Richard, is typical of the old ballade form.

5. *up so doun*, up as down and down as up. The modern "upside down" is popular etymology.

16. *dominacioun*, an astrological term.

VI. CHAUCER'S WORDS TO ADAM

This little poem possesses autobiographical interest, because in it we see Chaucer the workman, half-humorously and half-seriously reproving a careless scribe. The prose translation of Boëthius and the long *Troilus* seem to have given Adam the most trouble.

VII. CHAUCER'S COMPLAINT TO HIS PURSE

The charm of this little balade lies in the address to a purse in the manner used by conventional poets in their supplications to their mistresses. The same humor noted in the third roundel of *Merciles Beauté* is here, but there is a little seriousness also, for Chaucer was in financial difficulties and wrote the lines in the hope that a pension would be granted him. The poem belongs to the autumn of 1399 because King Henry was acknowledged by Parliament September 30, and awarded Chaucer the pension he desired October 3, of that year. These lines were written, therefore, at the very end of the poet's life.

22. *Brutes Albioun* the Albion (England) of Brutus. According to the old chronicles, Brutus, a descendant of Aeneas, was the conqueror of Britain. In his proclamation to the English people, Henry IV. laid claim to the throne, by right of conquest.

---

¹ *fòreign*.

GLOSSARY

The following abbreviations are used in the Glossary: P., the Prologue; K., Knight's Tale; N., Nun's Priest's Tale; M. P., Monk's Prologue; M., Monk's Tale; Pd. P., Pardoner's Prologue; Pd., Pardoner's Tale; 1, Roundel from the Parlement of Foules; 2, Merciles Beautè; 3, Truth; 4, Gentilesse; 5, Lak of Stedfastnesse; 6, Words to Adam; 7, Compleint to his Purs.

ger., gerund.
impv., the imperative mood.
impers., impersonal verb.
pl., plural.
pp., past participle.
pr., present tense.
pt., preterit tense.
s., singular.

A

A, on, in.
Able, fit. P. 167.
Aboghte (pt. of *abye*) paid for, atoned for. K. 1445, 2242; Pd. 41.
Abood, delay. K. 107.
Aboven, above. P. 53, etc.
Abrayde, started suddenly. N. 188.
Abregge, abridge, shorten. K. 2141.
Abyden, abide. K. 69; pp. K. 2124.
Abye, pay for. Pd. 294.
Accomplice, to accomplish. K. 2006.
Acorde, to agree. P. 830; suit. P. 244; pp. K. 356.
Acord, agreement. P. 838; N. 59.
Achaat, purchase. P. 571.
Achatour, purchaser, caterer. P. 568.
Acordaunt, according to, suitable. P. 37.
Actes, histories. N. 316.
Adoun, Adonis. K. 1366.
Adoun, adv., down.
Adrad, pp., in great dread. P. 605.
Afered, pp., afraid. K. 660; N. 566; *aferd.* P. 628.

Affeccioun, desire. K. 300.
Affermed, affirmed, fixed. K. 1491.
Affrayed, terrified, afraid. N. 458.
Affile, to file, polish. P. 712.
Afright, frightened. N. 75.
After, according to. P. 347; K. 1715. *After oon,* according to one (standard). P. 341; K. 923.
Agast, terrified. K. 1483; *agaste him,* was terrified. K. 1566.
Agayn, Ageyn, adv. and prep., again, against.
Ago, Agon, Agoon, pp., gone. K. 418, 924, 1965.
Agrief, in grief; *to take a.,* to take amiss. N. 73.
Al, awl. 3, 11.
Al, all, whole; quite, wholly; although. Pl. *alle.*
Alaunts, great boar-hounds. K. 1290.
Alderbest, see *Aller.*
Ale-stake, the horizontal bar from which hung the "bush" or sign of an ale-house. P. 667; Pd. P. 35.
Algate, always. P. 571. Any way. Pd. P. 6.
Alighte, alighted. P. 722; K. 125.

285

Alle, see *Al.*
Alle and some, one and all. K. 1329.
Allegge, to allege. K. 2145.
Aller, Alder (gen. pl. of *al*), of all; *our aller*, of us all. P. 823; *hir aller*, of them all. P. 586; *alderbest*, best of all. P. 710.
Alliaunce, alliance. K. 2115.
Also, as. P. 730; also. P. 64, K. 2246.
Amadrides, Hamadryads. K.2070.
Amblere, a nag. P. 469.
Amiddes, amidst. K. 1151.
Amonges, amongst. P. 759.
Amorwe, on the morrow. P. 822, K. 763.
Amounteth, amounts to, signifies. K. 1504.
And, if. K. 356.
Anhanged, pp., hung up. N. 242.
Anlas, knife. P. 357.
Anight, at night. K. 184.
Anoint, anointed. P. 199.
Apalled, become weak, pale. K. 2195.
Apayd, paid, satisfied. K. 1010.
Apes, dupes, gulls. P 706.
Apparailling, preparation. K. 2055.
Appetyt, desire, appetite. K. 822
Appropred, appropriated. 4, 17.
Apyked, trimmed. P. 365.
Aqueyntaunce, acquaintance. P. 245.
Arest, Areest, seizure, custody. N. 80; K. 452; *in arest*, couched. K. 1744.
Areste, stop. P. 827.
Arette, ascribe, account. P. 726; K. 1871.
Arm-greet, as large as a man's arm. K. 1287.
Armipotente, mighty in arms. K. 1124.

Array, dress, equipage. P. 41, 73; display. K. 1074.
Arrayed, pp. displayed, equipped. K. 1188; arranged in rows. K. 2009.
Arrerage, arrears. P. 602.
Arresten, to stop. N. 200.
Ars-metrik, arithmetic. K. 1040.
Artow art thou. K. 293.
Arwe, arrow. P. 104, K. 1500.
As, as if. P. 636, N. 570.
As, with the impv., denoting entreaty.
Ascendent, planetary influence. P. 417.
As nouthe, just now. P. 462; *as now*. K. 1406.
Aslaked, moderated. K. 902.
Asonder, asunder. P. 491.
Asp, aspen. K. 2063.
Aspect, the relation, in astrology, of a planet to other planets at a certain time. K. 229.
Assaut, assault. K. 131.
Assayed, tried. K. 953.
Asseged, besieged. K. 23.
Asshen, ashes. K. 2099.
Assoiling, absolution. P. 661.
Assuren, to confirm. K. 1066.
Assyse, assize. P. 314.
Asterte, to escape. K. 737; Pd. P. 86; pp. *astert*. K. 733.
Astoned, astonished. K. 1503.
Astored, stored. P. 609.
Asur, azure. N. 42.
Athamaunte, adamant. K. 447.
Atrede, outwit. K. 1591.
Atrenne, outrun. K. 1591.
Atte, at the, *atte beste*, in the best manner; *atte leste weye*, at least. K. 263.
Attempre, temperate. N. 18.
Atteyne, to attain. K. 385.
Auctoritee, authority (of a book). K. 2142.
Auctours, authors. N. 164.

GLOSSARY

Auter, altar. K. 1047.
Avaunce, be of advantage. P. 246.
Avaunt, boast. P. 227.
Avauntage, advantage. K. 435.
Avauntour, boaster. N. 97.
Aventure, adventure, chance, fortune. P. 25, K. 216, 648.
Avisioun, dream, vision. N. 294.
Avow, vow. K. 1379.
Avoy, fie! N. 88.
Avys, consideration. P. 786; opinion. K. 1010.
Axe, ask. K. 489; *axeth*, demands. 3, 16; *axing*, demand. K. 968.
Ayeins, against. K. 929.
Ayel, grandfather. K. 1619.

B

Bar, Baar, see *Bere*.
Bacheler, bachelor, aspirant to knighthood. P. 80.
Bake, pp. baked. P. 343.
Balled, bald. P. 198, K. 1660.
Bane, destruction. K. 239, 823.
Barbour, barber-surgeon. K. 1167.
Bareyn(e), barren. K. 1119; destitute. K. 386.
Barme, bosom. M. 449.
Baronage, assembly of barons. K. 2238.
Barres, ornaments of a girdle. P. 329.
Batailled, embattled, serrated. N. 40.
Bawdrik, baldrick, cord. K. 116.
Be, Ben, Been, to be; pr. pl. *been*, are. K. 76; *ben*. K. 85; impv. *beth*. N. 510; pp. *be*. P. 56; *been*. P. 64.
Bedes, beads; *peire of b.*, rosary. P. 159.
Beer, see *Bere*.
Beest, beast. N. 79; *best*. K. 1118; pl. *bestes*. K. 2071.
Beggestere, a female beggar. P. 242.

Bekke, nod, beckon. Pd. P. 68.
Belamy, good friend. Pd. P. 32.
Bemes, trumpets, horns. N. 578.
Bene, bean. 2, 39.
Bent(e), slope, open field. K. 1123.
Berd, beard. P. 270, K. 1272.
Bere, to carry, conduct oneself. K. 1398; pt. *baar*. P. 105; *bar him lowe*, conducted himself humbly. K. 511; pl. *baren*. P. 721; pp. *bore*. K. 684; *born*, carried. K. 1788.
Bere, a bier. K. 2013.
Bere, a bear. K. 782.
Berking, barking. N. 567.
Bern, barn. Pd. P. 69.
Berwik, Berwick-on-Tweed. P. 692; B. *unto Ware* (Hertfordshire), from end to end of England; cf. "from Dan to Beersheba."
Berye, berry. P. 207.
Bestes, see *Beest*.
Bet, better. P. 242.
Bete, to beat.
Bete, to kindle, to mend. K. 1395, 1434.
Beth, see *Be*.
Beye, buy. Pd. 383.
Bi-bledde, covered with blood. K. 1144.
Bifalle. K. 947; pp. *befallen*; pt. *bifel*. P. 19.
Biforn, Biforen, in front, before. P. 590, K. 518; 1189; ahead. P. 572.
Bigan, began. P. 44, K. 690; used as auxiliary with force of did. P. 827, K. 1573; pp. *bigonne*. P. 52.
Bihote, promise. K. 996.
Biknewe, pt. pl. acknowledged. N. 241.
Biknowe, to confess. K. 698.
Bile, bill (of a bird). N. 41.
Binne, bin, chest. P. 593.

Biquethe, to bequeath. K. 1910.
Biraft, bereft. K. 503.
Biseken, to beseech. K. 60.
Bisette, to employ. P. 279, K. 2154. (pt. *bisette,* pp. *biset.*)
Bismotered, smutted. P. 76.
Bisydes, near; *him b.,* in comparison with him. P. 402.
Bisynesse, care. P. 520; diligence. K. 149; anxiety. K. 1070.
Bit, bids (from *bidden*). P. 187.
Bithoght, *am b.,* have called to mind. P. 767.
Biwreye, to make known, to betray. K. 1371, N. 231, Pd. 361.
Blankmanger, capon served with cream sauce. (Skeat) P. 387.
Blent, blinded (pp.). 5, 18; also blinds (3rd. s. pres.). 3, 4. From *blinden.*
Bleynte, blenched, started back. K. 220.
Blyve, quickly. K. 1839.
Bocher butcher. K. 1167.
Boist, box. Pd. P. 21.
Bok, book (pl. *bokes*). P. 294.
Bokeler, small shield. P. 112, 471.
Bokelinge, buckling. K. 1645.
Boket, bucket. K. 675.
Boles, bulls. K. 1281.
Bond, (pt.) bound. K. 2133 (from *binden*).
Bone, boon, prayer. K. 1411.
Boon, bone. P. 546, K. 319.
Boras, borax. P. 630.
Bord, table. P. 52, N. 23.
Bore, (pp.) born. K. 684 (see *Bere*).
Born him wel, conducted himself well. P. 87.
Borwe, pledge. K. 764.
Bote, remedy. P. 424.
Boteler, butler. N. 314.
Botes, boots. P. 203, 273.
Botme, bottom. N. 281.
Bouk, body. K. 1888.
Bour, inner room. N. 12.

Bourde, jest. Pd. 316.
Bowes, boughs. K. 2059.
Box, boxwood. R. 578.
Bracer, an archer's arm-guard. P. 111.
Brak, (pt.) broke (from *breken*). K. 610.
Bras, brass. N. 578.
Brast, (pt.) burst (from *bresten*). N. 398.
Braun, brawn, muscle. P. 546, K. 1277.
Brede breadth. K. 1112.
Breed, bread. P. 147.
Breem, bream, a fish. P. 350.
Breke, to break. P. 551. M. P. 39.
Breme, fiercely. K. 841.
Bren, bran. N. 420.
Brend, burnished. K. 1304.
Brenne, burn. K. 1473; pp. *brende.* K. 1567; *brent.* K. 1159; pt. *brente.* K. 2088; *brenninge,* burning. K. 138, 1142.
Breres, briars. K. 674.
Brest, breast.
Bresten, burst. K. 1122; pr. s. *brest.* K. 1752; pt. s. *brast.* N. 398.
Bretful, brimful. P. 687, K. 1306.
Bretherhed, a religious brotherhood. P. 511.
Briddes, birds. N. 61. M. 424.
Britayne, Brittany. P. 409.
Brond, brand, fire-brand. gen. s. *brondes.* K. 1481.
Brood, broad. P. 155, 471.
Brouke, enjoy. N. 480.
Browding, embroidery. K.1640.
Browes, eyebrows. P. 627, K. 1276.
Broyded, braided. K. 191.
Bulte, built. B. 690.
Bulte, to bolt (grain), sift. N. 420.
Burdeux, Bordeaux.
Burdoun, burden of a song. P. 673.

GLOSSARY

Burgeys, burgess. P. 369.
Burned, burnished. K. 1125.
But, unless. P 582, 782; K. 262, 1387.
But if, unless. P. 351, 656; M. P. 25.
Buxumnesse, yielding, submission. 3, 15.
By and by, one by the other. K. 153.
Byjaped, befooled. K. 727.
Bying, buying. P. 569.
By weste, to or in the west. P 368.

C

Caitif, wretched. K. 694; captive. Pd. 206; pl. *caytyves*, poor wretches. K. 66, 859.
Cam, see *Come*.
Can, knows. P. 210; acknowledges. K. 922, 950, 2206; pl. *coune.* N. 501; pt. s. *coude*, knew. P. 327, 467; knew how. P. 713. The word is used in the modern sense also.
Cantel, corner. K. 2150.
Cardiacle, heart-pain. Pd. P. 27.
Care, sorrow. K. 463.
Careful, sorrowful. K. 707.
Careyne, carrion, carcase. K. 1155.
Carf, carved. P. 100, M. 467.
Carl, churl. P. 545, Pd. 255.
Carpe, talk, carp. P. 474.
Carte, cart, chariot. N. 198, K. 1164.
Cas, Caas, case, condition. P. 585, 844, K. 216; cases at law. P. 323. *Parcas,* by chance. Pd. 423.
Cas, case, quiver. K. 1500.
Cast, device, plot. K. 1610.
Caste, estimate, plan. K. 1314, 1996, N. 255.
Casuelly, by chance. N. 281.

Catapuce, spurge (an herb). N. 145.
Catel, chattels, property. P. 373, 540; N. 7.
Caughte, took. P. 498.
Caytyves, see *Caitif*.
Ceint, cincture. girdle. P. 329.
Celerer, cellarer, keeper of a cellar. M. P. 48.
Celle, branch of a monastery, religious house. P 172; cell (of the brain). K. 518.
Centaure, century (an herb). N. 143.
Cerial, the holme oak. K. 1432.
Ceruce, white lead. P. 630.
Chaced, chased. 2, 14.
Champartye, partnership in power. K. 1091.
Chaped, capped. P. 366.
Chapeleyne, chaplain. P. 164.
Chapman, merchant. P. 397.
Char, chariot, car. K. 1280.
Charge, care, matter for consideration. K. 426, 1429; P. 733.
Chasteyn, chestnut-tree. K. 2064.
Chaunterie, chantry. an endowment for the payment of priests to sing special masses. P. 510.
Chees, choose (from *chesen*). K. 737, 756.
Chepe, Cheapside.
Chere, fashions, manners. P. 139, 728; delight. K. 1825.
Cherl, churl. K. 1601. See *Carl*.
Chevetayn, chieftain. K. 1697.
Chevisaunce, gain, borrowing transaction. P. 282.
Cheyne, chain. K. 2130; 2. 16.
Chikne, chicken. P. 380.
Chirking, shrieking, confused cries. K. 1146.
Chivachye, cavalry expedition. P. 85.
Cipioun, Scipio Africanus. N. 304.
Citee, city. K. 81.

Citheroun, Cithæron, properly sacred to Apollo, but in Chaucer to Venus. K. 1078, 1085.
Citole, a stringed instrument like a psaltery. K. 1101.
Citryn, yellow. K. 1209.
Clarree, spiced wine mixed with honey, then strained. K. 613.
Clateren, clatter. K. 1501; pt. pl. *clatereden.* K. 1565.
Clennesse, cleanness of life. P. 506.
Clepen, to call. P. 643, K. 1872; pr. pl. P. 620; pt. *cleped.* K. 930, P. 121; pr. s. *clepeth.* Pd. 213.
Clerk, student, scholar. P. 285.
Clobbed, clubbed. M. 10.
Cloisterer, cloistered monk. P. 259.
Cloke, cloak. P. 157.
Clomben, climbed. N. 378.
Cloos, shut, close. N. 512.
Clos, enclosure, yard. N. 540.
Clothered, clotted. K. 1887.
Cofre, coffer. P. 298.
Cokewold, cuckold. Pd. P. 54.
Cok, cock. P. 823.
Col-blak, coal-black. K. 1284.
Colde, baneful. N. 436.
Cole, coal. K. 1834.
Colere, choler. N. 126.
Colered, collared. K. 1294.
Colerik, choleric. P. 587, N. 135.
Col fox, fox with black tips. N. 395.
Colpons, locks (of hair). P. 679; logs. K. 2009.
Comen, come. P. 671, K. 497; *cometh* (impv. pl.). P. 839; *com* (pt.). P. 672.
Commune, as in, generally. K. 393.
Communes, commoners. K. 1651.
Compaignable, companionable. N. 52.
Compeer, gossip, a near friend. P. 670.

Compleccioun, physical temperament. N. 104.
Compleynt, complaint. K. 2004; insurrection. K. 1154.
Composicioun, agreement. P. 848.
Condicioun, condition, quality. P. 38, K. 573.
Confiture, composition, mixture. Pd. 400.
Confort, comfort. P. 773, 776.
Conne, know, be able (see *Can*).
Conscience, sympathy, feeling. P. 150.
Conseil, counsel. K. 289; secret. Pd. 357.
Conserve, preserve. K. 1471.
Constellacioun, constellation, an astrological conjunction of stars. K. 230.
Contek, strife, contention. N. 112, K. 1145.
Contenaunce, countenance, general appearance. K. 1058.
Contrarie, opponent, adversary. K. 1001, N. 460.
Contree, country, region. P. 216, K. 355.
Conveyed, accompanied, escorted. K. 1879.
Cop, end. P. 554.
Cope, a semi-circular cloak. P. 260.
Coppe, cup. P. 134.
Corage, heart, spirit. P. 11, 22; K. 1087.
Coroune, crown. K. 1432, 2017.
Corny, strong of corn or malt. Pd. P. 29, 128.
Correccioun, pleyn, exemplary punishment. K. 1603.
Corrumpable, corruptible. K. 2152.
Cors, body. Pd. P. 18.
Corven, pp., cut. K. 1838.
Cosyn, cousin. K. 273; closely related, P. 742.

GLOSSARY

Cote, coat. P. 103, 612.
Cote, dungeon. K. 1599.
Cote-armure, a coat bearing the wearer's arms, worn over the body-armor. K. 158, 1282.
Couched, thickly embroidered. K. 1303; laid. K. 2075.
Coude, could. P. 236, 326; knew. P. 467; knew how. P. 95, 106. See *Can*.
Counseil, counsel, opinion. K. 283; adviser, confidant. K. 289.
Countour, treasurer. P. 359.
Countrefete, imitate. P. 139.
Courtepy, a short cloak of coarse stuff. P. 290.
Couthe, known, renowned. P. 14.
Coverchief, kerchief. P. 453.
Covyne, deceit, craft. P. 604.
Cowardye, cowardice. K. 1872.
Coy, quiet, modest. P. 119.
Cracchyng, scratching. K. 1976.
Crafty, skilful. K. 1039.
Crispe, crisp, curly. K. 1039.
Crokke, crock. 3, 12.
Croppe, top (of a tree), shoot. K. 674, P. 7.
Croys, cross. P. 699.
Crulle, curly. P. 81.
Cryke, creek. P. 409.
Cure, care, anxiety. P. 303; K. 149, 1995.
Curious, careful, skilful. P. 577.
Curs, curse, excommunication. P. 655.
Cursen, to impose penalties, to excommunicate. P. 486.
Cut, lot. P. 835.

D

Daliaunce, gossip. P. 211.
Damoysele, damsel. N. 50.
Dampned, condemned. K. 317.
Dan, Daun, lord, a common title (from L. *dominus*). K. 521, N. 492, M. 41.
Dar, pr. 1 s. dare. K. 293; 295. *darst.* K. 282; pt. subj. *dorste.* P. 454; pr. subj. *dare.* Pd. P. 52.
Darreyne, contest. K. 751.
Daun, see *Dan*.
Daunce, dance, tricks. P. 476.
Daunger, danger. P. 402; liability. K. 991; jurisdiction. P. 663; haughtiness. 2, 16.
Daungerous, stiff in manner, difficult. P. 517.
Daunte, subdue. 3, 13.
Daweninge, dawning. N. 62.
Daweth, dawns. K. 818.
Dayerye, dairy. P. 597.
Dayesye, daisy. P. 332.
Debonaire, gracious. K. 1424.
Dede, deed. P. 742.
Deduyt, pleasure. K. 1319.
Deed, dead. P. 145.
Deedly, deathlike. K. 55, 224.
Deef, deaf. P. 446.
Deel, Del, part, bit. K. 967, 1233; N. 14; P. 415.
Dees, dice. Pd. 5.
Defaute, default. Pd. P. 42.
Defended, forbidden. Pd. 48.
Degree, step, row of seats. K. 1033; rank. P. 40; K. 572, 576.
Del, see *Deel*.
Delen, to deal. P. 247.
Delivere, nimble, quick. P. 84.
Deliverly, quickly. N. 596.
Delve, to dig. P. 536.
Delyt, delight. P. 335, K. 821.
Deme, to judge. K. 1023, 4, 6.
Departe, to separate. K. 276.
Departing, separation. K. 1916.
Depe, deeply. K. 1782.
Depeynted, painted, depicted. K. 1169, 1173.
Dere, dear, dearly. K. 326, 2242.
Dere, to injure. K. 964.
Derke, dark. K. 1137.
Derre, dearer. K. 590.
Dertemouthe, Dartmouth. P. 389.

Desdeyn, disdain. P. 789.
Desiring, desire. K. 1064.
Despitous, merciless. P. 516; K. 738.
Despyt, spite. K. 83.
Destreyne, to vex. K. 597.
Dette, debt. P. 280.
Dettelees, debtless. P. 582.
Devoir, duty. K. 1740.
Devys, opinion, planning. P. 816.
Devyse, to direct, order. K. 567; tell, describe. P. 34; K. 190; N. 218; contrive, devise. K. 396.
Devysing, putting in order. K. 1638.
Deye, a dairywoman, female servant. N. 23.
Deyne, to deign. P. 361.
Deyntee, dainty. N. 15; fine. P. 168.
Deyntees, dainties. P. 346.
Deys, dais. P. 370, K. 1342.
Diapred, variegated, ornamented with figures. K. 1300.
Dich, ditch. N. 28.
Diched, ditched, moated. K.1030.
Dight, arrayed, dressed. K. 183; prepared. K. 772.
Dighte, prepare (to go). M. P. 26.
Digne, worthy. P. 141; K. 1358; Pd. 173; haughty. P. 517.
Dischevele, dishevelled. P. 683.
Disconfiture, defeat. K. 1863.
Disconfitinge, discomfiture. K. 1861.
Disconfort, discomfort. K. 1152.
Disconforten, to dishearten. K. 1846.
Disfigured, changed in appearance. K. 545.
Disherited, disinherited. K. 2068.
Disjoynt, dilemma. K. 2104.
Dispence, expenditure. P. 441, K. 1024.
Dispitously, cruelly, fiercely. K. 266.

Disport, diversion; *was of greet d.,* was readily amused. P. 137.
Disposicioun, astrological position. K. 229; disposal, guidance. K. 1506.
Disputisoun, disputation. N.418.
Distreyne, oppress. K. 958.
Divinistre, diviner. K. 1953.
Divisioun, distinction. K. 992.
Divyninge, guessing, predicting. K. 1663.
Doghtren, daughters. N. 9.
Doke, duck. K. 570.
Do, Doon, do. Used causatively. N. 200; K. 1047, 1055, 1763. M. P. 29.
Dokked, docked, cut short. P. 590.
Dong, dung. P. 530.
Donge, to dung, manure. N. 216.
Doom, legal decision, judgment. P. 323; M. P. 49.
Dormant, table, a fixed or permanent table. P. 353.
Dorste, see *Dar.*
Dowves, doves. K. 1104.
Drecched, troubled, distressed. N. 67.
Drede, dread, fear (personified). K. 1140.
Drede, to fear. P. 660; 3, 8.
Dredful, cautious, timid. K. 621.
Drenching, drowning. K. 1598.
Dresse, to set in order, prepare. P. 106, K. 1736.
Dreye, dry. K. 2166.
Dreynt, drowned. N. 262.
Dronkelewe, given to drink. Pd. 33.
Dronken, pt. pl., drank. P. 820; pp., drunk. P. 135, 637.
Drouped, drooped. P. 107.
Drugge, drudge. K. 558.
Duk, duke. K. 2.
Dure, endure, last. K. 1912; stay, remain. K. 378.

GLOSSARY

Dusked, pt. pl., grew dim. K. 1948.
Dwelle, stay, remain. K. 803. *dwelled,* lingered. K. 1946.
Dyen, to die. K. 251.
Dyere, dyer. P. 362.
Dyke, to ditch. P. 536.
Dys, dice. K. 380.

E

Ecclesiaste, ecclesiastic. P. 708.
Ech after other, one after another. K. 41; *e. other,* each the other. K. 1767.
Echon, each one. P. 820.
Eek, eke also, besides. P. 5, 41; K. 13, 31.
Eet, ate. K. 1190; *ete,* imp., eat. N. 147.
Eft, again. K. 811.
Eir, air. K. 388.
Elde, old age. K. 1590.
Elles, else. P. 375.
Embrouded, embroidered. P. 89.
Emforth, according to, to the extent of. K. 1377.
Empoysoning, poisoning. K. 1602.
Emprise, enterprise, undertaking. K. 1682.
Encens, incense. K. 1571.
Encombred, encumbered. P. 508; wearied. K. 860.
Encrees, increase. P. 275, K. 1326.
Endelong, lengthways, from end to end. K. 1133, 1820.
Endite, compose. P. 95, K. 522.
Engendred, engendered. K. 2139; produced. P. 4.
Engyned, tortured (an *engyn* was an instrument of any sort; in this case, of torture). N. 240.
Enhauncen, to raise. K. 576.
Enhorte, to encourage. K. 1993.
Enoynt, anointed. K. 2103.
Ensample, example. P. 496.

Entente, intent. K. 142.
Entree, entrance. K. 1125.
Entuned, intoned. P. 123.
Envyned, supplied with wine. P. 342.
Er, ere, before. P. 36, 835; K. 182, 297; N. 293.
Ere, to plow. K. 28.
Eres, ears. P. 556, K. 664.
Erly, early. P. 33, 809.
Erme, grieve, feel sad. Pd. P. 26.
Erst, first. P. 776; *erst than,* earlier than. K. 708.
Eschaunge, exchange. P. 278.
Eschue, to eschew, avoid. K. 2185.
Ese, pleasure. P. 768.
Esed, entertained. P. 29.
Esen, to entertain. K. 1336.
Esily, easily. P. 469.
Espye, discover, espy. K. 254, 562. *Spy,* Pd. 293.
Est, east. K. 1743.
Estat, estate, condition. P. 203, 522.
Estatlich, stately, dignified. P. 140, 281.
Estres, interior of a building. K. 1113.
Esy, easy. P. 223; moderate. P. 441.
Eterne, eternal. K. 251, 1132.
Even, just. K. 1006; *evene length,* medium stature. P. 83.
Evene, calmly, consistently. K. 665.
Everich, every. P. 241; each, P. 371; K. 790, 1269.
Everich a, every single. P. 733.
Everichon, every one. P. 31, 747.
Ew, a yew-tree. K. 2065.
Expouned, expounded. N. 295.
Ey, egg. N. 25.
Eyen, eyes. P. 152, 267.
Eyle, to ail. K. 223.

F

Fader, father. P. 100; gen. s. *fader.* P. 781; N. 148. M. P. 49.
Fadme, fathoms. K. 2058.
Fairnesse, beauty. K. 240; beauty of life. P. 519.
Falding, coarse cloth. P. 391.
Falle, befall. P. 585; pp. *falle.* P. 324, K. 1845; pt. *fil,* fell. P. 845; K. 176; pt. subj. *fille,* should fall. K. 1252.
Falwe, fallow, pale. K. 506.
Famulier familiar. P. 215.
Fare, affair, proceeding. K. 951.
Fare, Faren, go, proceed. K. 537; pr. pl. *faren.* K. 403; pp. *fare.* K. 1578; *faren in londe,* gone away. N. 59.
Farsed, stuffed. P. 233.
Faste, near. K. 618, 830.
Faught, fought. P. 399.
Fayn, fain, glad. P. 766; gladly, 399.
Feeldes, fields, or grounds of banners. K. 119.
Feend, fiend. N. 466, 569.
Fel, fell, cruel. K. 701, 1172.
Felawe, fellow, companion. P. 650, K. 766.
Feld, felled. K. 2066.
Femenye, the country of the Amazons. K. 8, 19.
Fen, section, chapter. Pd. 428.
Fer, far. P. 388, 491; comp. *fer.* K. 992; *ferre.* P. 48; *ferrer.* P. 835; superl. *ferreste.* P. 494.
Ferden, pt. p. fared. K. 514; acted. K. 789.
Ferforthly, far forth, to such an extent. K. 102.
Fermacie, a medicine, pharmacy. K. 1855.
Ferme, rent.
Ferne, distant. P. 14.
Ferre, Ferrer, Ferreste; see *Fer.*

Ferthing, a fourth part, a farthing, small part. P. 134, 255.
Festeth, feasts. K. 1335.
Fest, fist. Pd. 280.
Festne, to fasten. P. 195.
Fet, fetched, brought. P. 819, K. 1669.
Fetys, neat. P. 157, Pd. 16.
Fetisly, neatly, properly. P. 124.
Fettres, fetters. K. 421.
Fey, faith. K. 268, Pd. 300.
Feyne, to feign. P. 736; pp. 705; 2, 18.
Fiers, fierce. K. 740, 1087.
Fil, see *Fallen.*
Fillen, pt. pl., fell. K. 91. M. 3.
Finistere, Cape Finisterre, N. W. Spain. P. 408.
Fithele, fiddle. P. 296.
Flatour, flatterer. N. 505.
Flaundrish, Flemish. P. 272.
Flee, vb., fly. N. 122.
Fleigh, flew. N. 411, 519, 597.
Flete, float. K. 1539.
Fleting, floating. K. 1098.
Flex, flax. P. 676.
Fley, flew. N. 352.
Flikeringe, fluttering. K. 1104.
Flotery, disordered.
Flour, flower. P. 4, K. 124.
Flowen, pt. p., flew. N. 571.
Floyting, whistling. P. 91.
Folwed, followed. P. 528.
Folwinge, following. K. 1509.
Fomy, foamy. K. 1648.
Fond, pt. s., found. P. 701; provided for. N. 9.
Foom, foam. K. 801.
Foot-mantle, riding skirt. P. 472.
For, because. P. 443; in order that. K. 2021; against, P. 276, N. 297; in spite of. K. 1887; *for al,* in spite of, K. 1162.
Fordo, pp., *fordone,* destroyed. K. 702.

GLOSSARY

For-dronke, very drunk. Pd. 212.
Forgeten, Foryeten, forgotten. K. 1163.
Forheed, forehead. P. 154.
For-lete, forsake. Pd. 402.
Forn-cast, pp., forecast, preordained. N. 397.
Forneys, furnace. P. 202, 559.
For-old, very old. K. 1284.
For-pyned, greatly tortured. P. 205.
Fors, force. K. 1865; *do no f. of,* take no account of. N. 121.
For-sleuthen, lose by sloth. N. 276.
Forster, forester. P. 117.
Forther-moor, further on. K. 1211.
Forthren, to further, aid. K. 279.
Forthy, therefore. K. 983.
Fortunen, to predict, foresee (a fortunate 'ascendant'). P. 417; *fortunest,* allottest fortune (good or bad). K. 1519.
Forward, agreement, promise. P. 33, K. 1761.
Forwhy, because. Pd. 325.
Forwiting, foreknowledge. N. 423.
Forwot, foreknows. N. 414.
For-wrapped, concealed. Pd. 256.
Foryete, forget. K. 1024.
Foryive, forgive. P. 743, K. 960.
Fother, load, lot. P. 530, K. 1050.
Founden, ppl., found. K. 754.
Foundred, stumbled (cf. foundered, of a horse). K. 1829.
Fowel, bird. P. 190; K. 1579; pl. *fowles.* P. 9.
Foyne, p. subj., K. 1692; thrust. K. 2550; *foyneth.* p. indic., K. 1757; pr. pl. *foynen.* K. 796.
Fraknes, freckles. K. 1311.
Frankeleyn, franklin, freeholder, country gentleman. P. 331; pl., P. 216.

Fredom, freedom, liberality, frankness of manner. P. 46.
Free, frank and generous. N. 94.
Frendlich, friendly. K. 1822.
Frere, friar. P. 208.
Freten, inf., devour. K. 1161.
Fro, from. P. 324.
Fruytesteres, female sellers of fruit.
Fulfild, filled full. K. 82.
Fume, vapors arising from excess in eating or drinking. N. 104.
Fumetere, the herb fumitory. N. 143.
Funeral, adj., funereal. K. 2006, 2054.
Fyled, filed, smoothed. K. 1294.
Fynde, find, invent. P. 736; provide. K. 1555.
Fyr, fire. K. 2084, 2093.
Fyr-reed, red as fire. P. 624.

G

Gabbe, jest, lie. N. 246.
Gadered, pp., gathered. K. 1325; pt. s., *gaderede.* P. 824.
Galingale, sweet cypress root. P. 381.
Game, sport. K. 948, N. 442.
Gamed, it pleased. P. 534.
Gan, began, did, would; *gan preye,* would pray. P. 301, *gan espye,* did see. K. 254.
Gappe, gap. K. 781.
Gargat, throat. N. 515.
Garleek, garlic. P. 634.
Gat, got. P. 703.
Gat-tothed, having the teeth far apart (a sign that one will travel). P. 468.
Gaude, trick, toy. Pd. P. 61.
Gaude grene, light-green. K. 1221.
Gauded, furnished with beads called gauds. *g. al with grene,*

every eleventh bead was a large green one. P. 159.
Gaunt, Ghent. P. 448.
Gayler, jailer. K. 206.
Gayne, avail. K. 318, 1897.
Gaytre, dog-wood. N. 145.
Gentil, noble (by birth or breeding). P. 72; excellent. P. 718; good-natured. 647.
Gere, gear, armor. K. 1322; utensils. P. 352; apparel. 365; manners. K. 514.
Gerful, changeable. K. 680.
Gerland, garland. P. 666; K. 196, 2079.
Gerner, garner. P. 593.
Gery, changeable. K. 678.
Gesse, suppose, think. P. 82, 117; K. 1735.
Gete, get, obtain. P. 291.
Gigginge, fitting with straps. K. 1646.
Gilteless, guiltless. K. 454.
Ginglen, jingle. P. 170.
Gipoun, a short coat. P. 75, K. 1262.
Gipser, pouch, purse. P. 357.
Girles, young people of either sex. P. 664.
Girt, pierced. K. 152.
Gise, guise, way. P. 663.
Gladere, one that makes glad. K. 1365.
Glede, live coal. K. 1139.
Gnow, gnawed. M. 458.
Gobet, fragment. 696.
Godhede, godhead, divinity. 2381.
Goldes, marigolds. K. 1071.
Goliardeys, buffoon. P. 560.
Gon, walk, go. P. 12, 450, 771; N. 32.
Good, property. P. 581, 611.
Goost, Gost, spirit, ghost. P. 205; M, P. 46, 3, 20.
Goot, goat. 688.

Goune, gown. P. 93.
Governaunce, management of affairs. P. 281; control. K. 455.
Governing, control. P. 599.
Graunt mercy, many thanks. N. 150.
Graunting, granting. K. 1581.
Grece, grease. P. 135.
Gree, prize, superiority. K. 1875.
Greet, great. P. 84, K. 218; compv. *gretter.* K. 5; superl. *gretteste.* N. 164.
Grene, green. P. 103.
Grette, greeted. Pd. 252.
Greves, groves. K. 633, 783.
Greve, to grieve. K. 59.
Griffoun, griffin. K. 1275.
Grim, fierce. K. 1661.
Gronen, to groan. N. 66.
Grope, to test. P. 644.
Grote, groat (small coin). N. 138.
Groyning, murmuring, mutterings of revolt. K. 1602.
Grucchen, grudge, murmur. K. 2200; *gruccheth,* grudges. K. 2187.
Gruf, flat on the face, grovelling. K. 91.
Grys, gray fur. P. 194.
Gulty, guilty. P. 660.
Gye, to guide. K. 1957.
Gyle, guile, deceit. K. 1738.
Gyse, guise, fashion. K. 135.

H

Haberdassher, a seller of hats. P. 361.
Habergeoun, a coat of mail. P. 76, K. 1261.
Hakke, to hack. K. 2007.
Halt, holdeth. 2, 16.
Halwes, saints (cf. all hallowe'en), by metonomy, shrines. P. 14.
Hamer, hammer. K. 1650.
Han, see *Have.*
Hardily, certainly. P. 156.

GLOSSARY

Hardinesse, boldness. K. 1090.
Haried forth, dragged out roughly. K. 1868.
Harlot, fellow. P. 647.
Harlotryes, ribaldries. P. 561.
Harneised, equipped. P. 114.
Harneys, harness, armor. K. 148, 755.
Harre, hinge. P. 550.
Harrow, cry of distress. N. 225.
Hasardour, gambler. Pd. 289.
Hauberk, coat of mail. K. 1573.
Haunt, custom, skill. P. 447.
Hauteyn, proud. Pd. P. 2.
Have, Han, have. K. 19; pr. pl. *han.* P. 795, 849; pt *hadde.* P. 48; K. 55.
Hawe, hedge, enclosure. Pd. 393.
Heeld, see *Holde.*
Heelp, helped. K. 793.
Heep, assembly, crowd. P. 575.
Heer, here. K. 933.
Heer, hair. P. 589; K. 1148; pl. *heres.* K. 1276; N. 84.
Heeth, heath. P. 606, 606.
Hegge, hedge. N. 398.
Heigh, high. K. 207; great. K. 940; prominent. K. 1309.
Heigh and lowe, in, in everything, completely. P. 817.
Hele, health, well being. K. 413, N. 130.
Heled, healed. K. 1848.
Heled, hidden, concealed. N. 235.
Hem, them. P. 39, K. 89.
Hem thoughte, it seemed to them. N. 568.
Hemself, themselves. K. 396.
Heng, see *Honge.*
Henne, hence. K. 1498, Pd. 165.
Hente, seize, get. P. 299, 698; pt. s., took. K. 99; pt. pl. *henten.* K. 46.
Heraud, herald. K. 159, 1675.
Herbergage, harborage, lodging. N. 169.

Herberwe, harbor. P. 403; lodging, inn. P. 765.
Herd, haired. K. 1660.
Herde, herdsman, shepherd. P. 603.
Here-agayns, against this. K. 2181.
Hereos, Eros, Cupid; *the loveres maladye of h.,* love-sickness. K. 516.
Herknen, harken. K. 668; *herkneth,* imp. pl., harken, listen. P. 788, K. 1816.
Hert, hart. K. 831.
Herte-blood, heart's blood (*herte* is gen. s.). K. 1148.
Hertely, heartily, cordially. P. 762.
Herte-spoon, breastbone. K. 1748.
Hest, behest, command. K. 1674.
Hete, to promise. K. 1540.
Hethenesse, heathendom. P. 49.
Heve of, heave off. P. 550.
Hewe, color, complexion. K. 180; *hewes,* colors, paints. K. 1230.
Hewed, hued, colored. N. 49.
Hider, hither. P. 672.
Hidous, hideous. K. 1120; *hidously,* hideously. K. 843.
Highte, was called. P. 616; K. 1114; pl., were called. K. 2062.
Highte, on, aloud. K. 926.
Hipes, hips. P. 472.
Hir, her. P. 119, K. 11.
Hir, their. P. 586, Ki 320.
Hit, it.
Hold, in, in keeping, custody. N. 54.
Holde(n), to hold, esteem. P. 141; pp. *holde,* held. K. 832; esteemed. K. 1861; beholden. K. 449.
Hole, Hool, whole. P. 533, K. 2148.
Holm, evergreen oak, holm-oak. K. 2063.
Holpen, helped. P. 18.

Holwe, hollow. P. 289, K. 505.
Honest, fit, becoming. P. 246.
Honestly, in a becoming manner, honorably. K. 586.
Honge, to hang. K. 1552; pt., *heng.* P. 676; pt. pl., *henge.* P. 667.
Hooly, wholly. P. 599.
Hoom, home. P. 400; K. 1881; *hoomly,* homely. P. 328.
Hoot, hot.
Hoppesteres, female dancers; dancing ships. K. 1159. See note.
Hors, horse. P. 168; pl., *hors.* P. 74, 598; K. 1634.
Hostiler, inn keeper. P. 241.
Hote, hot. P. 394; hotly. P. 97.
Houndes, little dogs. P. 146.
Houped, whooped. N. 580.
Houres, (astrological) hours, P. 416.
Housbondrie, economy. N. 8.
Humblesse, humility. K. 923.
Hunte, hunter. K. 820, 1160.
Hunten, to hunt. K. 782; *on h.,* a-hunting. K. 829.
Hurtle, to push. K. 1758.
Hust, hushed. K. 2123.
Hye, to hasten. K. 1416; *in h.,* in haste. K. 2121.
Hye, high, K. 39, 1605; highly. P. 271, K. 1217.
Hyer, upper. P. 399.
Hyne, hind, servant. P. 603, Pd. 226.

I

Ilke, same. P. 64, 175.
In, Inne, inn. K. 1578; N. 206.
Infect, invalid, not binding. P. 320.
Infortune, misfortune. K. 1163.
Inne, adv., in. P. 41, K. 760.
Inned, lodged. K. 1334.
Inspired, quickened. P. 6.
Iordanes, chamber pots. Pd. P. 19.

Iren, iron. K. 218, 1134.

J

Janglere, jangler, loud talker. P. 560.
Jape, trick. P. 705; N. 271; Pd. P. 33, 66.
Jape, to trick, befool. K. 871.
Jeet, jet. N. 41.
Jet, fashion. P. 682.
Jolif, joyful. N. 254.
Jolitee, joyfulness, prettiness. P. 680, K. 949.
Journee, a day's journey. K. 1880.
Joynant, joining. K. 202.
Juge, a judge. P. 814, K. 854.
Jugement, judgment. P. 778.
Juste, to joust. P. 96, K. 1628.
Justes, jousts. K. 1862.
Juwise, judgment. K. 881.

K

Keep, care, heed. K. 1830, 531; P. 503, 398.
Kembd, combed. K. 1285.
Kempe, shaggy. K. 1276.
Kepe, to care. P. 130; K. 1380, 2102; pp. *kept,* held. P. 276; pt. *kepte.* P. 415.
Kervere, carver. K. 1041.
Kerving, cutting, sculpture. K. 1057.
Knarre, a thick-set fellow, literally, "a knot." P. 549.
Knarry, gnarled. K. 1119.
Knave, boy, servant. K. 1870
Knobbe, pimple, wen. P. 633.
Knowe, pp. known. K. 345, 1442.
Kyn, kine, cows. N. 11.
Kyn, race, lineage. N. 148.
Kynd, nature. K. 1593, N. 376.

L

Laas, Las, lace, belt, snare. P. 392; K. 959, 1093.
Lacerte, a fleshy muscle. K. 1895.

GLOSSARY

Lad, pp. led. K. 1762; pt. *ladde*. K. 588.
Lafte, pt. failed. P. 492.
Lak, lack. N. 24.
Lakke, to lack. K. 1422; *lakkide*. P. 756.
Langour, weakness, illness. M. 417.
Large, broadly. P. 734; *at hir l.*, at his ease. K. 1430; *at thy l.*, free. K. 425; *largely*, fully. K. 1880.
Las, see *Laas*.
Lasse and more, smaller and greater, high and low (of rank). K. 898.
Lat, impv., let. P. 188, K. 93, N. 623.
Latoun, latten, an alloy of copper and zinc. P. 699, Pd. P. 22.
Launde, an open space in a forest, K. 833.
Laurer, laurel. K. 169.
Laynere, strap, or laces for the armor. K. 1646.
Lazar, leper (from the name of *Lazarus* the beggar, Luke xvi: 20). P. 242.
Leche, physician. Pd. 394.
Lechecraft, medical skill. K. 1887.
Leed, a cauldron; *forneys of a l.*, fire under a cauldron. P. 202.
Leef, pleasing, dear. K. 979.
Leen, give, let (me) have. K. 2224 (impv., of *lene*).
Leep, lept. K. 1829.
Leet, let. P. 128; K. 348; see also *Lete*.
Lekes, leeks. P. 684.
Leme, gleam. N. 110.
Lene, to lend. P. 611.
Lene, lean, thin. P. 287, 591. 2, 28.
Lenger, longer. P. 330, 821; K. 1912.
Lere, learn. N. 286. Pd. P. 39.
Lese, lose. K. 357. N. 322.
Lesing, losing, loss. K. 849.
Lesinges, lies, leasings. K. 1069.
Lest, pleasure, desire. P. 132.
Leste, least. K. 263.
Lete, to leave. K. 477; pt. *leet*. P. 508; cause, *leet crye*, had announced. K. 1873; *leet brynge*, had brought. K. 2031.
Letten, hinder, prevent. K. 31; pt. *lette*. K. 1034; delay. N. 214, 264; *letten of*, refrain from. K. 459.
Letuaries, electuaries, sirups. P. 426; Pd. P. 21.
Leve, impv., leave. K. 756.
Leve, adj., dear. Pd. 269.
Levere, rather, liefer (comp. of *leef*); *hym was l.*, he had rather. P. 293, N. 300.
Leveth, impv., believe. K. 2230.
Lewed, unlearned. P. 574; *lewed man*, layman (necessarily ignorant, when few but priests were educated). P. 502.
Leyd, pp., laid. P. 81; *ley hond to*, impers., take hold (of the 'cuts'). P. 841; *ley on faste*, lay on stoutly. K. 1700.
Leyser, leisure. K. 330.
Licenciat, 'one licensed by the Pope to hear confessions in all places, and to administer penance independently of the local ordinaries' (established clergy), Skeat. P. 220.
Liche-wake, the watch (wake) over a dead body. K. 2100.
Licour, liquor, sap. P. 3.
Lief, beloved. N. 59.
Lifly, in a life-like, vivid manner. K. 1229.
Liggen, pr. pl., lie. K. 1347, N. 405; *lyth*, lies. N. 222; *lyth to wedde*, lies as security. K. 360.

Lightly, joyfully. K. 1012.
Ligne, verray, true descent, line. K. 693.
Likned, likened. P. 180.
Limitour, a friar licensed to beg within certain limits. P. 209.
Lind, linden-tree. K. 2064.
Lipsed, lisped. P. 264.
List, impers., it pleases. P. 583; K. 1092; *liste*, pt. s. P. 102; K. 194.
Listes, lists, enclosure for a tournament. K. 1687, 1808.
Litarge, white lead (as cosmetic). P. 629.
Lite, Lyte, little, small. K. 1769.
Lite, moche and, great and small. P. 494.
Lith, limb. N. 55 ('locked in every limb of hers,' cf. 'wrapped up' in a person).
Livestow, livest thou. Pd. 257.
Lode, load. K. 2060.
Lodemenage, steersmanship. P. 403.
Lodesterre, load-star, pole-star. K. 1201.
Logge, lodge, dwelling-place. N. 33.
Logged, lodged. N. 176.
Logging, lodging. N. 175.
Loken, locked. N. 55, see *Lith.*
Loking, sight, appearance. K. 1313.
Lokkes, locks (of hair). P. 81.
Lond, upon, in the country. P. 702; *londes*, lands. P. 14; *in londe*, into the country. N. 59.
Looketh, impv., look. K. 2215.
Longen, belong. K. 1420.
Longes, lungs. K. 1894.
Looking, glance. K. 1313, 1611.
Looth, loath, hateful, distasteful (with dat.). K. 979; *l. were hym*, it was distasteful to him. P. 486.

Lordings, sirs, masters. P. 761.
Lore, doctrine, learning. P. 527.
Los, loss. K. 1685.
Losengeour, flatterer. N. 506.
Lough, laughed. Pd. 14.
Luce, a pike. P. 350.
Lust, pleasure. P. 192.
Lustinesse, pleasure. K. 1081.
Lusty, pleasant, gay. P. 80, K. 655.
Luxurie, lechery. Pd. 22.
Lyde, Lydia. N. 318.
Lyf, life. P. 71, K. 1918.
Lyk, like. P. 590, K. 443.
Lykly, likely. K. 314.
Lymes, limbs. K. 1277.
Lynage, lineage. K. 252.
Lyth, lies. K. 360 (From *liggen*).
Lyves, (gen. s.) living. K. 1537.

M

Maad, Mad, pp. made. P. 394, 668.
Maat, dejected. K. 98.
Maist, mayest. K. 385; *Maistow*, mayest thou. N. 286.
Maister, master, chief. P. 261, 576; K. 2044.
Maistrye, skill, power, eminence. P. 165.
Make, mate, companion. K. 1698; 1, 9.
Make it wys, make it a matter of discussion. P. 785.
Maked, pp. made. K. 1666.
Male, bag, wallet, mail. P. 694, Pd. 458.
Manace, Manasing, menace, threat. K. 1145, 1178.
Maner, kind, sort of. P. 71, 858; K. 1077; N. 26.
Mantelet, short mantle. K. 1305.
Manye, mania. K. 516.
Many oon, many a one. P 317.
Marshal, marshal of the hall, who arranged the feast and seated the guests. P. 752.

GLOSSARY

Martirdom, torment, martyrdom. K. 602.
Martireth, torments. K. 704.
Mary, marrow. P. 380.
Mase, wild fancy. N. 273.
Matt, see *Maat*.
Matere, matter. P. 727, K. 401.
Maugree, in spite of. K. 311, 1760 (F. *malgré*).
Maunciple, caterer, steward for a college or inn of court. P. 544.
Mede, meed, reward. P. 770; 3, 27.
Mede, meadow, mead. P. 89.
Medlee, mixed in color. P. 328.
Meel, a meal. N. 13.
Men, one (cf. German *man*). P. 149, K. 2174.
Mene, to mean, intend. P. 793; pt. s. *mente*. N. 604.
Mene, means, way. 2, 36.
Mere, mare. P. 541.
Mervaille, marvel. N. 256.
Mery, Merye, merry. P. 757; pleasant. N 146; pleasantly. N. 251. *Mury.* K. 528.
Meschaunce, mischance. K. 1151.
Meschief, Mescheef, trouble, mischief. P. 493, K. 468; *at m.*, at a disadvantage. K. 1693.
Messager, messenger. K. 633.
Mester, need, necessity. K. 482.
Mesurable, temperate, moderate. P. 435, Pd. 53.
Met, pp. dreamed (from *meten*). N. 106.
Mete, meet, fit. K. 773.
Meth, mead, a drink. K. 1421.
Mette, pt. of *meten, me m.* I dreamed; literally, it dreamed to me. N. 74, 258.
Mewe, coop, mew. P. 349.
Meynee, household, suite. K. 400, N. 574.

Ministres, officers of justice. N. 223.
Misboden, insulted. K. 51.
Mishappe, to mishap, turn out badly. K. 788.
Mister, trade. P. 613; *what mister men*, men of what guild or trade. K. 852.
Mo, more. P. 576, K. 1077.
Moche, Mochel, Muchel, much, great. P. 132, 258, 494; K. 258, 1992.
Moder, mother. N. 476.
Moever, mover, first cause. K. 2129.
Mone, moon. P. 403, K. 1219.
Mone, moan. K. 508.
Mood, anger. K. 902.
Moorning, mourning. K. 2110.
Moot, Mote, may, must, should. P. 732, P. 753 K. 27; pl. *moote*. P. 232, 742; pr. subj. *mote*. P. 832; pt. *moste*. P. 712.
Moralitee, moral (of a story). N. 620.
Mordre, n., murder. N. 201; vb., to murder. N. 405.
Mordred, pp., murdered. N. 221.
Mordrer, murderer. N. 406.
Mordring, murdering. K. 1143.
More, greater (of rank). K. 898.
Mormal, open sore, or cancer. P. 386.
Morne, morning. P. 358.
Mortreux, a thick, highly seasoned soup. P. 384.
Morwe, morrow. P. 334.
Morwe-tyde, morning time. N. 196.
Morweninge, morning morrow. K. 204, N. 482.
Mosel, muzzle, of an animal. K. 1293.
Most, mostly, chiefly. P. 561.
Moste, highest, greatest. K. 37.
Moste, see *Moot*.

GLOSSARY

Mot, Mote, see *Moo..*
Mottelee, motley. P. 271.
Mountance, amount, value. K. 712, Pd. 401.
Mowe, pr. pl., may, are able. K. 2141.
Moyste, new. Pd. P. 28.
Murmure, murmurs, murmuring. K. 1601.
Mynde, remembrance. K. 544, 1048.
Mynour, miner, digger. K. 1607.

N

Nadde = *ne hadde*.
Nailinge, fastening, strengthening with nails. K. 1645.
Naker, kettle-drum. K. 1653.
Nam = *ne am*.
Namely, especially, K. 410, 1851; Pd. P. 74.
Namo, Namore, no more. P. 101, 544; K. 731, 1620.
Narette (*ne arrete*), ascribe not. P. 726.
Narwe, close, small, narrow. P. 625.
Nas = *ne was*.
Nat but, only. K. 1864.
Nath = *ne hath*.
Natheles, nevertheless. P. 35.
Neet, neat, cattle. P. 597.
Nercotikes, narcotics. K. 614.
Nere = *ne were*.
Neyles, claws. K. 1283.
Ne, not. P. 70; nor. P. 526.
Nede, needful. P. 304.
Nedely, of necessity. N. 424.
Nedes, needs, of necessity. K. 311.
Nedes-cost, of necessity. K. 619.
Nedeth, impers., it must needs be. K. 2170.
Neer, Ner, near. K. 581; comp. *neer*, nearer. P. 839; *ner.* K. 992 (see *Fer*).
Newe, recently. N. 229.

Nexte, nighest, nearest. K. 555, 1507.
Nigard, niggard. N. 95.
Nightertale, night-time. P. 97.
Niste, knew not (*ne wiste*). Pd. 25.
Nis = *ne is*.
Noght, not. P. 253. K, 1452.
Nolde = *ne wolde*, wished not. K. 166.
Nones, nonys, for the, for the nonce, occasion. P. 379, 523.
Nonne, nun. P. 118.
Noot = *ne wot*.
Norice, nurse. N. 295.
Norissing(e); *of greet n.*, very nutritious. P. 437; nurture, growth. K. 2159.
Nose-thirles, nostrils. P. 557.
Notabilitee, thing worthy to be known, wise saw. N. 389.
Not-heed, crop-head. P. 109.
Nothing, adv., not at all. K. 661, 896, 1647, N. 20.
Nouthe, as, just now. P. 462.
Ny, nigh. K. 472; nearly. P. 732; close. P. 588.
Nyce, foolish. N. 495, over-scrupulous, P. 398.

O

O, one. P. 304, K. 354, N. 170.
Obeisaunce, obedience. K. 2116.
Observaunce, respect. K. 187, 642 (*do o.*, render observance, pay respect).
Of (partitive), something of. K. 2227, *of smale*, some small. P. 146.
Of, concerning, in. P. 191, K. 2027.
Of (expressing agency or means), by, with. K. 420, 422, 745, 2023.
Of, off. K. 1818.
Offende, to injure, attack. K. 51.

GLOSSARY

Offensioun, offence, damage. K. 1558.
Offertorie, verse of scripture chanted during the offering. P. 710.
Office, business position. P. 292.
Offring, the offering collected at mass. P. 450.
Ofte sythes, oftentimes. P. 485.
Oghte, ought. P. 660.
Oo, Oon, one. P. 148; *ones*, once. P. 765; *oon and oon*, one by one. P. 679.
On lyve, alive. K. 2181.
Opie, opium. K. 614.
Oratorie, oratory, a small room for private prayers. K. 1047.
Ordinaunce, orderly plan. K. 1709.
Orgons, organ. N. 31.
Orisoun, orison, prayer. K. 1514.
Orlogge, horologue, clock. N. 34.
Oth, oath. P. 120, K. 101.
Ought, aught. K. 2187.
Ounce, small portion. P. 677.
Out of, without. P. 452, K. 765.
Outhees, outcry, alarm. K. 1154.
Outher, either. K. 627.
Outrely, utterly. K. 296, N. 409, Pd. 327.
Out-ridere, the monk who rode out to inspect farms, etc., belonging to the monastery.
Out-sterte, started out. N. 227.
Over, upper. P. 133; beyond. K. 2140; *overest*, uppermost. P. 290.
Overal, everywhere. P. 216.
Overal this, besides all this. K. 1992.
Overlad, overborne, put upon. M. P. 23.
Over-riden, ridden over. K. 1164.
Over-thwart, athwart. K. 1133.

Owher, anywhere. P. 653.
Oxenford, Oxford. P. 285.
Oweth, owneth. Pd. P. 33.
Oynement, ointment. P. 631.
Oynouns, onions. P. 634.

P

Pace, to pass. K. 744, 2140; tell on. P 36; surpass. P. 574.
Paleys, palace. K. 1341.
Palfrey, an easy-going road-horse. P. 207.
Pan, skull, head. K. 307.
Paraments, rich clothing or furniture. K. 1643.
Paramour, by way of love; as a lover. K. 297.
Paramours, passionately. K. 1254.
Pardee, *par dieu*, a mild oath. P. 563.
Pardoner, a seller of indulgences. P. 543.
Parfit, perfect. P. 72, 422, 532.
Parisshen, a parishioner. P. 482.
Parlement, decree. K. 448.
Parte, company. K. 1724.
Partrich, a partridge. P. 349.
Party, variegated. K. 195.
Partye, a part. K. 2150; partisan K. 1799.
Parvys, church porch, or the open space in front of a church. P. 310.
Pas, foot-pace, walk. P. 825; paces, yards. K. 1032.
Passe, to surpass. P. 448. *passant*, passing, surpassing. K. 1249, 2027.
Passed, surpassed. P. 448.
Patente, letter patent, authorization. P. 315.
Payen, pagan. K. 1512.
Pecok, peacock. P. 104.
Pees, peace. K. 589.
Peire, pair, set. P. 159.

Pekke, to peck. N. 147.
Penaunce, pain, sorrow. K. 457.
Penaunt, penitent. M. P. 46.
Perced, pierced. P. 2.
Perrye, jewelry, precious stones. K. 2078.
Pers, stuff of a blue color. P. 439.
Persoun, parson, parish-priest. P. 478.
Perturben, disturb, trouble. K. 48.
Peyne, pain, grief. K. 439; torture. K. 275.
Peyne hym, endeavor. N. 485; *peyned hir*, took pains. P. 139.
Peyre, a pair. K. 1263.
Pighte, pt. s., pitched. K. 1831.
Piled, stripped of hair, thinly haired. P. 627.
Piler, pillar. K. 1135.
Pilour, plunderer. K. 149.
Pilwe-beer, pillow-case. P. 694.
Pinche, find fault with. P. 326.
Pinched, pleated, fluted. P. 151.
Pitaunce, a mess of victuals or other gift. P. 224.
Pitous, compassionate. P. 143.
Pitously, piteously. K. 259.
Plat, flat, plain. K. 987.
Plentevous, plentiful. P. 344.
Plesaunce, pleasure. K. 713. Pd. P. 81.
Plesen, please. P. 610.
Pley, jest, fun. K. 267.
Pleyen, play. P. 236; make merry. P. 758.
Pleyn, fully. P. 327; full, P. 315; *pleyn bataille*, open or fair fight. K. 130.
Pleyne, to complain. K. 462; *pleynen*, pr. pl. K. 393.
Pollax, pole-axe, halberd. K. 1686.
Pomel, crown of the head. K. 1831.
Pomely, dappled. P. 616.

Poplexye, apoplexy. N. 21.
Poraille, poor folk. P. 247.
Port, carriage, deportment. P. 69.
Portreiture, portraiture, painting. K. 1057, 1110.
Portreyinge, painting, depicting. K. 1080.
Portreyour, painter. K. 1041.
Pose, to admit (for the purpose of argument). K. 304.
Post, pillar (as we say 'pillar of the church'). P. 214.
Poudre-marchaunt, a sharp flavoring powder. P. 381.
Pouped, blew abruptly. N. 579.
Poure, to pore. P. 185.
Povre, poor. P. 225.
Povrely, poorly, as a poor man. K. 554.
Poynaunt, piquant, highly seasoned. P. 352. N. 14.
Poynt o, a bit of (in any wise). K. 1908.
Poynt, in good (Fr. *embonpoint*), in good condition, fleshy. P. 200.
Poynt of his desir, object of his desire. K. 643.
Practisour, practitioner. P. 422.
Predicacioun, preaching. Pd. P. 79.
Prees, crowd. 3, 1.
Presseth, presses. K. 1672.
Preve, proof. N. 163.
Preved, proved. K. 2143.
Preye, to pray. P. 301; beseech. K. 625.
Preyeres, prayers. P. 231.
Pricasour, a hard rider. P. 189.
Priketh, pricks, incites. P. 11, K. 185; spur (a horse). K. 1820.
Priking, spurring, hard riding. P. 191, K. 1650.
Prikke, prick, thrust. K. 1748.

GLOSSARY

Prively, secretly, covertly. P. 652.
Privitee, privity, private affairs. K. 553.
Profreth, proffers. K. 557.
Propre, own. P. 540, 581. K. 2179.
Proprely, accurately. P. 729.
Prow, advantage, profit. N. 130, Pd. P. 713.
Pruce shield, Prussian shield (a small triangular buckler). K. 1264.
Pryme, the first quarter of the day, 6-9 A. M. K. 1331; (here six o'clock). Pd. 140.
Prys, price. P. 815; credit, reputation. P. 67, 237, K. 1383.
Pulled, plucked it. P. 177.
Pultrye, poultry. P. 598.
Purchas, occasional gains (as opposed to fixed income, *rente*). P. 256.
Purchasour, conveyancer. P. 318.
Purchasing, conveyancing. P. 320.
Pure, very. K. 421.
Purfiled, edged, bordered. P. 193.
Purs, purse. P. 656.
Purtreye, draw (probably used here of illuminating MSS.). P. 96.
Purveiaunce, foresight, providence. K. 394, 807, 2153.
Pykepurs, pick-purse. K. 1140.
Pyne, to torture. K. 888; pp. *pyned.* N. 239.

Q

Qualm, sickness, disease. K. 1156.
Quelle, to kill. N. 570, Pd. 392.
Queme, please. 4, 20.
Queynt, pp., quenched. K. 1463; pt. s. *queynte,* went out. K. 1476.
Queynte, strange, quaint. K. 673, 1475.
Quike, quick, alive. K. 157; *quiked,* made alive, revived. K. 1477.
Quitly, free, clean. K. 934.
Quod, quoth. K. 49, 376.
Quook, quaked. K. 718, 904.
Quyte, to free. K. 174; to requite, to repay. P. 770, Pd. P. 92.

R

Rad, pp. read. K. 1737 (from *rede*).
Rage, to romp, play wantonly. P. 257.
Rage, raging wind. K. 1127.
Ransake, to ransack, to search. K. 147.
Rape, haste. 6, 7.
Rasour, razor. K. 1559.
Raughte, pt. reached. P. 136, K. 2057 (from *reche*).
Raunsoun, ransome. K. 166, 318.
Ravenes, raven's. K. 1286.
Rebel, rebellious. P. 833, K. 2188.
Recche, reck, care. K. 1387; *rekke.* K. 1399; pr. s. *roghte.* N. 520; *recche nat to sterve,* care not though I die. K. 540.
Recchelees, reckless, careless of duty. N. 287, P. 179.
Reconfort, to comfort. K. 1994.
Recorde, to remember. P. 829.
Rede, to advise. K. 2213; 3, 7; explain. N. 76.
Rede, to read. P. 709; pp. *rad.* K. 1737; impv. *reed.* N. 310.
Redily, ready. K. 1418.
Redoutinge, reverence. K. 1192.
Redy, ready. P. 21.

GLOSSARY

Reed, counsel, plan, advice. K. 358, Pd. 222.
Reed, Rede, red. P. 90, 153, 458.
Reed, counsel, adviser. P. 665.
Registre, roll, register. K. 1954.
Regne, reign, kingdom. K. 8, 766.
Reherce, to rehearse. P. 732.
Rehersing, rehearsal. P. 792.
Rekene, to reckon. P. 401, K. 1075.
Rekening, reckoning. P. 600; bills. P. 760.
Remes, realms. N. 316.
Remenaunt, remnant. P. 724. N. 84.
Renges, ranks. K. 1736.
Renne, run. K. 2010; *renneth*, runs. P. 1777; pt. *ronnen*. K. 2067; *renning*. P. 551.
Rente, fixed income (cf. *purchas*). P. 256, 373.
Repleccioun, repletion. N. 17.
Replicacioun, reply. K. 988.
Reportour, reporter. P. 814.
Rescous, rescue. K. 1785.
Rese, to quake, shake. K. 1128.
Resons, opinions. P. 274.
Resoun, reason, right. P. 37, 847.
Resouneth, resounds. K. 420.
Respyt, respite, delay. K. 90.
Rethor, rhetorician. N. 387.
Reule, rule. P. 173; pt. *reuled*. P. 816; K. 814; *reulen* (inf.). N. 224.
Reve, steward or bailiff. P. 587.
Revers, reverse, contrary. N. 157.
Rewe, to rue, be sorry for. K. 1005, 1375. N. 277.
Rewfulleste, most sorrowful. K. 2028.
Rewthe, ruth, pity. K. 56.
Reyn, rain. P. 492, 595; *reyne*, to rain. K. 677.
Reyse, to make a military expedition. P. 54.
Richesse, riches. K. 397.
Ride, ride. P. 94; pr. s. *rit*. K. 116, 123; pt. *rood*. P. 328; K. 108; *riden*. P. 825, K. 2039.
Righte direct. K. 1881.
Rightes, rightly. *At alle r.*, rightly in all respects. K. 994.
Rit, see *Ride*.
Roghte, see *Recche*.
Roial, royal. K. 160; *roially*. K. 855; *roialliche* (royally). P. 378.
Rome, to roam, walk. K. 207, 670; *rometh*. N. 360.
Ronnen, see *Renne*.
Rood, see *Ride*.
Roos, rose. P. 823, K. 1356.
Roost, roast. P. 206.
Roste, to roast. P. 383; pp. *rosted*. P. 147.
Rote, a musical instrument with strings, a fiddle. P. 236.
Rote, rote. P. 327.
Rouke, to cower, crouch. K. 450.
Rouncy, a hackney, common cart-horse. P. 390.
Roundel, a song with several repeated lines and a refrain. K. 671.
Route, rout, company. P. 622, K. 31.
Rudeliche, rudely. P. 734.
Ruggy, rough, disordered. K. 2025.
Rumbel, rumbling. K. 1121.
Ryot, loud, boisterous conduct. Pd. 3.
Ryve, rive, thrust. Pd. 366.

S

Sad, sober, serious. K. 2127.
Sadel-bowe, curved pieces of wood at front and rear of saddle. K. 1833.
Sadly, firmly, determinedly. K. 1744.

GLOSSARY

Saffron, to color. Pd, P. 17.
Salueth, salutes, greets, hails. K. 634.
Saluing, greeting. K. 791.
Sangwyn, sanguine, ruddy. P. 333, K. 1310; blood red. P. 439.
Sarge, coarse stuff, serge. P. 1710.
Saufly, safely. N. 388; 4, 6.
Saugh, see *Se*.
Sautrye, psaltery. P. 296.
Save, sage. K. 1855.
Savour, taste, have appetite for (impv.). 3, 5.
Sawceflem, pimpled. P. 625.
Sawe, saying, saw. K. 305, 668.
Say, see *Se*.
Scalle, scab. 6, 3.
Scalled, scurfy. P. 627.
Scapen, to escape. K. 249.
Scarsly, sparingly. P. 583.
Scathe, a pity, too bad. P. 446.
Science, knowledge. P. 716.
Sclat, slate. 2, 34.
Sclendre, slender. P. 587; light (of a meal). N. 13.
Scole, manner, school. P. 125.
Scoler, scholar. P. 260.
Scoleye, to attend school. P. 302.
Scriptures, writings, books. K. 1186.
Scriveyne, scribe. 6, 1.
Seche, to seek. P. 784.
Secree, secret. N. 95.
See, Se, Seen, see. K. 56; ger. to *sene*. K. 177; pt. s. *saugh*, saw. P. 764; *seigh*. P. 193; *say*. N. 294; pt. pl. *syen*. N. 558; pp. *seyn*. N. 461; K. 1796.
Seet, sat. K. 1217; pl. *seten*. K. 2035.
Seege, siege. P. 56, K. 79.
Seek, sick. P. 18.
Seigh, see *See*. P. 193.

Seistow, sayest thou. K. 267.
Selde, seldom. K. 681.
Selve, same, self-same. K. 1726.
Sely, simple. N. 555, Pd. 6.
Semed, seemed. P. 39.
Semely, seemly. P. 751; properly, agreeably. P. 123.
Seeke[n] ... *to*, seek after. P. 13f.
Semi-cope, a short cape. P. 262.
Sendel, a light fine silk. P. 440.
Sene, visible. P. 134, K. 1107.
Sene, to, see *See*.
Sentence, thought, subject-matter. P. 306, 798; subject. N. 394; opinion. K. 2144.
Sergeant of the Lawe, a law officer for the crown. P. 309.
Serie, series (array of arguments). K. 2209.
Servant, K. 956 (used here technically for a lover; so also K. 1929).
Servage, bondage. K. 1088.
Servisable, willing to be of use, obliging. P. 99.
Sesons, seasons. P. 347.
Seten, pp., sat. K. 594.
Sethe, seethe, boil. P. 383.
Sette, put down, reckon at. K. 712.
Seurtee, security, surety. K. 746.
Sewe, follow. N. 517; 4, 4.
Seye, Seyn, Seyen, to say. P. 181, K. 410; pt. *seyde*. P. 183, K. 57.
Seyl, sail. P. 696.
Seynd, singed, broiled. N. 25.
Shake, shaken. P. 406.
Shal (used absolutely), must. K. 1696.
Shamfast, modest. K. 1197.
Shamfastnesse, modesty, bashfulness. P. 840.
Shap, shape. K. 1031.
Shape, Shapen, to purpose, plan.

GLOSSARY

Shaply, fit, suitable. P. 372.
Shave, shaven. P. 588.
Sheef, sheaf, a bundle of twenty-four. P. 104.
Sheeldes, crowns (coins). P. 278.
Shene, bright, beautiful. P. 115, K. 210.
Shent, pp., injured. K. 1896.
Shepne, sheep-folds. K. 1142.
Shere, shears. K. 1559.
Sherte, shirt. N. 300.
Shet, sheet. K. 1739.
Shirreve (sheriff), governor of a shire. P. 359.
Shiveren, to shiver, break in pieces. K. 1747.
Sho, shoe. P. 253.
Shode, parting of the hair. K. 1149.
Sholde, should. P. 249.
Shoon, pt. shone. P. 198.
Shorte, to shorten. P. 791.
Short-sholdred, stocky, short in the upper arm. P. 549.
Shrewe, to curse, beshrew. N. 607.
Shrewe, rascal. Pd. 34, 297.
Shrighte, shrieked. K. 1959, N. 542; *shryked.* N. 580.
Shul, shall. K. 889, 1498; pl. *shullen.* K. 2156.
Shulder, shoulder. P. 678.
Shyne, shin. P. 386, p. K. 421.
Sight, providence. K. 814.
Sike, to sigh. K. 682; pt. *siked.* K. 2127.
Siker, sure. K. 2191; *sikerly.* P. 137.
Sikes, sighs. K. 1062.
Sin, since. P. 601, 853, K. 415.
Singeth, impv. sing. N. 500.
Sit, sitteth, sits. K. 741, 942.

P. 772; arrange. P. 809; ordained. K. 250, 367, 534. M. 21; pt. *shoop,* Pd. 412.

Sith, Sithen, since, afterwards. K. 72, 434, 545, 663, 1244; Pd. 407.
Sithes, Sythes, times. P. 485, K. 1019.
Slake, slow, slack. K. 2043.
Slawe, see *Slee.*
Slee, Sleen, to slay. P. 661; K. 364; *sleeth.* K. 260; pp. *slawe.* N. 194; pt. *slough.* K. 122, *slow.* K. 1608.
Sleep, pt. slept. P. 98, 397. (From *slepen.*)
Sleere, a slayer. K. 1147.
Sleight, cunning, craft. P. 604.
Slepen, pr. pl. sleep. P. 10.
Sleping, sleep. N. 192.
Slepy, causing sleep. K. 529.
Sleves, sleeves. P. 193.
Slider, slippery. K. 406.
Slogardye, sluggardy, sloth. K. 184.
Slough, see *Slee.*
Slyly, cautiously, wisely. K. 586.
Smerte, smarting, sharp. P. 149.
Smerte, pain. K. 1367.
Smerte, to pain, hurt. P. 230, 534. K. 536.
Smoking, perfuming with incense. K. 1423.
Smoot, smote. P. 149, K. 846.
Snewed, snowed. P. 345.
Snibbe, to snub. P. 523.
Soberly, sad, solemn. P. 289.
Socour, succor. K. 60.
Sodein, Sodeyn, sudden; *sodeynliche, sodeynly,* suddenly. K. 260, 717.
Solas, solace, mirth. P. 798.
Solempne, important. P. 209, 364.
Solempnely, solemnly, pompously. P. 274.
Solempnitee, feast, ceremony. K. 12, 1844.

GLOSSARY

Som, some. P. 640. *som . . . som,* one . . . another. K. 397, 399, 2143, 2144.
Somdel, somewhat. P. 174.
Somer, summer. P. 394.
Somnour, apparitor, officer who summoned delinquents before an ecclesiastical court. P. 543.
Somtyme, formerly. P. 65.
Sond, sand. N. 447.
Sondry, sundry. P. 14, 347. N. 316.
Sone, soon. K. 1412, 1812.
Song, pt. sang. K. 197. *Songe,* pp. sung. P. 266, 711.
Soote, sweet. P. 1.
Sooth, truth. P. 284, K. 663.
Sooth, Sothe, true. P. 845, K. 767.
Soothfastnesse, truth. N. 508.
Soothly, truly. P. 117; K. 1078.
Sop, bread (dipped in wine). P. 334.
Soper, supper. P. 348; K. 33.
Sore, sorely. P. 230; K. 536.
Sort, lot, chance. P. 844.
Sorwe, sorrow. K. 361, 419.
Sorweful, sorrowful. K. 212.
Sory, sorry, doleful, sad. K. 1146, 1152.
Sotil, subtle, dainty. K. 196, 1172, 1191.
Soun, a sound. K. 674, 1654.
Souneth, tends, inclines. M, P. 79. See *Sowninge.*
Souple, supple. P. 203.
Sovereyn, high, supreme. P. 67. *Sovereynly,* surpassingly. N. 542.
Soun, to sound. P. 565.
Sowninge, tending to. P. 275, 307.
Space, course. P. 176; *as in so litel s.,* for so short a time. K. 1038. P. 87.
Spare, abstain from. P. 192, 737.
Sparre, bar, beam. K. 132, 218.

Sparth, double-edged battle-axe. K. 1662.
Sparwe, sparrow. P. 626.
Speces, species. K. 2155.
Special, in, specially. P. 444.
Spede, to speed, prosper. P. 769; pt. s. *speede,* hastened. K. 359.
Speken, speak. P. 142; pt. s. *spak.* P. 124, K. 54; pr. subj. *speke.* P. 734.
Spere, spear. K. 781, 795.
Spiced conscience, sophisticated conscience. P. 526.
Spicerye, spices (in the larger sense, including aromatic gums). K. 2077.
Springen, to spring. K. 1013, 1749; pp. *spronge,* become widely known. K. 579.
Spore, spur. K. 1745; *spores,* pl. P. 473.
Sporne, kick. 3, 11.
Sprad, pp., spread. K. 2045.
Squyer, a squire, an aspirant for knighthood. P. 79.
Staat, condition. P. 572.
Stablissed, established. K. 2137.
Stalketh, walks stealthily. K. 621 (cf. deer-*stalking*).
Starf, see *Sterve.*
Stemed, flamed, glowed. P. 202.
Stente(n), to stop, cease. K. 45; pp. *stente,* stopped. K. 510.
Stepe, protruding. P. 201.
Stere, rudder. 7, 12.
Sterres, stars. P. 268, K. 1179.
Stert, start. K. 847. Pd. 243.
Sterte, to start, leap. K. 186, Pd. 183.
Stertling, agile, spirited. K. 644.
Sterve, die. K. 286; pt. P. 123; Pd. 343; 2, 23; pp. *storven.* Pd. 426; pt. s. *starf.* K. 75.
Steven(e), voice. K. 1704; *at unset s.,* at a time not agreed upon. K. 666.

GLOSSARY

Stewe, fish-pond. P. 350.
Stille, at rest, quietly, still. K. 145, 2127; N. 401, 623.
Stinte, to stop; pt. *stint.* K. 1563; impv. *stint.* K. 1490.
Stith, an anvil. K. 1168.
Stiwardes, stewards. P. 579.
Stoke, to stick, thrust. K. 1688.
Stokkes, stocks, sticks. K. 2076.
Stole, pp., stolen. K. 1769.
Stomblen, stumble. K. 1755.
Stonden, to stand. P. 88; *s. at,* abide, by. P. 778; *stant,* standeth. M. P. 38; M. 419.
Stongen, stung. K. 221.
Stoor, store (of implements, etc.), stock (of a farm). P. 598. Pd. P. 37.
Stope, advanced. N. 1.
Store, telle no, take no account; have no opinion. N. 334.
Stot, a horse. P. 615.
Stounde, a moment, brief space of time. K. 354.
Stoute, bold. K. 1296.
Straunge, foreign. P. 13, 464.
Strecche, to stretch. N. 488; pt. s. *straughte.* K. 2058.
Stree, straw. K. 2060.
Streem, stream, river. P. 464; pl. *stremes,* currents. P. 402; beams (of light), rays. K. 637.
Streite, pp., drawn. N. 537.
Streite, closely, snugly. P. 457.
Streit(e), strait, strict. P. 174; narrow. K. 1126; *streit of herbergage,* limited in accommodations, lodgings. N. 169.
Strengthe, with, by force. K. 1541.
Strepe, to strip. K. 148.
Streyneth, constrains. N. 424.
Strike of flex, hank of flax. P. 676.
Strof, strove, vied with. K. 180.
Strondes, strands, shores. P. 13.
Stubbes, stumps. K. 1120.

Subtilly, craftily. P. 610.
Suffisaunce, sufficiency. P. 490; *hertes s.,* contentment of heart. N. 19.
Suffisaunt, sufficient. K. 773.
Surcote, overcoat. P. 617.
Sustene, to sustain, hold up. K. 1135.
Suster, sister. K. 13; pl. *sustren.* K. 161; *sustres.* N. 47.
Swelte, fainted. K. 498.
Swerd, sword. P. 112, K. 717.
Sweven(e), dream, N. 76; pl. *swevenis* (for the rime). N. 101.
Swich, such. P. 3, 243, K. 4., etc.
Swinke, to toil. Pd. 352, P. 186.
Swink, toil, labor. P. 186.
Swinkere, laborer. P. 531.
Swore, pp., sworn. P. 810.
Swough, soughing of wind. K. 1121.
Swowne, to swoon. K. 55, 1961.
Swyn, swine. P. 598.
Swythe, quickly. Pd. 334.

T

Tabard, short-sleeved coat, ploughman's coat. P. 541; an inn. P. 20.
Taffata, taffeta, a kind of silk. P. 440.
Taille, tally, account notched on pieces of wood. P. 570.
Tak, impv. *take.* K. 226.
Take, pp. taken. K. 1693, 1289.
Takel, tackle; an arrow or other implement or weapon. P. 106.
Talen, to tell stories. P. 722.
Tapicer, an upholsterer. P. 362.
Tappestere, a female tapster, barmaid. P. 241.
Targe, target, shield. P. 471.
Tars, cloth of, tartary silk. K. 1302.
Tas, heap. K. 147, 151, 162.
Teche(n), to teach, direct. P. 308; N. 129.

GLOSSARY

Temple, an inn of court, lodging place for lawyers. P. 567.
Tendite, to endite. K. 351.
Tene, vexation, sorrow. K. 2248.
Terciane, tertian. N. 139.
Teres, tears. K. 422.
Tespye, to espy. N. 468.
Testers, head-pieces. K. 1641.
Than, Thanne, then. P. 12, 535.
Thankes, (adverbial genitive) willingly. K. 768, 1249.
Tharray, the array. P. 716.
Thavys, the advice. K. 2218.
That, that which. K. 567.
Thee, to prosper, thrive. N. 615, Pd. P. 23.
Thencens, the incense. K. 1419.
Thencrees, the increase. P. 275.
Ther, where. P. 547, K. 1224.
Ther as, where, where that. P. 34, 172, K. 200, 1116.
Ther to, besides. P. 153, 757.
Thestat, the estate or rank. P. 716.
Thider, thither. K. 405.
Thikke, stocky. P. 549; thickly set. K. 217; crowded together. K. 1652; thick. K. 1660.
Thilke, that same, that. P. 182, K. 335, 1525.
Thinges, business affairs. N. 269.
Thinke, to seem. Often used impersonally. P. 37, 385, 682, 785.
Thirle, to pierce. K. 1852.
Thise, these. P. 701, K. 673.
Tho, those. P. 498, K. 265, 3495.
Tho, then. K. 135.
Thoughte, pt. from *thinken.*
Thombe, thumb. P. 563.
Thorisoun, the orison or prayer. K. 1403.
Thral, slave, thrall. K. 694.
Threste, to thrust. K. 1754.
Thridde, third. K. 605, N. 193.
Thriftily, becomingly. P. 105.
Throte, throat. K. 1155, N. 49, 66.
Thryes, thrice. P. 63, 463, K. 2094.
Thurgh, through. K. 362.
Thurghfare, thoroughfare. K. 1989.
Thurghgirt, pierced through. K. 152.
Thurghout, through. K. 238, N. 398.
Tikelnesse, instability. 3, 3.
Til, to. P. 180, K. 620.
To, at, gone to. P. 30.
To, toe. K. 1868; pl. *toon.* N. 42; *toos.* N. 360.
To-breste, burst asunder. K. 1753.
To-brosten, burst, broken in pieces. K. 1833, 1899.
Togidre, together. P. 824.
To-hewen, cut or hewn in pieces. K. 1751.
Tollen, to take toll or payment. P. 562.
Tombesteres, female tumblers, dancing girls, Pd. 15.
Tonge, tongue. P. 712.
Tonne-greet, as great as a tun in circumference. K. 1136.
Tool, weapon. N. 96.
Toon, see *To* (2).
To-rente, tear utterly. Pd. 247.
Torets, swivels (in a dog's collar). K. 1294.
Torne, to turn. K. 630.
To-shrede, to cut in shreds. K. 1751.
To-swinke, labor greatly. Pd. 57.
To-tere, to tear utterly. Pd. 12.
Toun, town. P. 478.
Tour, tower. K. 172, 419.
Touret, turret. K. 1051.
Trace, Thrace. K. 1114, 1271.
Trapped, having trappings. K. 2032.

GLOSSARY

Trappures, trappings. K. 1641.
Traunce, trance. K. 714.
Trays, harness, traces. K. 1281.
Trede, tread. K. 2164.
Tresoun, treason, treachery. K. 1143.
Tretee, treaty. K. 430.
Tretys, shapely. P. 152.
Trewe, true. P. 531.
Trewely, truly. P. 481.
Trompe, trumpet. P. 674, K. 1316.
Tronchoun, the butt (or part remaining in the hand) of a broken spear. K. 1757.
Trone, throne. K. 1671, Pd. 380.
Trouthe, truth. P. 46; pledge, promise. K. 752.
Trowe, believe. P. 155.
Trussed up, packed in. P. 681.
Trusteth, imper. pl., trust, believe. K. 1324.
Tukked, tucked up. P. 621.
Turneyinge, a tournament. K. 1669.
Tweye, two, twain. P. 704, 792, K. 40, 270.
Twinne, separate. Pd. P. 102.
Twyned threed, a doubled or twisted thread. K. 1172.
Tyde, tide. P. 401; time. N. 196.
Twynne (literally separate), depart, go on. P. 835.

U

Uncouth, unknown, strange. K. 1639.
Under the sonne, to the eastward under a low-lying sun. K. 839.
Undern, the time from 9 A. M. to 12 M. In N. 402 the time of the mid-day meal, about 11 A. M.
Undergrowe, undergrown, small of stature. P. 156.
Undertake, affirm, venture to say. P. 288, N. 391; to assume a responsibility. P. 405.
Unkindely, unnaturally. Pd. 23.
Unknowe, unknown. P. 126, K. 548.
Unkonning, ignorant, inexperienced. K. 1535.
Unnethe, scarcely, with difficulty. M. 431.
Unset, not appointed or planned. K. 666.
Unwist, unknown. K. 2119.
Unyolden, pp., not having yielded or surrendered. K. 1784.
Up, . . . armed, fitted out. K. 994.
Up-haf, uplifted, raised. K. 1570.
Upon, on. P. 617.
Up peyne, upon pain or penalty. K. 1685.
Up-right, full length, either standing or lying down. K. 1150, N. 222, Pd. 152.
Up-riste, rising. K. 193.
Up-so-doun, upside down. K. 519.
Upsterte, started up. K. 441.
Up-yaf, gave up, gave forth. K. 1569.
Usage, experience. K. 1590.

V

Vache, cow. 3, 22.
Vassalage, valiant and faithful service (to his feudal lord). K. 2196.
Vavasour, a sub-vassal, holding a small fief, a country gentleman. P. 360.
Venerye, hunting. P. 166, K. 1450.
Venim, poison. K. 1893.
Ventusing, cupping (in surgery). K. 1889.
Verdit, verdict. P. 787.

GLOSSARY

Vernicle (from Veronica), miniature picture of Christ, supposed originally to have been miraculously imprinted upon a handkerchief. (See note.) P. 685.
Verraily, verily, truly. P. 338.
Verray, true, very. P. 72, 422.
Vers, pl., verses. N. 493.
Vertue, power, virtue. P. 4, K. 1391; ability. K. 578.
Vertuous, efficient, (in begging). P. 251.
Vese, a gust or rush of wind. K. 1127.
Vestiments, vestments. K. 2090.
Veyl, vail. P. 695.
Veyn, vein. P. 3.
Veyn, vain. K. 236.
Veyne-blood, bleeding at a vein (surgical). K. 1889.
Viage, journey. P. 77, 723.
Vigilyes, vigils, evening services 'on the eve of a festival' (Skeat). P. 377.
Vileinye, coarseness (of language). P. 70, 740; churlishness, ill-breeding. P. 726; disgrace. K. 1871.
Vitaille, victuals. P. 569, 749.
Vouchesauf, vouchsafe, consent. P. 807.
Voyden, to expel. K. 1893.

W

Wafereres, makers of wafers, confectioners. Pd. 17
Wake-pleyes, ceremonies accompanying vigils for the dead. K. 2102.
Walet, wallet. P. 681.
Wan, won, conquered. K. 131. See *Winne*.
Wanhope, despair. K. 391.
Wanie, to wane, diminish. K. 1220.
Wantown, free in manners. P. 208.
Wantownesse, jollity. P. 264.
War, aware, cautious. P. 157, 309. K. 840.
War him, let him beware. P. 662.
Ware, a town in Southern England. P. 692.
Warente, warrant, protect. Pd. P. 10.
Waryce, heal, cure. Pd. 444.
Wastel-breed, fine quality of bread. P. 147.
Wawes, waves. K. 1100.
Wayke, weak. K. 29.
Waymenting(e), wailing, lamenting. K. 137, 1063.
Wayte, to watch. P. 571; K. 364, P. 525.
Webbe, a weaver. P. 362.
Wed, pledge, dat. *wedde*. K. 360.
Wedden, to wed. K. 974; pt. *weddede*. K. 10.
Wede, clothing. K. 148.
Weel, well. K. 68, 1265.
Weep, wept (see *Wepen*). K. 1487.
Wel, full, very. P. 614, K. 396, N. 56.
Welked, withered. Pd. 276.
Weylaway, alas, well-a-way. K. 80, N. 560.
Wele, weal, prosperity. K. 37; 3, 4.
Welle, well, source. K. 2179.
Wende, pt. weened, thought. K. 411, Pd. 260. (See *Wene*.)
Wende, to go. P. 16, 21, K. 1356, Pd. 465; pass away. K. 2167.
Wene, to ween, think. K. 797; pl. *wenen*. Pd. P. 21.
Wepe, to weep. P. 144; pt. *weep*. K. 1487; *wepte*, P. 148.
Wepne, weapon. K. 733.
Were, to guard defend. K. 1692.
Were, pr. pl., wear. K. 2090; pr.

subj.. sg., wear, 4, 7; pt. *wered*. P. 75.
Werre, war. P. 47, K. 429.
Werreye(n), to make war. K. 626, 686.
Werte, wart. P. 555.
Wesshe, washed. K. 1425.
Wete, wet. K. 422.
Wex, wax. P. 675.
Wexe, to wax, increase; *wexeth*, waxes, becomes. K. 2166; pt. *wex*. K. 504; *wexing*. K. 1220.
Wey, Weye, a way. P. 34, 467.
Weyeth, weighs, esteems. K. 923.
Weyle, to wail. K. 363.
What, why. P. 184, 854.
Whelkes, pimples. P. 632.
Whelpe, puppy. P. 257.
Wher, where. K. 1952.
Wher, whether. K. 1394. N. 311. M. P. 41.
Whether, whether, which of two. K. 998.
Which, what, *which a*, what a. K. 1817; pl. *whiche*. P. 40.
Whippeltre, cornel-tree. K. 2065.
Whyl, whilst. P. 35, 397.
Whylom, formerly, once. K. 1, 1545.
Whyt, white, P. 238.
Widwe, widow. P. 253.
Wight, person, any living creature. P. 71, 326.
Wighte, weight. K. 1287.
Wikke, wicked, evil. K. 229. N. 603.
Wilfully, willingly. N. 276.
Wilne, to desire. K. 751; *wilneth*. K. 1706.
Wiltow, wilt thou. K. 298.
Wilwe, willow. K. 2064.
Wimpel, wimple, covering for the face. P. 151.

Winne, win, conquer. P. 594; pt. *wan*. P. 442. K. 131.
Wirche, to work. K. 1901.
Wise, manner, fashion. K. 480, 882.
Wisly, truly, surely. K. 1005, 1376.
Wit, understanding. P. 279, 746.
Wite, to know; pr. pl. *witen*. K. 402; pr. 1, 35; *woot*. P. 389, K. 283; pr. 2. s.; *wost, woost*. K. 305, 1449; pr. subj. *wiste*. P. 766.
With, by. K. 1866.
Withholde, pp., maintained. P. 511.
Withouten, without. P. 538; besides. P. 461.
Withseye, Withseyn, to gainsay. P. 805, K. 282.
Witing, knowledge. K. 753.
Wlatsome, loathsome, hateful. N. 233.
Wo, woe. K. 1766; sorrow. K. 42; adj., sorrowful. P. 351.
Wodebynde, woodbine. K. 650.
Wofullere, the more sorrowful. K. 482.
Wol, Wole, will, P. 42; K. 880; 2 s. *wolt*. K. 766; pl. *woln*. K. 1263; pt. s. *wolde*, would. P. 144; pt. pl. *wolden*. P. 27; wished. N. 467.
Wolle, wool. Pd. P. 120.
Woltow = *wolt thou*. K. 686.
Wommanhede, womanliness. K. 890.
Wonder, adj., wonderful. K. 1215; adv., wondrous. P. 483, K. 796.
Wonderly, wonderfully, remarkably. P. 84.
Wone, custom, usage. P. 335, K. 182.
Woneden, pt. pl., dwelt. K. 2069; pr. pt. *woning*, dwelling, living. P. 388.

GLOSSARY

Woning, a dwelling, home. P. 606.
Wood, mad. P. 582, K. 471.
Woodly, madly. K. 443.
Woodnesse, madness. K. 1153.
Wook, awoke. K. 535.
Worship, honor, respect. K. 1065.
Worshipful, honorable. K. 577.
Worshipe, to honor, render due respect to. K. 1393.
Worth, was noght, was not worth while. P. 785.
Wortes, herbs. N. 401.
Wostow = *wost thou;* see *Wite.*
Wrastleth, wrestles. K. 2103.
Wrastling, wrestling. P. 548.
Wrecche, wretched. K. 248.
Wreke, wreak, avenge. K. 103, M. P. 7.
Wrethe, a wreath. K. 1287.
Wrighte, workman. P. 614.
Writ. writes. N. 303.
Wrooth, wroth, angry. P. 451.
Wyke, week. K. 681; Pd. P. 34; pl., K. 992.
Wys, adv., truly, surely. K. 1928; *as w. God helpe me,* as surely as God may help me. N. 588.
Wyte, to blame. M. 456.
Wyve, to, dat., to wife, as a wife. K. 1002.

Y

Y-, a prefix chiefly used with the pps. of verbs. It represents A.S. *ge,* which is cognate with the same prefix in Germ. e. g. *ge*habt, *ge*geben.
Yaf (pt. of *yeve*), gave. K. 583; cared. P. 177.
Y-been, been. N. 477.
Y-bete, beaten. K. 121; *newe y-b.* just forged. K. 1304.
Y-bore, Y-born, borne, carried. P. 378. K. 1836.
Y-born, born. K. 161.
Y-boundèn, bound. K. 291.
Y-brent, burnt. K. 88.
Y-broght, brought. K. 253.
Y-clenched, clinched. K. 1133.
Y-cleped, called. P. 410; K. 9; *y-clept.* P. 376.
Y-corve, cut. K. 1155.
Y-don, done. K. 167; *y-doon.* N. 600; *y-do.* K. 1676.
Y-drawe, drawn. P. 396. K. 86.
Y-dropped, bedropped, bedewed. K. 2026.
Yë, eye. P. 10; K. 238 (this is the form in rime; within the verse *eye,* pl. *eyen,* is common).
Yeddings, proverbial sayings. P. 237.
Yeer, Yer, year. P. 347; K. 523; pl. *yeer.* P. 82.
Yeld-halle, guild-hall. P. 370. (see P. 364, note.)
Yeldyng, yielding, produce. P. 596.
Yelleden, yelled. N. 569.
Yelpe, to boast. K. 1380.
Yeman, yeoman, commoner, retainer. P. 101; pl. *yemen.* K. 1870.
Yerde, stick. P. 149, K. 529.
Yerd, yard, enclosure. N. 27.
Yerne, eagerly, quickly. Pd. P. 70.
Yet now, even now. K. 298.
Yeve, to give. P. 223. Pd. P. 121.
Y-faille, fallen. P. 25.
Y-fetered, fettered. K. 371.
Y-go, gone. P. 286.
Y-hent, seized, caught. Pd. 406.
Y-holde, held, esteemed. K. 1516, 2100.
Yiftes, gifts. K. 1340.
Yif (impers. of *yive*), give. K. 1402, 1562.
Yive, to give. P. 225; pp. *yiven,* K. 57.

Yaf, gave. M. 466, Pd. 425.
Y-knowe, known. P. 423.
Y-lad, drawn. P. 350.
Y-laft, left. K. 1888.
Y-liche, alike. K. 1668.
Y-logged, lodged. N. 171.
Y-lyk, alike. P. 592; *y-lik.* K. 1876; *y-like.* K. 681.
Y-maked, pp., made. K. 1207, 1997.
Y-met, pp., met. K. 1766.
Y-meynd, mingled, mixed. K. 1312.
Y-nogh, enough. P. 373.
Yolden, yielded. K. 2194.
Yolle, to yell. K. 1814.
Yond, yonder. K. 241.
Yore agoon, a long time ago. K. 955.
Youling, loud weeping, yelling. K. 420.
Yow, you. P. 34, 38.
Y-payed, paid, rewarded. K. 944.
Ypolita, Hippolita, queen of the Amazons. K. 10, 827.

Y-preved, proved. P. 485.
Ypres, in West Flanders. P. 446.
Y-raft, bereft, plundered. K. 1157.
Y-ronne, run. P. 8 (*was y-r*); arranged, fell. K. 1307; had flowed. K. 1835.
Y-sene, adj., visible. P. 592 (see *Sene*).
Y-seyled, sailed. N. 279.
Y-shave, shaven. P. 690.
Y-shrive, shriven. P. 226.
Y-slayn, slain. K. 1850.
Y-spreynd, sprinkled. K. 1311.
Y-stiked, pierced, stuck. K. 707.
Y-stong, stung. Pd. P. 27.
Y-storve, dead. K. 1156 (pp. of *sterve*).
Y-teyd, tied. P. 457.
Yve, ivy. N. 146.
Y-wimpled, wimpled, wearing a wimple. P. 470.
Y-wis, certainly, truly. N. 379, 622.
Y-wrye, covered, hung. K. 2046.